# Jerry Baker's

# IT PAYS
# to be
# CHEAP!

## www.jerrybaker.com

**Other *Jerry Baker* home books:**

*Jerry Baker's Eureka! 1001 Old-Time Secrets and
   New-Fangled Solutions to Life's Everyday Problems*

***Jerry Baker* health books:**

*Oddball Ointments, Powerful Potions & Fabulous
   Folk Remedies*
*Jerry Baker's Kitchen Counter Cures*
*Jerry Baker's Herbal Pharmacy*

***Jerry Baker* gardening books:**

*Jerry Baker's Perfect Perennials!*
*Jerry Baker's Backyard Problem Solver*
*Jerry Baker's Green Grass Magic*
*Jerry Baker's Terrific Tomatoes, Sensational Spuds,
   <u>and</u> Mouth-Watering Melons*
*Jerry Baker's Great Green Book of Garden Secrets*
*Jerry Baker's Old-Time Gardening Wisdom*
*Jerry Baker's Flower Power!*

To order any of the above, or for more information on
*Jerry Baker's* amazing home, health, and garden tips, tricks,
and tonics, please write to:

**Jerry Baker, P.O. Box 1001, Wixom, MI 48393**

Or, visit Jerry Baker on the World Wide Web at:

# www.jerrybaker.com

Jerry Baker's

# IT PAYS
## to be
# CHEAP!

**1,973 of the Niftiest, Swiftiest, and Thriftiest Secrets on Earth for Spendin' Less and Savin' More on… Food, Clothes, Electronics, Furniture, Travel, Household Goods, Pets, Personal Care, and Almost Everything!**

by Jerry Baker

Published by American Master Products, Inc.

Copyright © 2002 by Jerry Baker

All rights reserved. No part of this book may be reproduced or transmitted in any form or by any means, including, but not limited to, photocopying, recording, electronically, via the Internet, or by any other information storage or retrieval system without the express written permission of the Publisher.

All efforts have been made to ensure accuracy. Jerry Baker assumes no responsibility or liability for any injuries, damages, or losses incurrred during the use of, or as a result of following this information.

**IMPORTANT**—Study all directions carefully before taking any action based on the information and advice presented in this book. When using any commercial product, always read and follow label directions. When reference is made to trade or brand names, no endorsement by Jerry Baker is implied, nor is any discrimination intended.

**Published by American Master Products, Inc. / Jerry Baker**

Executive Editor: Kim Adam Gasior
Project Editor: Cheryl Winters Tetreau
Writers: Vicki Webster, Melinda Whitteberry
Interior Design and Layout: Sandy Freeman
Cover Design: Kitty Pierce Mace
Indexer: Nan Badgett

**Publisher's Cataloging-in-Publication**

Baker, Jerry.
    Jerry Baker's it pays to be cheap : 1,973 of the niftiest, swiftiest, and thriftiest secrets on Earth for spendin' less and savin' more on — food, clothes, electronics, furniture, travel, houehold goods, pets, personal care and almost everything! / Jerry Baker. — 1st ed.
        p. cm.
        Includes index.

    1. Consumer education.   2. Shopping.   3. Home economics — Accounting.   I. Title.

TX335.B35 2002                     640'.42
                                   QBI02-200539

Printed in the United States of America
2 4 6 8 10 9 7 5 3   hardcover

# Introduction

When I was just a lad growing up with my Grandma Putt, we didn't have much money, but we sure had fun! Grandma never made a big fuss about "frugality." (In fact, I don't recall her ever mentioning the word!) She just went about life in her good old commonsense way—and enjoyed every single minute of it. In fact, I'd say she was a world champ at what folks today would call "livin' the good life on the cheap!"

It'll come as no surprise that this book is chock full of tips, tricks, tonics, and just plain good ideas that Grandma Putt passed on to me over the years. There's plenty more than that, though—after all, a lot of the things that put big holes in our bank accounts didn't even *exist* in Grandma's day! That's why, in these pages, I've taken her solid, down-home wisdom, and added some new-fangled angles of my own. Then, for good measure, I've tossed in a lot of money-saving brainstorms that folks have shared with me as I've traveled this great land of ours.

**PART I** of this book is all about spending money wisely—whether you're shopping for the basic necessities of life or heading off on the vacation of your dreams.

In Part II, we'll talk about saving money. How? By taking good care of all that great gear you've just bought! Besides time-tested techniques, you'll find formulas for cleaning, polishing, and keepin' up your whole house, and everything in it. Plus, I'll tell you how to cut the high cost of personal care for the entire family, including your four-footed pals. Take a look at the next page for one example of my Fantastic Formulas—they're guaranteed to save you money over store-bought solutions!

We'll start Chapter 1 in a place where most of us drop big bucks every week: the grocery store. (Even I can't grow everything I eat!) I'll clue you in on a whole slew of cost-cutting tactics that the corporate bean counters would rather you didn't know about, including how to make store geography work in your favor, not theirs, and how to read between the lines in ads and posters. I'll even tell you what you should never buy in a supermarket—not, that is, if you're looking for a bargain.

Movin' right along to Chapter 2, I'll give you my best advice on dressing like a king (or queen) on a pauper's income. Then, in Chapter 3, we'll enter that uncharted territory which strikes financial fear in lots of folks' hearts: appliances and electronics. I'll arm you with a bevy of facts and strategies that'll save you hundreds of dollars (or more) on stoves, refrigerators, and washing machines, as well as computers, VCRs, and other gadgets.

Chapters 4 and 5 really hit home—your home, that is. There, you'll find a

passel of ideas and strategies for saving money on decks, patios, and other building projects, whether you do the work yourself, have your neighbors lend a hand, or call in a pro. I'll also let you in on some inside secrets for landing the best deals on furniture, tools, and building supplies—including why you'll almost never find a real bargain at one of the big-box megastores!

Part I ends with luxury travel on a shoestring budget. That's where you'll discover my tried-and-true techniques for finding the best bargains in air fares, rental cars, and hotel rooms. Plus, I'll give you the inside scoop on havin' more fun for less money, no matter where you're headed.

**PART II** is all about hangin' on to your investments, large and small. We'll start in the kitchen. After all, it's great to get a steal of a deal on 10 pounds of potatoes. But if they go bad before you've eaten 'em all, you've thrown your hard-earned bucks right out the window! In Chapter 7, I'll share more moneysaving tactics than you can shake a grocery bag at—including how to store your food so it stays fresher, longer, and how to turn tired leftovers into

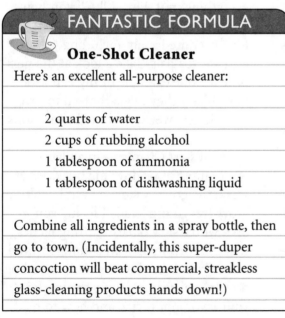

## FANTASTIC FORMULA

### One-Shot Cleaner

Here's an excellent all-purpose cleaner:

| |
|---|
| 2 quarts of water |
| 2 cups of rubbing alcohol |
| 1 tablespoon of ammonia |
| 1 tablespoon of dishwashing liquid |

Combine all ingredients in a spray bottle, then go to town. (Incidentally, this super-duper concoction will beat commercial, streakless glass-cleaning products hands down!)

## SUGAR, SUGAR

\* \* \* \* \*

Ah, the dreaded hard-as-a-rock brown sugar. Your brown sugar starts out just fine, but once you open up that box or bag, the contents turn to stone about as quickly as it takes liquid cement to harden. What to do? Here are a couple of options:

✦ Keep the box in the fridge. Believe it or not, it keeps the contents from hardening.

✦ Buy brown sugar only in plastic bags. Once you open the bag, fold down the top really tight and clip it shut (I use a large paper clip), then put it into another plastic bag with a zipper closure. Now it'll keep in the pantry for months without hardening.

✦ If it's too late and you're stuck with a brown sugar fossil, put it in a glass bowl, sprinkle a few drops of water over it, and put it in the microwave for 10 to 15 seconds. It should soften right up.

✦ Emergency Plan B: Put rock-solid brown sugar in a tightly covered container with a slice of white bread, and put it in the microwave for 30 seconds. Your sugar'll be as soft as the day you bought it (and you can feed that piece of bread to the birds).

meals you'd be proud to serve to Julia Child herself. For a taste of what you'll find, take a peek at "Sugar, Sugar," at left, for ways to "revive" rock-hard brown sugar.

Of course, spoiled food isn't the only culprit in The Case of the Runaway Dollars. Clothes, appliances, furniture, even decks and patios can go belly-up before their time. They won't, though, if you heed the helpful hints in Chapters 8 through 11. There, you'll find time-tested tips for keepin' everything inside and outside your house lookin' and workin' its best. What's more, I'll arm you with a slew of fantastic formulas that beat commercial cleaning products hands down, and at a fraction of the cost.

But wait—we're not through yet! To keep you lookin' and workin' *your* best, you need a little TLC, too, and so do your four-footed pals. In Chapters 12 and 14, you'll not only find some great health and fitness tips for you and your pets, but also some fantastic formulas for everything from mouthwash and hair conditioner to dog food and flea repellent.

Whew! As you can see, we've got a lot of ground to cover. So what are we waiting for? Let's get this show on the road!

# Contents

## Part I: Spending Money

# Part II: Saving Money

# Spending

# · PART I ·

# MONEY

# CHAPTER 1

# The Goods on Grocery Shopping

You know me—I'm as frugal and self-sufficient as they come. But even I need to go to the supermarket occasionally. And by the looks of it, I'm not alone. Government statistics say that we spend almost 10 percent of our yearly income at the supermarket! That adds up to a lot of dough, and I'm here to tell you that there's no good reason to give up one penny more than you have to. So in this chapter, I'll walk you through some of my favorite hints, tips, and secrets for spending a whole lot less at the grocery store.

I'll talk about ways to get yourself organized before you head out the door to shop, including the best ways to collect and use coupons. I'll also let you in on some of the tricks of the supermarket trade that are designed to get you to spend more time and money in the store—I call them "supermarket sand traps"—and some sure-fire ways to avoid them.

This chapter won't keep you out of the supermarket entirely, but if you follow my advice, you'll surely save plenty once you get there!

# Think First, Shop Later

Saving money at the supermarket starts long before you even leave your home. I'll show you how getting more organized in your moneysaving approach will keep you from spending a bundle on things you don't want or need. And did you know that making friends with the folks at the supermarket can add up to real savings? Well, that's just one of my many supermarket savings secrets. Read on to learn more.

## Getting Organized

**You wouldn't think that grocery shopping takes planning, but if you want to shop smart and save big, it pays to get yourself organized before you hit the stores. Here's how.**

## BOOK IT

Have you heard of something called a price book? It's a tool to help you keep track of how much your grocery items cost and which store usually has the best price. Make up a price book to take along to the grocery store and I *guarantee* that you'll save money.

One day, I sat down to make a list of all the products I regularly buy from the supermarket, from staples to snacks. My list had four columns: The first column noted the product (flour, for instance). The second column was the brand that I preferred (which, in my case, is usually the store brand). The third column noted the unit price of the product, and the fourth column was the name of the store that carried that item for the least amount of money. With this list, I knew exactly how much my regular items cost, whether a sale was actually saving me money, and which grocery store had the best price. Sure, this can take a little time, but the money you'll save in the long run will more than make up for it.

Now don't you dare go to the stationery store and buy a notebook to use for your price book! That would be wasteful, and there's really no need. Just look around the house for one of the following items:

★ An old spiral notebook. You've probably got several of these lying around. Some may contain half a book full of unused pages. Just rip out the used ones. Or you may have notebooks with pages that have writing only on one side. Just flip over the notebook so the back is now the front, and use the blank pages.

★ That little calendar book you got from your insurance agent or bank. If it's a monthly calendar, each page already has seven columns!

★ One of the extra check registers that your bank sends you with each box of new checks.

## DON'T MAKE DO— MAKE A SHOPPING LIST!

**D**on't get suckered into buying what the store wants you to buy rather than what you need. Supermarkets spend lots of time, money, and effort trying to get you to spend big bucks. The easiest way to avoid this hazard is to go into the store with a detailed game plan—in other words, a shopping list. That way, you won't be wandering the aisles aimlessly, buying products that you really don't need.

If that isn't a good enough reason to make up a list, here's another one: Those clever super-marketeers have found a great way to get you to traipse all over the store looking for the items you want. How? They

---

### NO STRINGS ATTACHED

If you're a senior citizen, you could qualify for free groceries every single week. There are several programs throughout the country—most at a local level—that offer this service. To find out if such a program exists in your town, contact a local senior citizen's center, community center, or food bank, all of which will be listed in your local Yellow Pages.

move them! That's right. Last week, the tomato soup was in aisle 3; now it's in aisle 7! Those clever folks who run the supermarkets hope that by making you search around for a bit, you'll (a) spend more time shopping (and buying), and (b) wander by a product that you've just gotta have. So avoid overspending by making, taking, and diligently sticking to a grocery list!

# TAKE STOCK

One week this month, make a list of what you throw out at the end of that week. If you're tossing out a half-pound of baloney, don't buy a whole pound. If you're dumping a bunch of carrots, choose broccoli this week. By keeping better track of what you're consuming, you can buy only what you need and use, and that's money in the bank!

# Avoiding Impulse Purchases

You know how it is. You go to the grocery store to get a roll of aluminum foil and you leave $60 poorer. *How the heck did that happen?* Well, supermarkets are designed to persuade you to buy items on impulse. They put the dip near the chips. They tuck the expensive salad dressing near the produce. They put those gourmet condiments and high-priced breads near the deli counter. That's a lot of temptation! But here are some sure-fire ways to get out of the store alive, with *only* what you want.

# LEAVE HOME WITHOUT 'EM

Here's one of my all-time favorite ways to avoid impulse purchases at the grocery store and save all kinds of money: Leave those credit and debit cards at home. That's right—after you've made up your list and gathered up all your coupons, take a minute or two and add up the cost of the items on your shopping list. Take enough cash to cover that total plus an extra $5 (just in case), but leave your cards at home. You might get caught a little short the first time you try this (okay, so leave behind that extra pint of

Häagen-Dazs), but after that, you'll hit your mark on the nose every time you shop—and you'll avoid needless purchases.

## HAVE A SMART SNACK

**A**nother quick-and-easy way to keep yourself from making impulse purchases (and wasting money) is to avoid shopping when you're hungry. It's a well-researched fact that the hungrier a person is, the

more he or she will spend in the supermarket. (Supermarket managers aren't dumb—they know that when you're hungry, everything looks a little more appetizing.) Here's how I banish the after-work munchies that sometimes plague me at the store. In the cooler months, I keep a small bag of energy bars in my car. When it's warm, I keep a bag of popcorn in the backseat ('cause it doesn't melt). As I head to the grocery store, I make sure to have a snack if I'm the least bit hungry. I just take a few minutes and munch in the parking lot before I enter the store. Believe it or not, those 59-cent snacks save me about $20 per shopping trip!

## A LITTLE LEEWAY CAN GO A LONG WAY

**$AVE** Now this may sound as though I'm contradicting myself, but as important as a shopping list is, don't use it with blinders on. I mean, if an item is on sale that's not on your list but that you might otherwise buy (and use), then by all means, buy it—if your budget allows and you have the room to store it. That way, you can take advantage of the sale price on an item that you would normally pay a lot more for.

But here's a sure-fire way to keep yourself from going overboard on those kinds of purchases: Set a limit. My personal policy is to limit unscheduled buys to three per trip. You might want to make that number smaller or larger, or even set a dollar limit—but no matter what your limiting method, stick to it.

# Learning the Inside Dope

I'll bet most of you don't often chat with the folks who work in your supermarket, but it's one of my favorite ways to get the best deals. As I always say, "It pays to be in the know." Here's how to get the know-how you need to shop smart.

## ASK THE BUTCHER

**Y**ou know that the steak you're eyeing today will be about half the price in a couple of days—but when is that, exactly? Talk to the guy or gal behind the meat counter and ask what day *and* what time that meat gets reduced. That way, you can be sure to be first in line and save as much as 50 percent on your meat bill.

## QUIZ THE MANAGER

**O**kay—you've done your homework and made up your shopping list, and it includes lots of generics (good for you!). But every time you go to your supermarket, it's out of at least one of your favorite items, and that means you have to buy a more expensive item. What's the solution? Talk to the department managers and find out when the manufacturer delivers the goods. That way, you can be at the store bright and early on those days to pick up your favorites—and beat the competition. Here are

three more reasons to quiz your managers:

1. **He or she knows when the produce is fresh.** For example, you can find out from the produce manager when the carrots are due to arrive, and you'll know that's the day that the older ones will be on sale. And keep in mind that slightly wilted produce is still terrific for soups and stews! Keeping tabs on produce deliveries also means you'll be one of the first to know when the freshest fruits and vegetables are available.

2. **The manager has coupons.** Store managers often get coupons directly from manufacturers or distributors to share with their customers. You won't get them if you don't ask.

3. **The manager knows when sales will be.** Supermarket managers know when promotions and sales are being planned. That means they can let you know about them in advance, which can help you plan your shopping—and save lots of money.

## LITTLE ONES EQUAL BIG TROUBLE

Supermarkets can be especially cruel to parents and grandparents. Placing items such as candy in the same aisle as cereal triggers the automatic, "I want it, I want it!" response in kids and forces parents to spend more than planned. (Talk about impulse buys— these are payola to get the kids to quiet down and behave.) Here are some ways to make shopping with kids or grandkids a bit easier on the pocketbook:

★ If it's at all possible, the simplest solution is to leave the kids at home when you shop. (Hey, that's why God created dads and granddads!)

★ The next-best idea is to give the little ones a snack before you go inside. That way hunger pains won't cause them to wail for a sugary treat.

★ If all else fails, get the kids involved with sorting coupons or adding up prices. Even a toddler in the grocery cart seat is at just the right height to grab unbreakable

### SENIOR SAVINGS

**$AVE** Did you know that some supermarkets offer discounts to senior citizens? That's right—usually around 10 percent off the total. So if you're a senior—and that often means over age 50—find out if your local grocer offers a senior discount program. Some stores offer discounts only on certain days of the week or at specific times of day, so do your homework before you shop.

items off the shelves for you. The idea here is that if kids feel they're part of the process, they might just calm down and help you cut costs.

## GET DOWN IN THE DUMPS

Wanna save up to 50 percent on your grocery items? Here's where to look. Many stores have what they refer to as a "dump" section. It might include items in dented cans, items with torn labels, or the last few boxes of a product that the store will no longer carry in stock. These items are always marked down, sometimes by as much as 50 percent.

Of course, they're usually tucked away in a back corner of the store. If you aren't aware of a dump section in your favorite grocery store, just ask at the courtesy desk if there are items that fall into that category. (The only catch: Be careful when it comes to dented cans, and make sure that they're not leaking. A leaking can may harbor dangerous bacteria that can cause food poisoning.)

# MAKE A COURTESY CALL

**A**ll supermarkets have a courtesy counter or customer service desk. That's where you can return items, cash checks, get change, and drop off film, among many other services. But you've probably never, or rarely, stopped by the courtesy desk unless you've needed help, right? Well, the next time you're in the store, take a stroll over to that area because you may be surprised to find manufacturer's coupons, rebate forms, and other giveaways that are there for the taking.

## THE 5 WORST TIMES TO HEAD TO THE GROCERY STORE

\* \* \* \* \*

Are you the type of person who stays away from a movie on its opening weekend and steers clear of "grand opening" events until the novelty has worn off? If so, then you're the kind of person (like me!) who would rather not be grocery shopping when the aisles are jammed full of shoppers or the shelves are practically bare. When's that? Any time listed here:

☞ Weekends

☞ Weekday afternoons between 4 and 7 P.M. That's when the hungry (and cranky) on-the-way-home-from-work crowd takes over.

☞ The afternoon before a holiday. (Do you really want to shop for a turkey the day before Thanksgiving? Or appetizers on New Year's Eve? I don't think so.)

☞ During or just before a holiday weekend (the Fourth of July, Memorial Day, and so forth).

☞ The day the weatherman predicts a really big storm. (You should have already been stocked up!)

# Shopping for Super(market) Savings

You know that you should trim the fat from a piece of meat, right? Well, think about trimming those extra dollars from your grocery bill the same way. Of course, you know that I'm just loaded with ideas on how to carve off a few bucks and put them back where they belong—in your pocket!

## DO A PERIMETER CHECK

**M**aybe you haven't given this much thought, but take a hard look at the layout of your grocery store. Chances are that the unprocessed foods (produce, meat, dairy) are on the perimeter of the store, while the higher-priced processed foods (canned, bagged, and boxed goods; junk food; frozen meals) are in the interior aisles. If you buy most of your groceries from the perimeter of the store, you'll not only save money, but you'll eat healthier, too.

## GIVE 'EM THE DEEP FREEZE

**I**f you bake or do a lot of cooking around the holidays, you know that supermarkets usually jack up the price of dairy products such as butter, margarine, and milk right around that time. So plan ahead and save some dough (ha ha). About a month before you start your holiday baking, buy your butter, margarine, and milk, then freeze them—and put the freeze on lower prices. Then, when it's time to make those cookies, you'll have provisions on hand without having to hand over a bundle.

## PASS ON THE PAPER

**D**o you purchase your paper and other nonperishable items—paper towels, toilet paper, trash bags, and the like— at your grocery store? If you do, you're making a big mistake! You're most likely paying way too much money for nonfood

items there. Instead, head to a local discount store for nonfood items and you'll probably pay a whole lot less.

## ASK AND YE SHALL RECEIVE

It's just you and your better half at home, but every time you go to the grocery store for chicken thighs, all you can find is the family pack with a whopping 4 pounds of meat! Are you out of luck? Not at all! Few people know that they can actually request that meat and poultry be repackaged in smaller (read: less expensive) portions. Just ring that little bell at the meat counter and tell 'em exactly what you want.

## HEAD FOR THE SALAD BAR

Now, I'm not usually a big fan of prepared foods—they're darned expensive. But here's an instance when it's okay to break the rules. If your grocery store has a salad bar, a visit there can save you a bundle. Next time you're making a soup or a stew (or anything else, for that matter) that calls for, say,

### A REAL CASH COW

\* \* \* \* \*

Here's something to sink your teeth into: According to the Tufts Nutrition Newsletter, if the average family were to reduce the amount of meat they eat at each meal from 11 ounces to 3 ounces, they'd save about $2,000 a year.
Now *that's* food for thought!

just a cup of carrots, don't get your veggies from the produce section, where that package of carrots will cost you $1.39. Not only will you end up with more than you need for your recipe, but you'll pay more for it, too. That same cup of carrots from the salad bar will cost a whole lot less—and they're already washed, peeled, and sliced, saving you time *and* money!

## STOCK UP—IN SEASON

Of course you know that it's a good idea to stock up on your favorite foods when they're on sale, but did you know that many grocery items are at their cheapest when they're "in season"? Here are a few examples:

**Apples:** Apples are at their peak harvest from October to March, so these are the months when you'll get the best buys.

**Ham:** When Easter rolls around, you're going to find ham on sale, so stock up on it then and freeze it.

**Sweet Potatoes:** You'll find great buys on these spuds from October through December. Store them in a cool, dry place and your sweets will keep for two months.

**Turkey:** Seems like they're practically giving turkeys away come November! Well, turkey freezes just fine, so buy a couple if you've got the freezer space, and celebrate turkey day well into the new year.

## NATIONAL SAVINGS MONTHS

Food marketers have thought of everything— now it seems that every kind of food has its own celebratory month. The good news is that during a food's national savings month, it may be on sale—so mark your calendar accordingly. Here are just a few of the foods that we'll "celebrate" in the coming year:

**January:** Hot Tea Month, Soup Month

**February:** Canned Food Month, Snack Food Month

**March:** Peanut Month, Frozen Food Month, Noodle Month

**May:** Salad Month

**June:** Iced Tea Month, Turkey Lover's Month, Dairy Month

**July:** Ice Cream Month

**September:** Chicken Month, Honey Month

**October:** Pretzel Month

# Supermarket Sand Traps

Supermarket managers are pretty sharp cookies, if you know what I mean. Over the years, they've developed plenty of ways to attract your attention and get you to buy and spend more of your hard-earned dough than necessary. Here are some of the most common schemes they've come up with—along with some clever ways to outwit them.

## Interpreting the Signs

From the signs in the store windows to the circulars in your mailbox, your friendly neighborhood grocers are out to lure you in. So you need to know just how to interpret those "sales" and "specials" the stores are always advertising. And once you get inside the store, you need to keep on reading—and not only the in-store signs, but product labels, too. Here's how to read between the lines.

## READ IT AND REAP THE SAVINGS

They're right there, as big as they can be in the windows of your local supermarket—huge signs with the names of products and their prices, usually in big red letters and numbers, just screaming for attention! And those big ol' signs are designed to make you think that what's being advertised are great bargains. Well, my friends, don't be duped by this old marketing trick. Those prices may be accurate, but they may not necessarily mean that they're showing a sale price.

The advertisements in the mailbox or newspaper circulars work the same way, too. You may think that the reason they exist is to tell you about all of the great sale items (and to lie on your front porch and clog your mailbox), but that's not always the case. The only sure way to know if you're getting a better price is to know what the regular price was in the first place. (Remember that little price book I told you to carry? If not, turn to "Book It" on page 3 to refresh your memory!)

# DO THE MATH

**D**on't get caught by labels that claim you get "10 Percent More Free." Check the unit price that's listed on the shelf. The unit price tells you the cost per unit (such as ounce, pound, or sheet) of that product. The unit price can be found on a shelf display label

right below the product. If the unit price is missing, you can easily calculate it yourself. Simply divide the price by the number of units. For example, a 12-ounce bag of pretzels that costs $1.29 costs about 11 cents per ounce. Compare that to a 16-ounce bag that costs $1.40 to see which is the better buy (the larger bag, in this instance). But don't automatically assume that all larger-size products are cheaper in the long run. Sometimes a larger package is much more expensive than the slightly smaller no-name brand, or is actually more expensive than buying two smaller packages of the same brand. So always be sure to calculate the unit cost!

# DON'T BE FOOLED BY THE WORD "NEW"

**E**ver wonder what, exactly, it means when one of your favorite products sports a label proudly proclaiming "New and Improved"? Well, it usually means that the product has been *needlessly* improved (New color! New scent! New size!),

## KNOW YOUR GENERICS

Everyone knows that store brands are cheaper than nationally advertised brands, but many people don't like trading quality for economy. The good news is that you don't have to. Many stores now carry more than one variety of house brand, and some have as many as three quality levels. Look for these:

**Generics.** These usually have black-and-white labels and are the lowest-quality product for the cheapest price.

**House brands.** These are equivalent to the better-known "name" brands, but at a price that's about 20 percent less.

**Premium store brands.** These deluxe items are the equivalent of gourmet products for around 25 percent less.

which means that the manufacturer has decided to charge more for it, too. It's almost like they were looking for an excuse to raise the price, and so they created one.

## Navigating the Aisles

**Okay, so now you're savvy to the ways of advertising specials and tricky product labeling. But do you really know how to cruise through your grocery store and keep your expenses to a minimum? The managers are betting that you don't. Here's how to prove them wrong!**

## MAKE AN END RUN

**D**on't be fooled by those big displays they set up at the ends of aisles. They sure do catch your eye—I mean, they're right there for you to see as you turn the corner into the next aisle, and they're beckoning to you while you cool your heels in the checkout line. But I'll bet dollars to donuts that most

times those items are not on sale. (It's just like those big signs I talked about earlier.) Just because an item is singled out *does not* mean that it's specially priced. Look carefully for a sign that states the price. If it's less than usual, great. If not, then walk on by.

## ON THE (EYE) LEVEL

**Y**ou know the old joke about the guy who says he's on the "seafood" diet? (When he sees food, he eats it. Ha ha.) Well, the supermarket pros know that most folks are on the "see" food diet, too. That's why the marketers place their most expensive items smack-dab at eye level. That way, they're the first items you see and they're easy to get to, so you grab 'em. And manufacturers pay dearly for that exclusive piece of real estate, causing their prices to be even higher. But guess what? Chances are that if you look just a little higher or lower on the shelves, you can save quite a bundle. Who knew that a simple squat could save you a bunch of money at the store?

Another thing to remember is that this eye-level marketing

can get pretty sophisticated, especially when it comes to products for kids. Their eye level is a lot lower than yours is, and it's at *their* eye level where you'll find the most expensive (and usually least nutritious) children's breakfast cereals.

## LEAVE THE ENTERTAINMENT BEHIND

**D**o your television watching at home, and read your newspaper at home, too, and you'll save yourself some money

---

### SHOP SMART AND SAVE

Here's a recap of the savings strategies I've told you about so far. Put these into practice every time you shop, and I guarantee that you will come home with money in your pocket!

✦ Shop alone. It cuts down on distractions and impulse buying.

✦ Stick to your list. Allow yourself only a set number of unplanned purchases.

✦ Snack first. A quick snack before you enter the store will keep you focused on the stuff you need, not on what you crave.

✦ Don't forget your price book. You won't know if a "bargain" is real if you don't have your price book with you.

✦ Carry your coupons. No point in spending time clipping, sorting, and filing if you leave them at home!

✦ Buy a larger-size item only if the unit price indicates that it's a better deal than the smaller-size package.

✦ Buy generics. "Premium" store brands are comparable to gourmet brands, but at prices that are 25 percent less.

✦ Stick to the perimeter. If you limit the majority of your purchases to the outer store aisles, you avoid traipsing through the prepared foods sections, where prices are highest.

✦ Cash is king. Leave your credit and debit cards at home, and you'll only be able to buy what you can afford.

✦ Check the circulars and newspaper inserts every week for specials and sales.

on groceries. How's that? You see, supermarkets these days do all they can to get you to linger in the store and (they hope) spend more money. Some larger stores even have televisions set up and newspapers available in seated café areas, all with the thought of keeping you in the store a little while longer. So the long and the short of it is, don't get comfortable if you want to save money!

## IT'S MUSIC TO YOUR EARS!

**W**earing a Walkman or other personal stereo while you're shopping will save you money. You're probably scratching your head at that one. Well, you see, not only are supermarkets a feast for the eyes and nose, but those rascally grocers attack your ears, too, to get you to buy more!

How do they do that? Just listen to the music playing in the supermarket—it's music in a major chord range because market researchers have found that people tend to buy more (and therefore spend more) when happy, bright music is playing.

Another ploy supermarkets use to get you to linger and spend more is to play a selection of music that includes lots of top favorites and golden oldies. That way (they reason), you'll stay a little longer to hear the end of the song and—oh yeah—buy something else while you're standing there.

## Checking Out

**If you've been following any of my advice, you're probably already an expert shopper. So let your expertise carry you quickly through the checkout. If I have a choice (and I usually do), I won't shop in a supermarket with fewer than five regular and two express checkout lanes open during my regular shopping hours, for two reasons. First, remember that time is money: The longer you wait in line, the more money it's costing you. The second reason is that the more overworked the cashier is, the more likely it is that mistakes will be made—and not necessarily in your favor! Here are some other tactics for making your next checkout experience as painless as possible.**

## THE LONG AND SHORT OF IT

**D**on't automatically go for the shortest checkout line. First, check out the cashiers for a moment or two. Are they paying attention to what they're doing, or do they seem to have their heads in the clouds? Are they courteous and helpful, or are they just looking to move on to the next customer? Also be alert for "traffic jams." A line may be short because the cashier is waiting for a price check or some other time-consuming task to be done before she can finish up with the person at the head of the line. That makes the line shorter as people get impatient with the wait and move to other checkout lanes. Dash into this kind of short line, and you may be the last one out the door!

## SCAN THE SCANNERS

**I** have to chuckle every time I see a sign in a supermarket that says "We guarantee our scanner price is correct or you get the product free," because I know that the store could be—but isn't—giving away a lot of free groceries. Why not? Because most shoppers don't pay attention to the screen as the prices get scanned, so they never realize they're being overcharged.

Errors often occur when the prices are being entered into the computer system to begin with. That often happens on the first day of a sale, when the system may not have been updated thoroughly. So how do you avoid this trap? Paying attention to the screen is key, but only if you know what you're looking for. You must also jot down the prices of sale items on your grocery list. That way, you'll know there's been a mistake when the scanner charges you $3 for an item that's on sale at two for $1.

---

### RAIN CHECKS ARE WORTH THE WAIT

\* \* \* \* \*

Missed a sale because the sale item was sold out? You may have a second chance at saving some money. By law, products advertised as being on sale must be available or the store must give you a rain check for that item at the sale price (unless the advertisement clearly states that there are limited quantities). If the item is sold out by the time you get to the store, ask for a rain check at the customer service counter. Take it with you the next time you go shopping, and use it then.

# Ready, Set, Clip!

Y ou heard it here first, folks: There is some controversy about using coupons, refunds, and rebates. Some folks swear by 'em, while others won't touch 'em with a 10-foot pole. I think they're great, if you know *how* to use 'em and, just as important, when *not* to use 'em. So get out your scissors, and let's clip!

## Gathering Up the Savings

You probably already know that the Sunday papers are a treasure trove of coupons. But here are a few more ways to add to your coupon supply and save big.

## FIND THE COUPON

H ere are some obvious, and not so obvious, places to search for those clippable tickets to savings:

**Check the mail.** Yes, most of it is useless—after all, that's why they call it junk mail! But at least *some* of the advertising circulars that you receive contain valuable coupons and refund or rebate offers. Give those circu-

lars a second glance before you transfer them to the trash heap or recycling bin.

**Scan the shelves.** Supermarkets often display coupons and refund or rebate forms right on the shelf where the product is displayed.

**Don't forget your receipt.** These days, many supermarkets issue coupons on the backs of register receipts. Have you looked at them lately? If your store doesn't offer these coupons, switch to one that does (if it's convenient and the prices are competitive). These coupons usually work by tracking your purchases and making you offers accordingly. Say that you buy a few cans of tuna. When the cashier rings it up, the cash register prints out a money-saving coupon for the same (or a competing) brand of tuna. So you're almost always guaranteed to get a coupon for a product you want. And by the way, if you're not already scrutinizing your register receipts for mistakes, you're really missing out on a chance to save money!

**Read the package.** That's where you'll often find the manufacturer's toll-free number. Give the company a call and tell the operator how much you love the product, then ask about any discounts or coupons. Did

you know that 35 percent of all manufacturers send coupons to consumers who request them? Don't be left out!

**Be a scavenger.** If it's not against the regulations at your local recycling center, you can find a slew of coupons for the taking right there. Rummage through the stacks of store fliers, newspaper inserts, and junk mail, and you're sure to find coupons for just about any product you like. Wear gloves if you're squeamish about rummaging through someone else's trash. I always bring some string or packing tape to retie the bundle after I'm done.

## FUN COUPON FACTS

\* \* \* \* \*

☞ More than 80 percent of all shoppers in the United States use coupons of some kind. That's a lot of savings!

☞ Each year, nearly 5 billion coupons are redeemed by manufacturers.

☞ In 1999, manufacturers distributed 256 billion coupons. Shoppers saved $3.6 billion using coupons that year.

☞ The average face value of those coupons was 73 cents. (Sounds high to me!)

☞ With all that coupon clipping going on, you'd think that there would be only a few left over, but in fact, 96 percent of coupons are never used. And that's like throwing money away.

# COUPONS ON THE GO

I've discovered a great way to collect manufacturer's coupons that aren't distributed where I live. I collect them whenever I travel! Some of the best places to find them are in shopping malls and in the ATM vestibules of banks.

## LET YOUR FINGERS DO THE WALKING

**D**id you ever think about checking the phone book for savings? Well, take a look at your local Yellow Pages. Chances are, tucked inside is a section that includes money-saving coupons from local merchants. Most people skip right over these!

## OH, PAPERBOY!

**W**ouldn't it be great to get twice as many, or more, of those valuable newspaper coupon inserts delivered right to your door? Just ask your paperboy or papergirl to save any extra inserts and include them with your paper delivery. To make it worth his or her while, increase the tip from your savings.

ONLINE STEALS & DEALS

**What could be better than free coupons** just for the asking? How about free coupons for the *exact* products that you want? Here's how: Get online and go to **www.valupage.com.** There you'll find a list of supermarket products. Just select the ones you're interested in and print out your selection. Take the list along with you when you go shopping. When you buy anything on that list, the cashier will scan the bar code on your printout and you'll get Web Bucks, which are coupons good for items on your next shopping trip!

Free products, samples, rebates, and discounts are just a click away when you contact your favorite manufacturer's Web site (the address is usually posted on the side of the package). You'll frequently find offers for free samples and refunds listed at the site.

*A word of advice:* The way Web sites come and go these days, there's no guarantee that the sites mentioned here will still be in existence by the time you read this. So to save yourself some aggravation—and find new sites—start by searching the Web for "manufacturer's coupons" or "product discounts," and see what comes up.

## START A SWAP MEET

**G**et two, three, or even more friends together to start a coupon swap club. Have everyone collect as many coupons as they can, then once a week (or however frequently you choose) meet and exchange coupons. If you can't get your friends interested in joining your coupon crusade, don't give up. There are plenty of folks like you out there. Ask the manager of your local supermarket if he or she will allow you to set up a coupon box. That way, like-minded customers will have a place to drop off their unused or unwanted coupons and pick up someone else's discards.

---

### COUPONS: A BRIEF HISTORY

**\* \* \* \* \***

You know, coupons are a relatively young phenomenon. Here's a timeline to ponder while you plan your next visit to the supermarket.

**1894: Things Start with Coke.** Asa Candler, the wily druggist and entrepreneur who bought the formula for Coca-Cola, distributes handwritten tickets offering a free glass of his new fountain tonic.

**1895: Nuts to You.** C. W. Post, the cereal manufacturer, distributes the first grocery coupons, worth a whopping one cent each, for his new health cereal, Grape Nuts.

**1930s: Coupons Catch On.** During the Depression, everyone needs to save money wherever possible, and clipping coupons cuts family grocery costs.

**1965: It's Fifty-Fifty.** Half of all the people in the United States are regular coupon users.

**1995: Cyber Savings Begin.** The first coupons are offered on the Internet.

---

## CONTROL COUPON CLUTTER

**I**f you've fallen for coupon clipping in a big way, you may soon find yourself drowning in these small scraps of paper! And all the coupons in the world won't do you a bit of good if you don't have them organized for easy access. Here are some ways to keep yours where you want 'em—and easy to find when you need 'em:

**Use double-duty envelopes.** You know you need two things when you go grocery shopping—your list and your coupons. Be smart and stay organized by saving used envelopes. When it's time to make up your grocery list, write it on the back of one of those envelopes. Then grab the coupons you'll need and tuck them right inside. You're ready to shop and save! (I've also used an old leather billfold to hold my shopping list and coupons.)

**Create a filing system.** I keep my coupons in an old tax folder in my office at home. (It's one of those expanding folders with spots for different labels.) My coupons are organized alphabetically by product type. When I need a coupon for, say, frozen spinach, it's very easy to find, right there under "Vegetables, Frozen."

**Root out the old ones.** Don't become a pack rat. Go through your coupon stash regularly to remind yourself of what's in there and to check the expiration dates. Anything that's of no use or has expired—trash!

## LEAVE YOURSELF A CLUE

You can save even more money on your groceries by leaving a small border around your coupons when you cut them out. No, I'm not kidding! I'm very particular about which coupons I use at which store. I always want to use my coupons where the item I'm shopping for is already cheap. But I've found that once I clip a coupon and file it away, I often forget which store I designated that coupon for. (My memory's not as good as it used to be.) But I came up with a truly clever, simple, and free solution. These days, every time I clip a coupon, I just leave a little extra border along one side. That's where I jot down the name of the store I'll use it at!

## HIT A DOUBLE

Shop around for a store that accepts manufacturers' coupons and the supermarket's own coupons for the same products—at the same time. It's like doubling your money! Also, be on the lookout for stores that double coupons. Many no longer do, but sometimes they'll have a special "double coupon week," so be sure to check the fliers.

## KEEP IT COURTEOUS

It's no fun when the person in front of you in the checkout line hands over a big wad of coupons, then finds out that the store doesn't accept them, or that some of the coupons have expired. And it's *really* no fun (and can be downright embarrassing) when it happens to you. So please, when you use coupons, use some common courtesy. Tell your cashier up front—before she or he starts to ring you up—and hand over the coupons right then and there. That'll save you a lot of time, money, and unnecessary hassle, and will earn you thanks from your fellow shoppers!

## Raking in the Refunds

**Using coupons isn't the only way to spend less at the supermarket. There are two other moneysaving methods you should know more about and use whenever possible. Or maybe it's just one more, 'cause I can hardly tell them apart. I'm talking about refunds and rebates. A refund or rebate is money back, a gift, or a free product that you get from a manufacturer in return for**

**buying its product. But don't jump at every refund or rebate offer you see. Read the requirements carefully and make sure it's worth your time and effort. If you follow my advice, you'll never miss a worthwhile refund opportunity again!**

## IN GOOD FORM

**M**ake sure that you have the right form to get your refund or rebate. Sometimes the form is on a pad hanging from the shelf near the product or attached to an aisle display case. Once in a while, you need to ask for the form at the courtesy desk. Sometimes you can send away to the company for a form, via the post office or through e-mail.

### HAVE POSITIVE PROOF

* * * * *

Most every rebate or refund offer requires a proof of purchase. That usually means you must supply one (or more) of the following: the bar code from the package, a box top, or the cash register receipt.

## THE ENVELOPE, PLEASE

**I**f you need more than one proof of purchase (say, several box tops), keep them in an envelope with the rebate address on it, and pencil in the expiration date (if there is one) and prod- uct name in an inconspicuous spot. (You can erase it later.) Put a stamp inside the envelope, and paper-clip the envelope closed. Then put the whole thing somewhere you can find it. Once you have all of the required stuff inside, stamp and seal the envelope and drop it in the mail.

# Alternative Saving Strategies

**N**ow that you've conquered the challenge of saving big at the grocery store, you may want to set your sights on some alternative shopping arenas— namely, buying clubs and food co-ops. While they're not everyone's cup of tea, the savings can be substantial. To find out if they're right for you, read on.

## Shopping the Clubs: Is It Worth It?

These days, it seems that just about everyone's joining a buying club—you know, one of those warehouselike super-supermarkets where you can buy everything from groceries to vitamins in bulk quantities. But is it as great a deal as it seems? Well, as with almost everything else in life, it depends. Let me play devil's advocate for the moment and offer some things you should consider before you go clubbing.

## TOO MUCH OF A GOOD THING?

Sure, you might eventually use three tubes of toothpaste, but will you really use up three tubes of antibiotic ointment before they expire? Three reams of paper for your printer might be nice to have on hand, but what about 300 ballpoint pens? Where are you going to put them all? Bulk prices may seem great, but the catch is that you can't buy just one of anything, or if you can, you can be sure that it'll be a big one—like that platoon-size jar of mayonnaise! So before you plunk down your hard-earned cash on 24 dozen eggs, ask yourself:

**Where's it gonna go?** Do you have the closet space for 140 rolls of toilet paper? Or a 25-pound bag of white rice? Do you have access to smaller storage containers to break down larger packages if you need to?

**Will you use it quickly enough?** Many items spoil or reach their expiration date long before you get a chance to use them. Some things don't store well to begin with. (On the other hand, some items, such as toilet paper, never get old—but that leads us back to the first question.)

**Are you just in it for the thrill?** Some folks just can't turn their backs on a bargain—even when it means purchasing quantities of items they will *never* use! How else can you explain the buying habits of the bachelor who took home a dozen 10-pound bags of potato chips? Or the retirees who found themselves staring at three cases of tuna, when they only ate a tuna sandwich about once a month? Don't be lured into buying in bulk just because it's a bargain!

## GET FRIENDLY

If you're determined to join a buying club and purchase in bulk, be sensible and split the membership fee with a friend or family member. Since most

clubs give you a photo ID, you'll need to be the one who actually gets out and does the shopping for the two of you. But think of the savings: Not only does this halve the storage problem, but it can also halve your shopping bills if you go in on the same item (say, 10 pounds of Cheerios) and split the product into smaller containers at home.

## SHOPPING THE CO-OP WAY

The problem with most supermarkets is that someone else controls the price of the groceries. Wouldn't it be great if you had a say in that decision? Well, if you're a member of a food cooperative, or co-op, you do. As a co-op member, you also get a say in what the store carries, who works there, and who gets to shop there!

So what exactly is a food co-op? Well, it's a company owned and managed by its members. Those members pool their money and purchase goods in bulk to resell. In addition to financing purchases, members of a co-op are responsible for managing it, too, and most times that means the members must work in the co-op a certain number of hours each week or month. The co-op can sell whatever merchandise the members

agree to, and that can include products other than groceries. Some co-ops are strictly members-only, while others allow nonmembers to shop—but they usually have to pay a little more.

All in all, I'm a big fan of food co-ops, and if it sounds like a good idea to you, check your local Yellow Pages to find out whether there's one in your neighborhood. If not, get some friends together and start one yourself!

You can also go online to locate your nearest food co-op. Set your browser for **www.cooperativegrocer.com/coopdir.html;** that is where you'll find a search engine that gives you the names and locations of nearby co-ops by searching your zip code. The site is run by the folks who publish *Cooperative Grocer Magazine*, a bimonthly trade magazine for food cooperatives.

# CHAPTER 2

# Get Dressed for Less

They say that clothes make the man; I guess that the same applies to the ladies, too. And it's true: From a distance, you can recognize your neighbors and friends by the clothes they wear even before you notice the way they walk. And when you meet someone for the first time, you can tell a lot about him or her just by the way they're dressed.

When I was just a wee lad living with my Grandma Putt, we didn't have very much money, but we were always among the most well-dressed folks in town. Many of the clothes I wore came from the local second-hand store. That's not to say that we didn't have fine clothes for dressy occasions. Grandma had a keen eye for quality and a sharp mind for a deal. (You might say that she was the original cheapskate!)

In this chapter, you'll find some clever ways to think about how, where, and when to spend less on clothes. Remember: You don't have to break the bank to look like a million bucks!

# Clothing Know-How

**B**efore you can get a good deal when buying clothes, you have to know just what makes an article of clothing worth buying. (A cheap price can be a real bargain—or the sign of a cheaply made suit.) I'll show you how to find the bargains without compromising quality. I'll also let you in on my secrets for shopping success. Hint: It all starts with a plan.

## Getting What You Pay For

A brand-new $1 shirt (if there were such a thing!) would last about a week before coming apart at the seams—and that's exactly what you'd expect for your dollar. But if the same thing happens to a $30 shirt—*arrrgh!*—you've been had. You may think that sticking to big-name labels ensures good-quality clothes, but don't let those designer labels fool you. When it comes to buying new or used clothing, quality depends on who did the sewing and what the garment is made of.

Here's how to make sure that what you pay for is the longest-wearing, best-made piece of clothing your money can buy.

## STITCH AND TELL

**R**emember that a garment is made of many parts, and those parts are all held together by stitches. The closer, neater, and stronger the stitching is, the better-made and longer-lasting the garment will be.

If you see hand stitching somewhere on a previously owned garment, it might indicate a repair, but it also could mean that the garment was custom made (ooh la la!) or has been altered. As long as the stitching is straight, strong, and doesn't look like an emergency patch job, then don't worry about it.

## BODACIOUS BUTTONS

**W**hen you're considering buying an article of clothing, give the buttons a tug. Are they sewn on securely? Is there a button for every hole? (Of course, even if a button is missing, it's not

such a big deal—you may even get a discount because of it.)

Take a look at the buttonholes. If they're not reinforced (that is, sewn through both sides of the fabric), they'll fray and look terrible in no time at all. If that's the case, give that piece of clothing a pass.

## SEAMS OKAY TO ME

**T**ake a look at the seams where the parts of a garment are joined together, such as where the arm meets the shoulder. Those seams should be flat, not all bunched up.

All the hems, whether on a cuff or a pant leg, should be straight, and you shouldn't see the stitching on the outside of the garment (unless that's the style, of course).

## LOOK OVER THE CLOSURES

**A**re you eyeing a shirt that has snaps down the front instead of buttons? Be sure that the snaps line up and that each one snaps securely. Close the snaps and give a gentle tug. If they pop right open, that shirt will be embarrassing to wear!

If a garment has a zipper, check to see that the zipper is

---

### HOW LONG WILL IT LAST?

\* \* \* \* \*

You've just spent big bucks on a new suit, and you're wondering just how long it will look good. Well, check out the figures below. These estimates, which come from clothing manufacturers, are for how long frequently worn clothing will last. If you take proper care of your clothing—keep it clean, hang it up, and wear it less frequently—who knows? You might be able to pass it along to the next generation!

| Item | How Long It Will Last |
|---|---|
| Coat, cloth | 3 years |
| Coat, leather | 4 years |
| Dress, casual/work | 2 years |
| Dress, eveningwear | 3 years |
| Shirt, cotton or cotton blend | 2 to 3 years |
| Suit, lightweight | 2 years |
| Suit, wool or wool blend | 4 years |
| Sweater | 4 years |

## DRY-CLEAN ONLY—
## IT'LL CLEAN YOU OUT!

There's nothing worse than bringing home a bargain only to find out that it costs a lot more in the long run than you originally thought. That's the case with most clothing that needs to be dry-cleaned.

So a word of advice: Always check the labels and be on the lookout for the dreaded "Dry-clean only" tag. Even if the price of the garment is right, having to professionally dry-clean it several times a year can double its cost—after all, dry cleaning a basic skirt or blouse can cost several dollars at a crack. In fact, over time, you may find that you spent more money on the dry cleaning than you paid for the clothes in the first place!

Of course, some items (such as suits and blazers that you wear to the office, or special-occasion clothing) must be dry-cleaned. But it's simply not cost-effective to buy casual clothing that needs any sort of special treatment.

sewn in straight and securely. Zip it open and closed a few times to be sure it closes smoothly. If you have to tug and pull to get it to close, put that garment back on the rack!

## PERFECT POCKETS

If the garment has pockets, they should be flat and have reinforced corners. And if you ask me, they should be functional—not just for show—and big enough to actually use.

## FABULOUS FABRIC

Take a good look at the fabric from which the garment is made. It should look flat and evenly woven (or knit) with no flaws—unless it's made from a fiber such as wool or raw silk that will have natural flaws.

## PREDICTABLE PATTERNS

Plaids, pinstripes, and checks should match at the seams and not look like a crazy quilt, going in all different directions. On long-sleeved garments, check under the arms and down the sleeve seams. On short-sleeved shirts, pants, and skirts, check that plaids or stripes match from front to back at the side seams. And be especially vigilant when scoping out the back center seam of pants. There's nothing worse than plaids, stripes, or checks that go haywire right on your rear end, where it's most noticeable!

## SHOP FOR STRENGTH

**I**f you're a high-paid, high-fashion model, then you probably don't worry much about how long your clothes last. (Of course, if you're a high-paid, high-fashion model, what the heck are you doing reading this?) For the rest of us, it matters a great deal that the clothing we buy with our hard-earned cash lasts as long as possible.

Here are some long-wearing fabrics to look for when you shop for new duds:

**Acrylic is A-1.** When it comes to items like socks and sportswear, you can't beat acrylic. It lasts and lasts, and it's resilient, too, which means it keeps its shape, doesn't shrink, and won't wrinkle. (Okay, so it does pill a little, but nobody's perfect!)

**Choose chambray.** Chambray is a 50-50 blend of polyester and cotton. It's a bit lighter than twill (see below), but it resists wrinkles and is a good choice for casual clothing.

**Kudos for cotton.** I'm a natural-fiber kind of guy, and that means I like cotton. Cotton clothes of all types tend to be pretty durable. Oh, they wrinkle, of course, but nothing feels better against your skin.

**Nylon is nifty.** Nylon is as tough as nails and it's easy to care for. It doesn't wrinkle, either. It's a popular fabric for sportswear, pants, jackets, skirts, raincoats, windbreakers, and kids' clothing.

**The thrill of twill.** Twill is a blend of 65 percent polyester and 35 percent cotton and it's darned durable—that's why I like it for my work clothes. Even better is that it's already preshrunk, which means my size 38-waist trousers don't become a size 34 after the first washing.

**Want free clothing,** like maybe some T-shirts? Go online to **www.freeclutter.com.** That site is updated every day with all sorts of offers for free stuff, from baby gear to software to books. Just go to the site's main page and click on clothing. That'll take you to a page with a list of companies that are giving away free T-shirts, hats, and the like. Most times, all you have to do is submit your name and address; other times, you'll need to fill out a brief survey. But isn't five minutes of your time worth some free stuff?

*A word of advice:* There's no guarantee that the sites mentioned here will still be in existence by the time you read this. So to make the most of your Web search—and find some new sites—start by searching the Web for "free stuff" and see what comes up.

**Be bully for wool.** I love wool. It's warm, even when it gets wet; it's durable (I have some *really* old sweaters and coats); and it just plain looks and feels good.

## BE CHEAP—NOT SILLY

**N**ow that you know what makes a good piece of clothing, don't disappoint me by running out to the five and dime to do your shopping. Sure, discount stores have their advantages, but they're *not* where you're going to find the best, longest-wearing clothing. Go ahead and shop for socks, underwear, and the like at the discount chains, but for a quality wardrobe, you should scout around a bit more.

## Make a Plan, Stan

Before I shop for clothing—or groceries, or anything else, for that matter—I start off with a plan and a budget. I decide at the outset what I'm looking for and how much I'm prepared to spend on that item. I try not to give in to impulses. (Okay, there *was* that pair of red suspenders that looked really sharp in the store!) That way I never feel like I got taken, and if I spend less than my maximum amount, I leave the store feeling like I really got a bargain. Here are some of my sure-fire planning tips to make your next shopping excursion more productive.

## RECYCLE THE MISFITS

\* \* \* \* \*

I know, this chapter is about *acquiring* clothing, but I can't resist this one. I'm the guy who's always saying, "Don't throw it away!" And the same is true when it comes to clothes—especially those that, when they were given to you, you opened the box and thought, "Oh no!"

Let's say you received a perfectly icky tie from Aunt Mabel last Christmas, and you want to get rid of it and buy one that actually matches your wardrobe and your taste. Well, there's a wonderful way to do that without hurting ol' Aunt Mabel's feelings. Just take a snapshot of yourself wearing that dreadful tie and send it to Aunt Mabel with a nice thank-you note, then promptly drop off the tie at the local Salvation Army store. No harm done—in fact, you've done a good deed. Same goes for that dreadful sweater your sister knitted for you or those pj's from cousin Joe that you wouldn't be caught dead in. Send a thank-you photo, then find a good home for the items.

What if Aunt Mabel (or any of your other gift-givers) happens to drop by and ask you about the item they so lovingly presented? Well, just say it's at the dry cleaner's!

# TAKE YOUR SWATCHES SHOPPING

Say you're at the department store and you find the perfect blouse to match the blue skirt you have back home. *And* it's on sale at a bargain-basement price, so you decide to buy it. But what's this: All sales are final? And are you absolutely *certain* that the blouse matches the skirt?

Here's an ingenious way to always know. Go into your closet and take out every piece of clothing that needs a matching or coordinating item—let's say you have a pair of trousers and a skirt that you can't wear yet because you need tops for them. Now get yourself a sharp pair of scissors, some household glue, and an index card. Turn the clothing inside out and snip a small piece of fabric from inside a seam on each garment. Glue that fabric to the index card, let it dry, and then put it in your purse or wallet so you'll always have it with you when you're shopping.

You'll know exactly what color and fabric you're trying to match, and you'll never waste another cent—or shopping trip.

# DRESS FOR SHOPPING SUCCESS

Shopping can be tough on even the most experienced shopper, but you can make things a little easier for yourself by putting on the right clothes before you head out the door. That means wearing comfy clothes and shoes that are good for pounding the pavement. If you plan to try stuff on (and I recommend that you do because it saves you the hassle of having to return ill-fitting clothes), wear clothing that's easily removed. Here's the perfect shopping-wear: stretch pants or a skirt with an elastic waistband, a shirt that doesn't need to be tucked in, and slip-on shoes—clogs are great, lace-up boots aren't. With this easy-on/easy-off ensemble, you'll be able to try clothes on quickly.

# STAY AWAY!

Ready to head out to the store? Wait just a minute and check your calendar. Here are the top four times to avoid:

1. **Weekends.** They're made for Michelob—*not* shopping. Whenever possible, schedule your shopping trip for a weekday.

2. **Middle of the day.** Most days there will be a crowd between noon and 4 P.M. Luckily, most shopping centers are open from 10 A.M. to 9 P.M. Heck, some are even open 24 hours! So plan your shopping trips for weekday mornings or evenings.

3. **The day after Thanksgiving.** Black Friday, as it's called, is the traditional "kickoff" of the holiday shopping season. But wouldn't you rather stay home and watch a kickoff on TV than fight the hordes?

4. **The day after Christmas.** I know this is *the* day for bargains, but it's also *the* day for crowds. You choose.

Of course, you can avoid all the crowds all the time by shopping online or through a mail-order catalog!

# Ready, Set, Shop!

Okay, I'll confess it: I hate to shop for clothes. (Why should I be unlike most other guys?) I like to spend as little time on that particular activity as possible, so I've gotten my clothes shopping down to a science. Here are my best tips for getting the best bargains on new clothes!

## Saving a Bundle on Everyday Clothing

You're pretty sure that you're going to have to spend a bundle on fancy-schmancy clothes (you won't, but that's later in this chapter), but you're usually surprised to find that the stuff you wear every day is darned expensive, too. Ah-ha—not anymore! Here are some of my favorite (and most inventive, if I do say so myself) ways to stay within your budget.

## TAILOR-MADE SAVINGS

Never turn your nose up at hand-me-downs that are in good shape—especially if they're just a little too big. If the garment is a style that you like, take it to a tailor for a consult.

He or she might have a nifty idea for altering the garment or even just taking it in. (You'll find tailors and seamstresses listed in the Yellow Pages, or you can take the garment to your local dry cleaner. They sometimes do alterations, too.) With just a small investment, you might find yourself well-vested. Here are some ideas to take along with you:

**Men's or women's shirt.** Remove the sleeves and collar and turn it into a tank top. Or just trim and hem the sleeves and turn a long-sleeved shirt into a short-sleeved shirt.

**Men's shirt.** Remove the collar and give it a Nehru look.

**Shorts.** Sew up the leg openings, and turn them into a handy clothespin holder!

**Skirt.** Make a long skirt into a shorter skirt.

**Trousers.** Turn them into a pair of shorts.

# STOCK UP ON STAPLES

**M**y approach to clothes shopping is the same as my approach to grocery shopping: I stock up on staples when there's a good sale. By staples, I mean the basics like socks, T-shirts, underwear, and work jeans. And for those items I head to the discount store, *not* the department store, where they'll cost an arm and a leg.

# SOCK IT TWO 'EM!

**T**ired of ruining (or losing) one sock and getting stuck with the orphans? Here's how I cope: Every time I need a pair of socks, I buy two pairs in each color. That way, whenever one sock gets a hole or is eaten by the washer, I still have a complete pair. Here's how it works.

## 5 FOR THE PRICE OF 1

**$AVE**

No woman's closet should be without at least one 36 × 60-inch rectangle of hemmed fabric. Why? Because it serves so many purposes.

**1.** Drape it around your shoulders as a wrap.

**2.** Wrap it around your head as a stylish headband.

**3.** Tie it around your neck as a decorative scarf.

**4.** Twist it up and use it as a pretty belt.

**5.** Take it to the beach and tie it around your waist as a cover-up.

Let's label the socks A, B, C, and D. I take A and B out of the pack and wear them. Soon enough, A gets a hole or disappears. So I take C out of the second pack. Now I'm wearing B and C while D patiently waits its turn. Eventually B (the oldest sock) gets worn out, so I grab D. C and D are nearly the same age and wear out at about the same time—provided one of them doesn't disappear while traveling between the washer and the dryer!

## CORRAL THE CLASSICS

**D**on't you hate having a shirt or tie that doesn't match anything else that you own? You never get to wear it and it just sits there in the closet, taking up space. That's a real waste of money. For my basics (suits and pants), I always buy classic colors:

black, brown, dark green, and navy. That way, I know that whatever I buy will match what I already have in my closet. (See "The Frugal Gentleman's Closet," at right, for more tips.)

## TURN THE TABLES

**W**hen I shop for clothing in the menswear department of an expensive department store, I bypass the store's aggressive sales practices. Here's how:

You'll often see tables piled high with accessories such as ties, belts, and socks. The idea is that you'll come in, buy an expensive suit, then see the table full of items and think, "Gee, I need a tie, too." The store is counting on you making an impulse purchase (you know, the same way you decide you "need" things like candy at the checkout counter in a grocery store). You've already spent $400 on a suit—and now you've just spent another $100 on ties, a belt, and a handkerchief that you didn't need!

Because of that, I never buy accessories when I make a major purchase— I always make a separate trip for them when I know they'll be on sale.

---

### THE LONG AND THE SHORT OF SAVINGS

Say you're buying a pair of work trousers and you'll need them to last a long time. Here's a clever way to do just that. Buy the pants with the waist size you want, but in a length 4 or 5 inches longer than you need. (Of course, they'll cost the same as the shorter pair.) Now take the pants home and hem them yourself, saving the fabric you cut off the bottom of the pant legs. When it comes time to patch those work pants (and believe you me, that time will come!), you'll have an exact match for the fabric. (Though if the pants have been washed many times, the extra fabric will be darker.) The best part is, those perfect patches won't cost a cent more!

# THE FRUGAL GENTLEMAN'S CLOSET

* * * * *

Of course you choose your clothes with an eye toward looking good and feeling good in them. But if you're a guy like me, you like to keep things simple: not too many choices, and nothing that costs too much.

It's a good feeling to be able to reach into the closet and pull out just the right outfit to wear, whatever the occasion may be. And it's an even better feeling when you know that you chose your clothes frugally and carefully. While you can pick up some of these items at the local thrift store or bargain outlet, you may want to invest a little more in them because they're the basics and you'll be wearing them for a long time. Notice, too, that most of the clothes in this section can be worn throughout the year, both casually and formally. Pretty smart, huh?

Keep in mind that this is just a basic list. It doesn't take into account your own personal preferences or specialty clothes, like athletic wear, but it's a darned good place to start. (See page 43 for "The Frugal Woman's Closet".)

**A dark-color, medium-weight suit.** It can be worn to special occasions like weddings and funerals.

**Black leather shoes.** These can be worn with any item of clothing in your closet. A decent (read: more expensive) pair of shoes will last for years as long as they're properly cared for. Resole and reheel them when necessary, and polish them regularly.

**Gray flannel pants of medium weight.** These wear like iron, look dressy or casual, and their medium weight and color means that you can wear them in spring, winter, and fall.

**Navy blue blazer.** Fashions come and go, but the classics last forever. Men have been wearing navy blue blazers for years, and you will, too, if you invest in a well-made one.

**Seersucker jacket.** Now this might seem like a frivolous addition to your wardrobe, but there's nothing like it for making a pair of jeans and a T-shirt look dressy or a pair of dress pants look more casual and comfortable in the good ol' summertime.

**White and light blue button-down Oxford shirts.** White and light blue will go with anything in your wardrobe, and you can jazz them up with the addition of a colorful tie—or dress them down by going tieless and leaving the collar open. Look for shirts made of 100 percent cotton; they'll wash well and you'll get years of wear out of them.

## GET CARDED— SAVE MONEY

The next time you're shopping at a clothing store, ask the sales clerk if you'll get automatic savings if you apply for the store's credit card. Sometimes you can save 30 percent just for applying! I usually do this once or twice a year, then I just cut up the card when it arrives at my house.

**Note:** Don't do this too often, because too many credit applications can negatively affect your credit rating.

## IMPERFECT PIECE, PERFECT PRICE

Found a new item of clothing in a department store that has a missing button, slight stain, or other minor imperfection? *Always* ask a manager for a discount—believe you me, he or she is authorized to give it and would probably love to get rid of the merchandise. Ten percent is reasonable. Just make sure it's an imperfection that you can live with or fix cheaply at home!

### NO STRINGS ATTACHED

Research shows that *half* of all gift certificates are never redeemed— that's free money in the pockets of clothing manufacturers. So the next time you get a gift certificate, mark your calendar, leave yourself a note, do whatever it takes—just use it!

## LAY IT AWAY

Even in this day and age of the almighty credit card, there's an old-fashioned way to buy clothing without going into debt—it's the layaway plan. It seems like some folks have forgotten about it, but it's frugal and smart. Here's how it works: You pay a little up front, say 10 or 20 percent of the total cost, then pay an agreed-upon amount every week or month until your item is paid off.

Layaway beats credit cards hands down because you pay no interest. And Grandma Putt approved of layaway because it reinforced her old-fashioned values: You don't take something home until it's paid for.

Layaways will really save you a bundle if you can time your purchase to coincide with a particularly low price. For instance, one November I had my eye on a winter coat that cost $200. That price seemed a little steep, and I knew that my old coat had one more winter in it. In February, the store marked down the coat 10 percent to $180. I was tempted to buy it right then and there, but I decided instead to put it on lay-away. I paid my 20 percent ($36), then paid $16 every month. By the following December, I had a brand-new coat. The best part was that by

## SHOP FOR SEASONAL SAVINGS

\* \* \* \* \*

Did you know that the best time to buy summer clothing is in late July, August, and September? And the best time to buy winter clothes is in February. The stores are looking to clear out their winter inventory by then to make way for their spring lines.

Here's a month-by-month rundown of best buys:

| Month | What to Shop for |
| --- | --- |
| January | Summer sports clothes (like camping gear) and winter clothes |
| February | Look for Presidents' Day sales on winter clothing |
| March | Spring clothing and shoes, and winter outdoor clothing |
| April | Heavy woolen suits, heavy-weight dresses, and other winter stuff |
| May | Lightweight clothing and accessories |
| June | Summer clothes start to go on sale already! |
| July | Now's the time to look for big-time sales on summerwear, including bathing suits |
| August | Jackets and other outerwear goes on sale |
| September | Time for those back-to-school sales, but not for the very best deals; some summer clothing may be on sale, too |
| October | Now's the time to shop for back-to-school clothing—it's drastically reduced |
| November | Winter-is-coming sales on boots, gloves, and the like (but the best deals are to be had in January and February) |
| December | 'Tis the season to stock up on holiday-theme clothing for next year |

**BARGAIN ALERT!**

One day, a friend of mine went shopping at a department store and she found a special on slippers—the store was selling them at two pairs for the price of one. Well, she couldn't pass up that deal! The problem was, she really needed only one pair. But she came up with a clever solution, one that you should keep in mind if you come across the same situation: She stopped the first lady she saw walking by and offered to go halves with her on two pair of slippers. It worked!

that time, the store had jacked up the price to $220, but I got mine at the bargain price!

## SHOP WITH THE BIG BOYS

**A**ttention all you small-size ladies out there! Are you tired of paying top dollar for items such as T-shirts, casual shirts, and even jeans? Then, depending on how petite you are, head to the boy's or the men's department. The large-size boy's duds and the small-size men's clothing may be just the ticket—and they'll cost you a whole lot less than the ladies' equivalent!

# Shopping the Malls

Hate mall shopping? You're not alone. There are many of us (including yours truly) who just cringe at the thought of tramping through a crowded mall, dodging and weaving between the crowds, the crying babies, and the hordes of teenagers just hanging out. Well, if that's the way you feel, too, then try some of my strategies to help you deal with your next trip to the maul, um, I mean, mall.

## CHART YOUR COURSE FOR SAVINGS

**Y**ou organize your grocery shopping list in the same way your grocer's shelves are arranged, so why not organize your mall shopping list the way the stores are arranged? Gotta make five stops? You'll save time—and avoid impulse purchases—if you plan your route. First stop: shoe store for Timmy's new loafers. Second stop: pharmacy to pick up the prescription. Third stop: card shop for Grandma's birthday card. Fourth stop: department store for new towels. Final stop: gourmet shop for smoked sausage. Bam—you're done!

## TRY TANDEM SHOPPING

**Y**ou can't be in two places at once, but two shoppers can work as a team and shop more efficiently. For instance, you

---

### THE FRUGAL WOMAN'S CLOSET

\* \* \* \* \*

Ladies, do you often find yourselves buying items that you like, but that just don't go with anything else in your closet? Here's my sure-fire way to avoid that while saving money and looking beautiful: Create a Frugal Woman's Closet. It has only a few items, but you can mix and match all of them to get you through many, many weeks of wear without repeating the same outfit.

First, choose two colors from the so-called classics: beige, black, brown, camel, gray, green, navy, and tan. These two colors will form the foundation of your wardrobe.

Next, start shopping for key pieces of clothing. To my mind, it's wiser to spend more on these items because they're going to be the things you wear often, and you want good quality that will last.

**Black pants.** They'll go with everything and can look elegant or casual.

**Khakis.** All-cotton khaki slacks are great because they can look dressy or casual.

**Suits.** If you work in an office, you ought to have one or two suits in either or both of your colors.

**Skirts.** Choose skirts in two different colors and a couple of different lengths, too.

Now, to fill in the holes, buy your tops—each one should go with everything else you have. For instance, a white blouse will go with both of your suits, the black pants, the khakis, *and* both the skirts.

Does this wardrobe sound boring? It's not! Once you own the basic pieces (which will last for years), you can go nuts accessorizing with scarves, hats, jewelry—even loads of wild, inexpensive tops.

and a friend could take turns running packages out to the car. Or if the checkout lines are getting long, you could send your partner to wait in line for you. If the crowds are really large, your pal could do the shopping while you look for a parking spot! And let's face it: Having an objective second person by your side can help you make tough decisions. (Make sure to set up a time and meeting place, just in case you get separated.)

# Dressing Fancy for Fewer Dollars

Got a wedding coming up? Or maybe your daughter or granddaughter has a date for the prom? Well, here's good news. You don't have to pony up big bucks to go in style. Here are several ways to get those special-event outfits for a whole lot less.

## SHOP AND SWAP

**M**ost women I know have at least one perfectly wearable bridesmaid's dress collecting dust in the back of the closet. And that means all of your friends do, too. Those dresses can come in mighty handy for you or someone else, so get all of your friends together and start a dress-lending library. Whenever anyone in the group needs a fancy dress, let her go through all the bridesmaids' dresses and find just the right one!

---

## MAKE YOUR LIFE A LITTLE LESS TAXING

Now I'm not saying you should travel cross-country to save 8½ percent on that new dress or a pair of pumps, but if you happen to find yourself in or live near any of these states that don't charge sales tax, it's time to stock up.

✦ Alaska

✦ Delaware

✦ Montana

✦ New Hampshire

✦ Oregon

Some states (Massachusetts, Pennsylvania, and New Jersey, for instance) don't charge sales tax on clothing purchases under a certain amount—that could be anywhere from $75 to $500. So before you go discount (ha ha!) shopping in a certain city or state because you think it has a sales tax, call ahead just to make sure.

## RENT, DON'T BUY

**S**ure, you know you can rent a tux if you need one, but did you know that you can also rent wedding gowns and other formalwear for women? And don't limit yourself to the usual rental stores. If you live in a community that has a costume rental shop, you just might find a stunning outfit there!

## SHARE AND SHARE ALIKE

**S**pring and summer mean weddings, right? And you probably have a friend (or two) who has a wedding (or two) to attend. If you're all the same or nearly the same size and you're not going to the same events, why not go shopping together, and buy one dress to share for the season? You may be able to split the cost of one dress two or more ways! (Of course, this doesn't go just for weddings, but for any occasion that calls for an expensive outfit.)

## BREAK OUT THE GLUE GUN

**O**ne way to turn a dime-store bargain into an elegant treasure fit for the fanciest of occasions is to attach small accessories to it with fabric glue (available at craft stores). Those old pumps will come alive with the addition of some spangles. Some faux pearls will really liven up the neckline and hem of that old gown. Heck, even those rubber flip-flop sandals will look marvelous with some plastic flowers!

---

### NOT JUST FINANCIAL SUPPORT!

\* \* \* \* \*

My wife says that it was probably a man who invented pantyhose, because no woman would invent such a torturous device. Well, I can't say for sure who did invent them, but I know a way to make paying for hose a little less painful.

How? Always opt for support pantyhose. Why? The nylon in support pantyhose has a tighter weave, so the pantyhose is more durable and lasts longer—even through repeated washing and wearing. And that's something you can't say about your garden-variety hose!

# Saving Big on Little Clothes

You can invest in good clothes if you're an adult. After all, you're probably not going to outgrow them in a few years! But what about the young whippersnappers? Are you doomed to spend a fortune keeping your kids well dressed, only to have them grow out of their clothes before they can wear them out? Not if you follow the advice in this section.

## STAY A YARD AHEAD OF GROWING KIDS

**K**ids grow like weeds—and that's exactly what makes yard sales such a terrific source of kids' clothes. Clothing doesn't sell well at yard sales to begin with, so it's extra cheap. And

---

## COSTUMES ON THE CHEAP

\* \* \* \* \*

Does the price of store-bought Halloween costumes make you cry boo (hoo)? Well, here's a tip for those of you who don't have the time or the talent to make Halloween costumes for your kids or grandkids: Give 'em your old castaways.

Before you relegate your old clothes to the recycling bin, take a hard look at them. Wouldn't that old peasant blouse make a great costume for a Halloween gypsy? And a man's suit jacket is big and long enough to stuff with newspaper to fill out your little Frankenstein.

Be creative—lots of "ordinary" clothes can be turned into frighteningly terrific costumes with just a few easy alterations.

since your kid (or grandkid) is going to grow out of it anyway, it doesn't need to be perfect—especially if you're shopping for play clothes.

## A UNIFORMLY GOOD IDEA

**D**o you cringe when the September back-to-school clothes shopping season rolls around? Here's one way to avoid it altogether—try to get your school to adopt uniforms. Bring it up at the next school board meeting—you may be surprised at how many other parents are dying to save big bucks on kids' clothes.

If you don't think the uniform idea would fly, try to get your kids to adopt an "unofficial" uniform: maybe two or three pairs of pants and coordinating shirts that they immediately change out of once they get home from school. It'll save some of the "what-do-I-wear?" whining that usually takes place on school mornings, and you'll save the clothes from wear and tear. (This will work better with little ones than it will with teens, of course.)

## START A LENDING LIBRARY

**C**hances are, if you have rugrats of your own, then you know other parents, too. And just think of all those kids at the local school. What am I getting at? Well, why not start a clothing library? Get a group of parents together and ask everybody to wash, iron, and fold any clothes their kids have outgrown. Put all the clothes together grouped by size and gender. Then, when anyone needs an outfit or an item of clothing for their little one, they go to the "library" and take out an item. If the clothes are still wearable once that child outgrows them, the parent washes, irons, and folds the clothes and returns them to the library!

### ASK AND YE MIGHT RECEIVE

\* \* \* \* \*

Do you have a friend who knits? Ask them to knit your child a sweater. Or two. Folks who knit will tell you that making kid-size clothes is a breeze—it takes less than half the time of making regular adult-size garments.

# Thrifty Threads

You already know that thrift stores, yard sales, secondhand shops, and outlets are great sources for inexpensive clothing, but here are my tried-and-true tips to help you save even more!

## Exploring Thrift Shops

Do you think that your local secondhand shop is nothing more than a junk store? Think again—there are hundreds of bargains to be found in those shops. All it takes is a little know-how!

## SET YOUR SIGHTS ON SWANKY SAVINGS

If you're going to shop in thrift shops, head to the most upscale neighborhood near yours. Rich folks tend to purchase high-quality clothes—and they trade them in more often than we ordinary folks do.

## THE EARLY BIRD GETS THE DEAL

**$ BARGAIN ALERT!**

Here's an amazingly clever way to find really cheap clothing—if you're looking for large sizes, that is. Visit your local gym or diet center, and find out if it has an announcement or bulletin board. Add your own posting that says you'll be willing to buy dieters' clothing after members have shrunk out of it. The successful dieters will most likely be pleased as pie (sorry) to earn some money for their now-oversize clothes, and you'll get a new wardrobe for a song.

Weekends are the best time to shop in a thrift shop, right? Nope. The days for the biggest selection are Monday and Tuesday. Why? Well, most folks clear out their closets (and take clothes to thrift shops) on the weekends—and that means they'll be put out and ready for sale early in the week.

# GARDEN-VARIETY DUDS

**A**s you may know, I spend a lot of time out in the garden. How do I keep from destroying my everyday clothes when the sudden urge to whack a weed hits me? Well, right by the door that leads to the garden, I keep a set of old mechanic's coveralls on a hook. I just step into them, zip 'em up, and then I can get down and dirty without worrying about my good clothes.

But for the times when I'm *planning* to be out there, or for any other project that's going to get messy, I make sure that I'm wearing my cheapskate clothes—in other words, items that I've bought in thrift shops. That way I know that whatever I'm working in has been broken in and didn't cost me very much to begin with. It doesn't get any better than that!

## IS THAT BARGAIN REALLY A BARGAIN?

\* \* \* \* \*

You've set your sights on that leather blazer at the thrift shop, but the elbows are a little worn. So do you pass it up or snap it up? Here's what to be on the lookout for to help you decide whether your next find is trash or a treasure:

☞ **Worn elbows.** If they're on a woman's blouse or man's shirt, pass it up; but keep in mind that it's easy to patch the elbows of a blazer or sport jacket with store-bought leather or fabric patches.

☞ **Too short.** There's an easy way to lengthen kid's jeans. Just cut them off at the knee, sew on a band of colorful fabric, and reattach the bottom denim portion; or just add the fabric to the bottom of the pant leg. Unless you're shopping for "kickin' around the yard" clothing, pass on adult-size trousers that are too short.

☞ **Missing buttons.** That's a no-brainer— it's easy to replace buttons. But torn or misshapen buttonholes are another matter completely. Steer clear of any garment that has buttonholes in bad shape.

☞ **Ragged or frayed hem.** As long as you can rehem a garment to make it shorter (and you don't mind the work), a ragged hem shouldn't make much difference, be it on a skirt, dress, or pair of pants. Fixing a ragged hem on a coat can be tricky to do yourself, but any good seamstress should be able to do the job fairly inexpensively.

# Hitting the Outlets

**Just because that blouse is for sale in an outlet store doesn't mean it's cheap (or even cheaper than in a department store). Outlets can offer good buys, but getting them takes some shopping savvy. Your best bet for outlet savings is to combine a really good price with a store credit or gift certificate. Here are some other ways to save.**

## LEARN THE LABEL LINGO

**B**affled by the tags on the merchandise you find at outlet stores? How can you tell if you're getting a bargain if you don't even know what you're buying? Here's the lowdown on label lingo:

**Irregular.** Merchandise marked irregular is slightly imperfect. That means maybe the stitching is off a bit on the hem of a pair of pants, but it's not bad enough that anyone would notice.

**Seconds.** Anything marked a second is flawed—and proba-

bly noticeably so. When I go outlet shopping, I head for the seconds when I'm buying socks, underwear, casual clothing, towels, and linens, or anything else that I'm not too concerned about.

**Samples.** These can mean a style that the manufacturer was just trying out, or it could be display merchandise. These items can be real oddballs— shoes in size 5 only, or clothing in strange colors and sizes.

**Past season.** Last year's styles are this year's best buys. As long as it's in good shape, past season merchandise can be some of the best clothing bargains around.

**Discontinued.** This merchandise is stuff the manufacturer has just stopped making—maybe it's updating the style or color for next season. The items may be of first quality, but sizes may be limited. You might find only really large or really small sizes.

**Overstocks.** What happens when a manufacturer makes 50,000 pairs of mauve slippers,

## IS IT A KNOCKOFF—OR THE REAL DEAL?

* * * * *

Years ago, you could be pretty sure that the items you found at outlet stores were first-rate garments at terrific prices. These days, it's hard to know whether an item of clothing really is a great find that's been marked down or a cheapo piece of clothing made especially for the outlet store. Well, take a tip from the Better Business Bureau and look for items that have sewn-in labels that have been cut or marked. You can be fairly sure that those items are not second-rate.

but only 25,000 people buy them? You guessed it—the leftovers become overstocks. Those items are generally first quality and a first-rate buy.

## Shopping for Shoes

**Last, but not least, are shoes. When your shoes fit, it's easy to forget you even have feet! But when your shoes pinch and rub, well, you know how that is. So next time you head for the shoe shop, keep these tips in mind and you'll get the very best shoes for your money.**

## SEE THE REVEALING HEEL

Look at the heel of the shoe you're considering buying and notice how it's attached to the body. If the shoe is new, does the heel look sturdy? If the shoes have been previously owned, is the heel so worn that you'll need to have it replaced? That should affect the price.

## MAKE SURE ALL'S WELT

Examine the shoe's welt, which is the seam where the upper part attaches to the sole. Give it a tug to see if it's well attached. Is it stitched, or is it just glued? As you may have guessed, stitched is better!

## GET THE INSIDE SCOOP

**P**lace your hand inside the shoe: You shouldn't find holes or deeply worn grooves. Of course, if the shoe is used, there might be slight signs of wear, but avoid shoes that look worn out or abused.

## DISCOVER A COVER-UP

**M**any women's pumps have heels that are covered in the same material as the upper. Make sure that the material is in good shape and is not fraying around the bottom of the heel or at the inside seam. That material is usually impossible to repair.

## PERFORM RESCUE AND RECOVERY

**I**'m always shocked when I see people throwing away perfectly good shoes. I mean, don't they know that they could *double* the life of their shoes just by visiting the neighborhood shoe repair shop? Of course, not all shoes are salvageable. Those $10 sneakers with a hole in the sole belong at the dump, but "hard" shoes such as loafers, pumps, and bucks can all be repaired.

---

### IT'S HARD, BUT TRUE

\* \* \* \* \*

Isn't it funny how shoes often seem more comfortable in the shoe store than at home? It's no accident. You might notice that most shoe stores have really thick, cushy carpeting; usually it's so thick that it could make a pair of tight wooden clogs feel like slippers! So the next time you're shopping for shoes, walk off of that carpet and onto a hard floor or even out onto the sidewalk (if they'll let you), so you can make sure that those shoes are *really* comfortable.

---

Keep that in mind when you're visiting the local thrift shop and you walk past the shoe aisle. Those once-proud pumps you're eyeing can regain their former glory for just a few dollars!

## CHECK THE LOST AND FOUND

**B**y the way, when you stop by your local shoe repair shop, ask if he or she has any shoes for sale. That's right— most shoe repair shops have a policy stating that the shop is not responsible if a customer leaves a pair of shoes for more than a specified number of days (usually 30). And most shops are willing to unload those freshly repaired shoes for a song. After all, these shops are in the business of repairing shoes—not warehousing them.

Don't forget that the same policy usually applies to dry cleaners, too. So next time you stop by, ask if they have any clothes hanging around that are for sale!

## NIGHTTIME IS THE RIGHT TIME

**D**on't shop for shoes early in the day. Why? Because by evening, they might not fit.

You see, your feet actually swell as the day progresses, so you're better off buying your shoes in the late afternoon or early evening, when your dogs are at their largest.

### Pennypincher's Hall of Fame

Now I'm not one to discuss politics, but I have to admit that when it comes to being, um, tightfisted, Ralph Nader is a man after my own heart. According to a woman who used to work for Nader, he once showed off a pair of socks he was wearing and exclaimed, "See these socks? I've had these for 20 years! Army surplus. They're cheap and they last forever!"

Now *that's* cheap!

# CHAPTER 3

# Appliances and Electronics on the Cheap

Everyone knows I'm a smart shopper. Lessons on being frugal, informed, and just plain dogged in getting top-quality for low prices were taught to me by my Grandma Putt when I was just a pup, and they've stuck with me for a lifetime. I've had to learn my lessons the hard way and on my own, though, when it comes to shopping for appliances and electronics. Most of the "plug in" things I shop for—computers, printers, VCRs, microwaves, and so on— are things my greatest advisor on frugality never dreamed of owning. Grandma Putt did her dishes by hand, she wouldn't have known a VCR if she met one in a dark alley, and she darned sure never had (or had a need for) a home computer.

For lots of folks—me included—appliances and electronics are the two things we're intimidated about buying. But, it doesn't have to be that way. If you know what you want, how it works, and what you intend to pay for it, you *can* purchase appliances and electronics on the cheap.

# Know Before You Go

O kay, shoppers, here's the thing to focus
on when heading out to shop for electronics and appliances: Why do you want
it? It's such a simple question, but the fact is,
stores and salespeople everywhere are hoping
that before you make your purchase, you'll forget what
you came for. For example, you want a television—so you
can watch television, of course! But if a smooth salesman
can make you believe you want a *60-inch* television with
*surround sound* that can broadcast *two channels at once,*
then you'll be leaving a lot more of your hard-earned
dough behind when you walk out the door with your new
purchase. Or you may go looking for a dishwasher and
come home with a machine that warms plates and bakes a
turkey, too! These are the pitfalls of big-ticket shopping.

But don't get discouraged. Just follow my advice on
preparing for the big purchase, and you'll not only get
what you want, but you'll pay less for it, too!

## Doing Your Homework Pays Off

Before you set foot in an
appliance or electronics store,
it pays to do your homework.
Read on for tips on the best
times to shop, how to get
expert advice and information on your potential purchases, and why a used item
may be your best bet.

## MIND THE SEASON

M ost of us think of shopping in season as some-
thing we do only for fresh fruit
and seasonal clothes. But there
are seasons for appliances and
electronics, too. You'll usually
find these items offered during
two kinds of sales: clearance
sales (because no one is buying
an item) and competitive
sales (because everyone

wants one). I always wait for the clearance sales because, in my experience, they save you more money. But that may not always be practical—especially if your washing machine just spun its last cycle! Here's a rundown of when to look for what:

**November:** Heating appliances go on sale, spurred by lots of competition.

**December:** You'll find good buys on "gift" appliances and electronics, such as vacuum cleaners, microwaves, televisions, and computers. But if you can wait until after Christmas, the sales are often the best of the year, as stores look to clear out the old in anticipation of upgrading their stock for the coming year. Don't forget to look for open-box and scratch-and-dent returns during the first three weeks after Christmas, since stores want to unload holiday returns as quickly as possible.

**January and February:** This is traditionally a dry period for retailers, and there are good sales on appliances and electronics. Look for clearance on last year's models. These may not be the latest and greatest, but they are top-of-the-line,

fully warrantied versions of last years' must-haves.

**May and June:** Spring cleaning sales offer low prices on vacuum cleaners. Competitive reductions on air conditioners and refrigerators kick in just before Memorial Day and last well into June.

**July:** Of course, if you can hold out until July for your new AC, prices will start heading toward clearance levels by mid-month.

## KEEP IT SIMPLE

I try to look at it this way— every button and function on an appliance or piece of electronics is a potential malfunction. Does the usefulness of that switch outweigh the risk of it breaking and needing repair? (In other words, do you really need 16 different slider switches on the front of your stereo to adjust the treble and bass?) If the answer is no, then I look for a more streamlined (that's pronounced "less expensive") model. A good friend once told me that the secret to good appliance and electronics buying was just to stick with KISS. "It stands for 'Keep It Simple, Sweetie,'" she said. That's one of the best bits of advice I've heard yet!

# DO A LITTLE DIGGING

**M**ost of the time we spend shopping for new big-ticket plug-in items would be better spent in the library. The biggest problem shoppers face when making this kind of purchase is being overwhelmed with too many choices (all of which add to the purchase price, of course). Here's a guide to digging up the information you need to make a smart purchase:

**Ask an expert.** Is there a serviceperson who's been coming to your house for years, someone you count on? Ask for that person's opinion on which brand to choose before you head to the stores. (Be sure you get someone who services *all* brands.) Among service technicians, it is usually common knowledge which brands and models need the most frequent and serious

## 3 REASONS TO BUY NO-FRILLS MODELS

**1. They cost less!** Take the $80 printer and leave the $350 one on the shelf—the cheap one will print your letters and greeting cards just fine. The $1,000 computer will serve your needs just as well as the $3,000 one. That $800 refrigerator is going to keep your food just as cold as the one that costs $2,500. The differences in the prices of these machines isn't due to their basic functions—they all do the job they're designed to do. The differences are in fine details that, frankly, you're never going to miss.

**2. They break less often!** Every button, switch, and special feature is a potential breaking point on your new purchase. Choose machines that have only the features you really want and need, and you'll reduce the potential for mechanical failure.

**3. They're easier to use!** So you have a TV, VCR, stereo, computer, dishwasher, microwave, washing machine, and dryer—the works. They probably have 100 function options between them, maybe even more. As a man who has only just learned how to program the VCR but who still can't set the clock, I know I don't need any more extra options. Choose appliances and electronics that make your life easier, not more complicated.

service—and how much replacement parts cost, too.

**Get the scoop from Uncle Sam.** To find out if the product you're considering buying has any recalls or blemishes on its safety record, contact the Consumer Products Safety Commission. This government agency has an extensive site at **www.cpsc.gov**. From there, click on the "recalls" link to search by the product or manufacturer name. If you don't have access to a computer, no problem—call the CPSC's consumer hotline at (800) 638-2772 or (800) 638-8270 (for the hearing impaired). Records go all the way back to 1972, so this is a good resource to tap into before making used purchases, as well.

**Read all about it.** Before you make a commitment to a new appliance, take a quick trip to the library to read about the models and brands you have in mind. Now I know that time is money, but in this case, it's well worth the effort. The last thing you need is a washer, dryer, or vacuum cleaner with a record of not washing, drying, or vacuum cleaning! Check out the

*Consumer Reports* annual buying guide in the reference section of your library to get information on the latest and greatest models the electronics and appliances industries have to offer. You'll get an honest report from people who put all that stuff through its paces.

**Scan the ads.** If you're in the market for any major appliance or electronics equipment, you'll save yourself a lot of trouble by studying the ads in the Sunday paper for three or four weekends in a row before making a final decision. If you know what you want, you can price that item at several different stores, then make a beeline for the store that offers the best price.

# BEST BEEN-USED DEALS

To be sure, there are some fantastic deals sitting in the classified section of your local newspaper, just waiting for you. But it's also a sure bet that there's a lemon (or maybe two) for every one of those deals. If you're going to buy used appliances or electronics, here are some points to ponder:

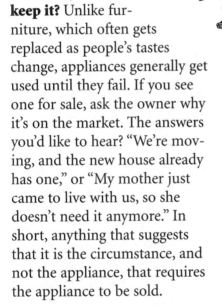

**If it's so great, why don't they keep it?** Unlike furniture, which often gets replaced as people's tastes change, appliances generally get used until they fail. If you see one for sale, ask the owner why it's on the market. The answers you'd like to hear? "We're moving, and the new house already has one," or "My mother just came to live with us, so she doesn't need it anymore." In short, anything that suggests that it is the circumstance, and not the appliance, that requires the appliance to be sold.

**Does it work?** This may sound really obvious, but you'd be surprised at the number of folks who don't bother to find out before they buy. As for me, I'd never buy an appliance or piece of electronics equipment that I couldn't plug in and try out first. If the sellers have nothing to hide, they'll be more than happy to show you that the item they're selling works just fine.

**How does it compare?** If you have a talent for appliance or electronics repair, you risk much less when buying used. If you don't have the skills to make at least minor repairs, be sure to compare the price you're looking to pay for a used machine with a similar machine from a used appli-

---

## ALL IN THE FAMILY
### * * * * *

Over the years, the number of manufacturers who make major home appliances has dwindled down to just a handful. The companies that remain produce appliances that bear several different names. Why should you care? Because many low-end appliances are made from the same components as their high-end cousins. So consider this when you're shopping:

✦ GE makes its own mid- and top-range products, and also the stripped-down Hotpoint models.

✦ Whirlpool makes not just Whirlpool and the more-expensive KitchenAid, but also the cheaper Roper line.

✦ Maytag makes the high-end Jenn-Air and the less-expensive Magic Chef.

So when you get ready to shop, try comparing a manufacturer's products to its own cheaper versions. You may be pleasantly surprised at how they measure up.

ance dealer. Most dealers offer a warranty on their used appliances—something you'll never get from a classified ad. (Be sure to ask whether that warranty includes labor or just parts. The labor hours are often the biggest repair expense.)

# WHEN USED IS ALMOST USELESS

While used appliances can often work just as well as their newer siblings, be wary of buying high-tech products—especially computers and "digi-

tal" anything—that are more than two years old. Technology is developing so quickly in this area that even recent models won't hold up to the standards of the near future. So while last year's TV or dishwasher, warranties and all, can be a fantastic buy for a smart shopper, an older computer or digital camera may not be compatible with today's technology, let alone with programs and upgrades coming down the line in the near future.

# SLOW THE FLOW...

Of electricity, that is. It pays to look at any appliance in terms of two kinds of costs: what you pay to get it out of the store and what you pay to run it once you're home. If you pay a small premium on an energy-efficient model, you may well recoup that cost during the first

---

**$ BARGAIN ALERT!**

Some utility companies will actually *pay you* to replace your old appliances. In many areas of the country, utility providers pay rebates when their customers replace older-model refrigerators, washers, dryers, and dishwashers with new, energy-efficient models. To find out if your utility company has such a program, call and ask before you shop for your appliance. Sometimes you have to preregister for the rebate before you make your purchase. The utility company can give you a list of products that meet their guidelines. Rebates can be as low as $20 and as high as $100 or even more on large appliances.

year of use. Keep in mind that the biggest energy-users are refrigerators, air conditioners, and dryers, in that order, so be sure to check the energy ratings on these items *before* you buy.

## DON'T CRY OVER SCRATCHES AND DENTS

**Y**ou know, I love an orderly house and all things in their place. It'd probably be fair to call me a perfectionist. But as far as I'm concerned, there's being particular, and then there's being wasteful. If I ever turned my back on a scratched, dented, or—better yet—open-box-but-otherwise-perfect appliance, I'd be passing on a great opportunity. So follow my example and don't shy away from these "blemished" items.

The best time to get open-box deals, as you might guess, is right after Christmas. All of the returned appliances and electronics stack up, and most stores are very eager to get rid of them to make room for new stock.

Most stores have a scratch-and-dent corner, but some warehouse and outlet stores specialize in carrying scratch-and-dent models. They may also specialize in fixing things like broken glass or cracked panels to bring the appliances back to almost-new quality. Just be sure that your item comes with the complete manufacturer's warranty on its performance. An appliance without a warranty isn't such a great deal, unless you can live without the appliance if and when something goes wrong.

## SIMPLE SWITCHES, PLEASE

**A** friend of mine who spent years as an appliance repairman confirmed what I'd always thought was true: an electronic keypad is the last thing you want on your shiny new appliance. You see, if a simple switch, dial, or button fails on your appliance, it's a cheap, easy fix for you or the repair person. But if an electronic keypad goes, parts and labor will run you a fortune. So whenever possible, go for the model with the clunky knobs instead of the cool keypad.

# WHEELING AND DEALING

**W**hen it comes to making big purchases, sometimes I feel a lot like a gambler. I've got to know when to push for a better deal and when to take what I've got and make tracks. The rules are a bit different depending on where you shop, so here's a guide to help you play your best hand:

**Retail stores.** Most appliance and electronics retailers won't deal on price, but many will throw in something extra if they think you're going to walk away. On big appliances, push for free delivery, no sales tax, or both. If you're going to transport it yourself, don't be afraid to ask to have an accessory thrown in (some places even sell the power cord separately!). The exception to this rule is on scratch-and-dent and open-box merchandise. These goodies have already been given up as not worthy of their original retail price, so the chances are fairly good that your salesperson or the sales manager has room to negotiate.

**Wholesale and discount centers.** You may be expected to handle your own delivery, but you can probably deal on price here. Offer 20 percent less than the asking price (or even less, if you think it's overpriced), and work from there.

**Dealing one-on-one.** Of course, no one needs to tell you to deal your heart out in person-to-person transactions. Private sellers know they're going to have to negotiate, and most take that into account when they set their asking price.

---

## AT YOUR SERVICE

**\* \* \* \* \***

Just how long can you expect your new appliance to last? Here's a rundown. Keep in mind, though, that an appliance that's well maintained could last almost forever, so don't lower your expectations!

- ☞ Washer: 8–12 years
- ☞ Dryer: 8–12 years
- ☞ Dishwasher: 5–10 years
- ☞ Refrigerator: 15–20 years
- ☞ Stove: 15–20 years

## A WORD ABOUT WARRANTIES

There are two kinds of warranties that you'll have to consider for any major appliance: the one that comes with your purchase and the one the salesperson will try to sell you. I highly recommend that you get the most complete, extensive warranty possible with your purchase, but never pay a single penny for an extra one. Those add-on warranties are money in the salesperson's pocket, but they're not likely to do you one bit of good.

# Appliance ABCs

To tell you the truth, an appliance in my house has to be completely belly-up before I'll replace it. I keep up the maintenance on all of our machines, make repairs when needed, and am not above using a little old-time ingenuity if it'll keep the dishwasher washing dishes or the VCR playing tapes. When I do have to bite the bullet and buy an appliance, I pity the poor salesperson who stands between me and my best deal! Here are my suggestions for getting the most bang for your appliance buck.

## Getting the Dirt on Washers and Dryers

We all need clean clothes, but boy oh boy, when it comes time to buy a washer or dryer—new or used—the costs can really add up. Here's how to get a good deal on these appliances.

## IT'S OKAY TO BE USED

Of all the appliances that can be purchased used, washers and dryers are the ones I'd be quickest to consider. Though there have been recent advances in the water efficiency of washers and the ability of dryers to stop when your clothes are dry, these appliances have largely remained similar to the ones made 5, 10, and even 15 years ago. Here's what to look for:

**Rust free for me.** If you're thinking about buying a used washing machine, be sure to carefully check for rust in the washer tub. If there is any, the tub must be replaced. But keep in mind that rust may not be limited to just the tub. If that's the case, the whole machine will have to be replaced in the not-too-distant future.

**Water-waste warning.** Be sure that any used washing machine you're considering allows you to adjust for the size of the load—you don't want to use a full tub of water if you're washing only half a load of clothes.

**Dryer beware.** When shopping for used dryers, make sure the air gets hot. The heating element is usually the first thing to go, and it can be costly to replace.

## PAY NOW OR PAY LATER

It's true that front-loading washers are more energy efficient than top loaders, but they cost hundreds of dollars more up front. It will likely take several years for you to make up the difference you'll pay to purchase a front-loading machine.

On the other hand, gas dryers, which cost up to $100 more than electric, are energy efficient enough to make up that cost difference quickly.

## IT JUST MAKES SENSE

When buying a new dryer, look for one with a moisture sensor. It will automatically

**$ BARGAIN ALERT!** ↓

Is there an appliance repair shop in your neighborhood? It might be a terrific place to do some shopping. You see, most repair shops have a policy that the shop is not responsible for items left after, say, 90 days. That means your local shop may have a supply of appliances—freshly repaired—for a song.

shut the dryer off when your clothes are dry, saving on your electric bill and making your clothes last longer by not burning them to a crisp.

# Finding a Fridge

**Your fridge is probably your most expensive appliance, and it's also the one that uses the most energy—by all estimates, it accounts for between 10 and 15 percent of the average utility bill. Follow these tips if you want to maximize your refrigerator dollar both when you make your purchase at the store *and* in your monthly tab to the utility company.**

## SOMETIMES NEWER IS BETTER...

Every season brings increasingly efficient refrigerator models to the stores. In fact, if you have a refrigerator that's more than 10 years old, you could probably run two of today's models for what it will cost to run just one older, less-efficient machine. To compare models, just read the yellow-and-black efficiency sticker that's on every fridge. It details the projected monthly energy use of each appliance.

## ...AND SOME THINGS WORK BETTER THE OLD-FASHIONED WAY

Don't automatically drift to the newer side-by-side models if you're hoping to get the highest energy efficiency from your refrigerator. Models with the freezer on the bottom are the cheapest when the utility bill rolls around, while models with the freezer on top come in second. Side-by-side models end up last.

## HOW MUCH IS THAT WATER WORTH, ANYWAY?

The world of fridge and freezer manufacturers would have us believe that there really is no greater convenience than water and ice that flow freely from their appliances. How great to fill your glass from that slot in the door, eh? Well, actually, in

# KEEP YOUR COOL
# WITH A USED REFRIGERATOR

Now you and I both know that there are times when a new refrigerator—good deal or not—is not in the budget. If a used fridge has to do the job, here's how to make sure you get a good one:

✦ **Go for youth.** Find out exactly how old the fridge is; the newer the model, the more energy efficient it will be.

✦ **Take its temperature.** Call ahead and ask the seller to have the refrigerator plugged in for you, then bring along a thermometer when you go to check it out. (In all fairness, give the seller at least 24 hours' notice—that's how long it can take for the temperature in a fridge to regulate after the unit has been shut off for a while.) Measure temperatures while you and the seller make small talk. Refrigerating compartments should be between 38° and 40°F. The freezer should be between 0° and 10°F.

✦ **Give it the paper test.** Close the refrigerator door on a sheet of paper or a dollar bill. If the paper falls out or slips, either the seal or the door hinges (or both) need repair.

✦ **Don't forget the yardstick.** The only feeling worse than hearing your old refrigerator take its last gasp is arriving home with a new one that doesn't fit in its appointed spot. Carefully measure your refrigerator space and your new appliance to make sure you've got a good fit.

✦ **See the rear view.** Make sure the coils are clean on the back of the fridge. If it works great and they're not, make a note to clean them the minute you get home. Just vacuum them, then wipe them with a damp cloth.

✦ **Clean it later, alligator.** If the refrigerator seems sound, don't let its lack of cleanliness turn you away. There won't be a slime, stain, or crumb in it that can't be easily removed with a little bleach or baking soda. In fact, you'll probably get a better deal on a dirty fridge than a clean one.

my kitchen, the tap is pretty darn close to the fridge, and I can just as easily fill my glass there. As for ice, I've been making it in ice cube trays for about 40 years now, and I don't see any compelling reason to stop. The fact is that fridge-produced water and ice come right out of your wallet, in three ways:

1. The day you buy the appliance, you'll pay a premium for built-in water and ice.

2. The fridge, of course, doesn't actually make the water. It comes from the very same pipes that run to your tap. Unfortunately, to get it into the fridge, you have to pay someone to run a water line. Average cost: about $100.

3. A fridge with an ice maker and a waterspout costs as much as 20 percent more to run than one without them.

# Dealing for Dishwashers

**If you've done your homework, you probably already know that almost all dishwashers are equally capable of washing a load of dirty dishes. What**

**you might not know is how to distinguish between the different models on the showroom floor. Here's a rundown of the features that make a difference and those that add big bucks to the cost, but very little to function.**

# HEAT IS NEAT

Ever wonder just how your dishwasher manages to get dishes so clean without the aid of scrubbing hands? The answer is the combination of extremely hot water and the abrasiveness of the dishwashing detergent—neither of which your bare hands could handle! But it's wasteful to set your hot water heater high enough to get really clean dishes (ideal washing temperature is about 140°F) and dangerous, too, because water that hot coming out of the tap can scald you. So pick a dishwasher with a temperature-boosting feature for the water. That one feature will do the job of most of those extra cycles dishwasher manufacturers offer and will allow you to keep your water heater at an economical lower temperature.

## IT'S UNI-CYCLE FOR ME!

The options on new dishwashers can be mind-boggling. There may be six or seven different wash cycles, depending on whether you're washing pots and pans, china, crystal, dishes with baked-on foods, and so on. But think twice before you invest more in a machine because it offers half a dozen different ways to wash your dishes. If you already have a dishwasher, ask yourself how often you run anything other than the "normal" cycle. If you're like me, the answer is probably never. I load the thing up, turn it on, and take the dishes out when it turns off. If you have one cycle you depend on, too, then don't waste your hard-earned money on features you don't need.

The same goes for the "dirt sensor" option that some manufacturers are offering. What the heck is that all about? Of course the dishes are dirty— that's why we're washing them! The adjustment that the dishwasher makes for dishes that are dirtier than others will probably never justify the extra cost of the machine.

## STEEL'S NOT A GOOD DEAL

Stainless steel cases may be the decor option of the moment, but they add big bucks to the price of a dishwasher, running up to $150 or more than other models. A stainless steel box can allow your washer to hold heat a bit better than a standard one, and I've been told that it will resist cracking. But if the case cracks on your new dishwasher, regardless of the make and model, you're entitled to a replacement. Most cases are warrantied for longer than most users keep the appliance.

---

### SILENCE REALLY IS GOLDEN

* * * * *

Or at least that's how it's priced. It may be worth it to some folks to pay the extra bucks for a truly quiet dishwasher, but know that the quietest models can cost twice as much as the standard loud ones. If you don't mind a little noise, you can save a lot of money on your dishwasher. Just think of that *swish-bang* ringing from the kitchen as the sweet sound of savings!

# Saving Big on Small Appliances

Microwaves, vacuums, air conditioners, and other small appliances can make a big dent in your wallet. But take my advice here and you'll learn how to shop smart and save a bundle!

$ BARGAIN ALERT!

Moving sales and garage sales are great places to find working microwave ovens at good prices. More and more new homes are coming equipped with built-in microwaves, and that leaves lots of working spares looking for new owners. To make sure a used microwave works, ask the seller to heat a cup of water in it for 2 minutes. The water should come out close to boiling hot.

## MINIMAL MICROWAVES

Some have turntables, others have meat probes. Some are compact enough to tuck into a tiny space, while others are big enough to bake a buffalo! (Just a slight exaggeration, of course.) But if all you really want to do is pop some popcorn and heat up small entrées, bypass the big, the option-filled, and the fancy designed, and feel free to buy the cheapest microwave you can find.

## GET AIR CONDITIONING DOWN TO SIZE

The size of your room, that is. I'm willing to give up just about any convenience except having a cool room on a hot day. But that room won't be very cool if the air conditioner that's cooling it isn't up to the job. The most important thing to do is measure the room area you want to cool *before* you start shopping. Believe it or not, a too-large capacity air conditioner won't cool your room any better than one that's too small. So get out your tape measure and know your square footage before you buy.

## CLEAN UP ON VACUUMS

Of all appliances, vacuums may have the biggest price range for the least difference in performance. You can literally spend thousands of dollars on a vacuum cleaner that cleans little or no better than a $200 model. Like the bigger appliances, this is an area where I prefer to go with the names I know. Companies like Hoover make vacuums in a wide range of prices, and in my experience, the low-end models from a good company like Hoover compare very well with the top-of-the-line models.

## TUNE IN TO TVS

There's good news on the entertainment front for bargain shoppers: The fact is, the industry has got itself twisted into knots trying to decide which makers and what machines will adopt new digital technology as standard, and which won't. For the clear-headed buyer, that means fantastic deals on the "old" technology that's been the standard for the last 10 to 15 years. If you're like me, you'll be very happy to watch the best picture last year's models can provide for a long time to come—after all, customers were beating down

## VCR VALUES

When it comes to VCRs, you can buy anything from a $70 model to one that will run you $300. Consider what you need from it: If you're just going to watch tapes, get the cheap model! If you want to record, too, you might want to spend a little more to get a model with VCR Plus—a feature that makes it much easier for technologically challenged folks like me to tape our favorite programs.

doors to get it just a year ago!

Another trend in TVs that's making many models less pricey is a leaning toward bigger and bigger sets. If you'll be happy with a 25- or 27-inch set, you can get a great deal—either on a new TV from a retailer or discounter or on a used one from someone who's decided to trade up.

# NO DVD FOR ME!

S omeday, the VCR will sing its swan song and just roll over for the DVD. But that day is a long way off. Right now, VCRs are inexpensive when you buy them right off the retailer's shelf. (Try buying them at a good discount store and you'll get an even better price.) They are probably the best buy in entertainment today. Meanwhile, the DVD—a CD-like, digital answer to the VCR—is still in its technological growth spurt. These machines are expensive and changing dramatically from year to year. For the time being, even if you opt for a DVD, you'll still need a VCR to watch many movies. While the studios are churning out their latest releases on DVD as well as video, most of their older movies (even those just a few

## TVS AND STEREOS AND VACUUMS, OH MY!

* * * * *

When you're shopping for hi-tech, relatively low-cost machines like small televisions, VCRs, and vacuum cleaners, buying used usually just doesn't pay. That's because the cost for a single repair on a used model can add up to almost as much as the cost of a new model. Take the repair on my last VCR (please!): $17 for parts and $54 for labor brought the total to $71. Sticker price for a new model on sale at Wal-Mart the same week: $79. Unless you're facing the garage-sale steal of the year—say $15 for a functioning vacuum cleaner, or $20 for a working, under-a-year-old TV—watch out for those deals on secondhand small electronics and appliances. They're not built to have long life spans, and more often than not, these plug-ins will soon give out.

years old) are still available only on video. And your local video store may not have many DVD offerings yet. Personally, I'm going to wait a couple of years to see how this all sorts out before I make any investment.

# The Digital Age

**W**elcome to the wonderful world of home computers. Well, maybe "wonderful" is an overstatement, but for sure, we are now living in a world of A-drives and C-drives, e-mail, and online everything. If you have children at home, no doubt you've either already bought a personal computer or you're being pressured to do so at every turn. For the rest of us, the demands may not be as insistent, but that sense that we're not keeping up with the Joneses unless we, too, can visit **www.jerrybaker.com** (or any other worthy Internet location!) is definitely there. If you've decided to jump in and see how your life might change with a computer, here's some advice I had to learn the hard way.

## Calling All Computer Shoppers

The good news is that even the most basic new computer system on sale at your local electronics retailer can do everything most first-time computer users want it to do. Technology for these machines gets better every day, and in a strange but pleasant twist of fate, the prices continue to come down.

A word to the wise, though: No matter what kind of system you buy, look for a deal that includes free technical support. If your system develops kinks, you don't want to be stuck paying $50 an hour to have it looked at or to have your questions answered.

## BUY IN BUNDLES

**C**omputer manufacturers and retailers like to sell you the whole enchilada, and they're willing to make you a pretty good deal to do so. If you buy your hard drive (the computer's "brain"), monitor, and printer together, you'll get a good discount on the three pieces and, on most packages, get hundreds of dollars in software thrown in for free. Check your Sunday newspaper ads for complete systems at good prices. Usually these prices include rebates, so you'll have to wait for your refund to get the whole deal.

## USE YOUR CALCULATOR

There are plenty of "alternative" means of buying a computer besides paying for it all up front. For example, some-times you can get a "free" computer when you commit to a particular online access provider for a three-year stint. Now, keep in mind that the fees for that online service run an average of $24 a month. Sounds great? Not necessarily, once you consider the fact that $24 times 36 months adds up to $864. But no matter what, you're going to end up paying for your Internet access, so look into what other Internet access providers are charging before you make up your mind.

## THE DIGITAL CAMERA DILEMMA

* * * * *

Digital cameras seem to be everywhere—in magazines and television ads and in the hands of your friends and neighbors, too. Don't rush out shopping for one of these gizmos, though, unless you've carefully considered how you'd use it. My guess is that you can probably do without one for a few more years, and here's why:

☞ If you just want to take more pictures and not save the ones you don't like, a digital camera that will produce prints of as high a quality as your 35 mm camera will cost you several hundred dollars.

☞ If you want to e-mail snapshots to friends or post them on a Web site, Wal-Mart or just about any other film processor can put your 35 mm shots on a disc for you for a couple of dollars.

☞ Lastly, keep in mind that these cameras are on the cutting edge of technology, but they're already starting to come down in price. Wait a couple of years, and I'd bet dollars to donuts that they'll soon be priced more in line with "old-fashioned" cameras.

## WEIGH THE WARRANTY

**I**f you're pretty lax about reading the warranties on most of your purchases, break that habit NOW! Of all the purchases you need to read the warranty on, a computer is the most important. You don't want to get stuck with this very foreign and perplexing machine on your desk—not working—and find out there's no one to help you fix it. Make sure you're getting technical support with your purchase; unfortunately, there's a very good chance you'll need it. And be sure to read the fine print. Is the support for a specific time period, say the first 90 days, after which you pay a per-hour or per-phone-call rate? Is the tech-support number toll-free? Can you get tech support free via e-mail?

## HOW MUCH COMPUTER DO YOU NEED?

**I**f you're a *real* computer newbie, you may be saying to yourself, "How can I decide what I want to use a computer for when I don't even know what the possibilities are?" Here's a clever way to figure out what you need—and best of all, it's free.

Get yourself a pen and pad and on one page make two columns. Next, with pen and pad in hand, head to a local computer store—the bigger the better—and browse the software titles. Look for any programs that sound useful or fun to you. Don't limit yourself—you're not spending any

## NO STRINGS ATTACHED

Believe it or not, for the smart shopper, there are lots of freebies to be had in the world of electronics. Computer keyboards, disks, mice, and all kinds of software turn up every week in national chain stores like Office Depot, Office Max, CompUSA, and many others—for free. Check out the electronics ads in your Sunday paper, and most weeks you'll find a few items being sold as "Free After Rebate." Manufacturers count on consumers not sending in those rebates, but smart shoppers like us wouldn't think of passing up a freebie!

money yet, so go wild.

For each program that appeals to you, copy the title in the first column on your pad. Next, look on the product packaging for a section that says "System Requirements" or "Minimum System Requirements." (If you can't find that information, ask a sales clerk to point it out to you.) That section will say something like "Pentium 90 Mhz Processor, 16 Mb RAM, 40 Mb available hard disk space, CD-ROM drive." Copy that information next to the software title in the next column.

When you've copied all the information for each of the titles you're interested in, you'll probably start to see a pattern. Pretty soon you'll realize that most of the programs you'll

want to use will require, say, 20 Mb RAM, a 90 Mhz processor, 40 Mb available hard disk space, and a CD-ROM drive. Those are your basic requirements for a computer.

Now take that list with you when you go shopping for a computer. This will give you a basis for comparison when you look at systems from several computer manufacturers. Don't be afraid to show the salesperson your specifications and ask how their computer system compares to it.

# CONSIDER RECONDITIONED MODELS

The best way to get your new computer on the cheap is to buy a reconditioned system. I know what you're thinking—"reconditioned" makes me think of something that's been beat up, too. But in the world of home computers, "reconditioned" usually means somebody sent it back—or better yet, cancelled their order—and the maker can't sell it as "new" anymore. Here's what you need to know if you're thinking of buying a reconditioned system:

**Stick with a name you know.** If you buy a reconditioned computer direct from a major manufacturer, you'll have a much easier time getting help if you need it. Companies like Gateway and Dell sell their refurbished models direct to consumers and sometimes sell them through retailers. Either way, you'll get a discount in the neighborhood of 20 to 30 percent off the new price.

**Read every word of the warranty.** Yes, I said it before, and I'm saying it again. That 30 percent savings wouldn't

be such a big deal if it didn't come with a good company to back it up. Most of the big-name makers cover their refurbished machines with complete one- to three-year warranties and technical support. Don't settle for a 90-day warranty; it's not enough.

**Make sure there's a return clause.** In general, refurbished computers are in great shape and have no running problems. They've been completely tested, but if it's just your luck to get the computer that lies lifeless on the desk when you hook it up, be sure you can return it for a refund or a replacement.

# CHAPTER 4

# Great Furniture Finds

Furniture: You can't live well without it, but how come it costs so dad-burned much? Well, did you know that the standard markup on new furniture is somewhere in the neighborhood of 300 percent? And if you shop in a high-end store, you'll see many pieces marked up 400 percent or even more! Now if that doesn't rile up the cheapskate in you, nothing will.

Lucky for us, there are plenty of ways to get around that heavy-duty profit margin—even on new, top-quality furniture. And since some folks' taste in furniture changes as often as their preference in breakfast cereal, there are always plenty of great deals to be had on used furniture, too.

This chapter will show you how to get the best deals on new and not-so-new furnishings so your home will look like a million bucks. They say a man's home is his castle—so here's how to decorate yours with quality furniture without paying a royal fortune.

# Know a Good Thing When You See It

**W**hen I was a lad, I made a cape out of an old blanket and practiced "flying" from the dining room chairs to the floor. My Grandma Putt didn't think much of that. She told me that those chairs had already been around a lifetime—and if I didn't abuse them quite so much, they just might last another one. Judging by the shape they're in today at my house, I guess she was right.

Buying furniture that will last for generations takes a little bit of know-how and a good eye for detail. But you don't need to be an expert appraiser—I'll tell you what to look for when you go furniture shopping. That way, when you bring home your furniture, you'll know that the only thing cheap about it was the price!

## Getting the Goods on Wood

First off, let's talk a little bit about what furniture is made of. You'll hear the term "cased goods" thrown around a lot when you're shopping, and that just means that the furniture is wood (as opposed to upholstered). As America's Master Gardener®, I have more than a little knowledge to share about trees and wood. Here's how to make sure you're getting the best deal on wood furniture.

## HOW MUCH WOOD WOULD A WOODCHUCK CHUCK?

**N**ot much, if it's a rock-hard hardwood like oak, cherry, maple, walnut, or mahogany. That would be too much work for the little furry fellow, and that's why these types of wood make top-quality, enduring, and fairly expensive furniture. They're tough to scratch and dent, and they're resistant to warping, too. Just be prepared to pay a pretty penny for any furniture you find made from these kinds of wood.

On the other hand, softwoods like pine, cedar, and poplar can make beautiful furnishings, but they wear and show their age sooner than hardwoods. At the same time, they can cost considerably less than their hardwood cousins. So if you're looking for furniture that isn't going to have to stand up to heavy use, you can save big by going with the softwoods.

## VENEER VALUE

**A** veneer is composed of either thin sheets of wood that are glued together like a wood "sandwich" or one sheet attached to a solid wood core. The method is a time-tested way for craftsmen to make furnishings from several pieces of wood instead of just one;

### GO NATIVE

* * * * *

The most popular hardwoods for furniture are cherry, maple, oak, mahogany, walnut, and teak. Now, the first three—cherry, maple, and oak—all grow beautifully and plentifully right here in sunny North America. Walnut does, too, but when it comes to furniture, imported English walnut is what people look for. The other woods have to be shipped from Africa, Asia, or South America, with the cost going straight to the bottom line of the sticker price. So stick with the "local" woods and you'll save yourself a bundle on top-quality furniture—and that's even before you start wheeling and dealing.

otherwise, we'd never have large furnishings—like tables and armoires—from trees that don't grow very big (such as cherry).

Now veneers have gotten a bad rap in recent years because some manufacturers put them on particleboard—and some don't even attach them very well. So when you shop for veneered furniture, find out what both the veneer and the material beneath it are made of. If both are hardwoods, there's nothing to worry about. In fact, quality veneered pieces often outlast solid wood ones because the veneering process makes them extra strong.

## PARTICLEBOARD PRAISES AND PITFALLS

* * * * *

Like a certain comedian we all know, particleboard gets no respect. The reason, no doubt, is rooted in the fact that this material really isn't a "board" at all, but a bunch of fused wood particles that are veneered to look like a board. Now, this type of construction doesn't look as good or last as well as true hardwood furniture. But if you're just looking for something to meet a temporary need or a very utilitarian one (such as shelves for your pantry or a child's bookshelf), there's no reason to rule out this very cheap material.

There is, however, every reason to double-check every new piece of furniture you buy to be sure particleboard isn't being misrepresented and sold to you for more than it's worth. To make sure, take a close look at the nooks and crannies that manufacturers don't expect to be seen. The backs and ends of drawers and shelves and the parts of furniture that will rest on the floor are all good places to check. Hidden particleboard is a mighty good reason to turn and run—or at least to drop the bottom out of your highest offer.

## FINISHING OUT

The finish is the manufacturer's last chance to make a good impression on you, so be sure to check on what kind of effort they've put into it. Is the whole piece finished, or just the front and top? If the latter, watch out for those! Does it feel smooth (it should), or rough and gritty? Are there any visible bubbles, blisters, cracks, or flaws in the finish? If there are, you can ask for a discount—or keep on searching for a piece that's "perfect," instead.

## FINISH FUNNY BUSINESS

One important thing to remember about finishes is that a label that says a chair has an "oak finish" doesn't mean that chair is made of oak. It means it is the *color* of oak. Not all furniture dealers are honest enough to point this out to their customers.

## THE DRAWERS HAVE IT

If there's one feature in a new piece of furniture that gives away more information about its quality than anything else, it's a drawer. It has all the elements in one small piece, and it's relatively easy to thoroughly inspect. Here's how:

1. **Roll it out.** Well-made drawers slide easily in and out on guides or rollers. They also have built-in stops, so you

won't accidentally pull them out and drop them on your toes—ouch!

2. **Peek out back.** The joints in the drawers tell you how much pride and effort manufacturers put into their work. Dovetailed drawers (they have a pattern of interlocking wood that looks a bit like puzzle pieces) and drawers joined by wooden dowels show up in well-made pieces. Drawers joined with nails or glue *may* last just fine, but they don't take as much time, energy, or craftsmanship to make. Drawers joined with staples are a sure sign of a shoddy product.

3. **Look for the dust panel.** If you're looking at a well-made piece of furniture, you'll find a dust-catching panel between the drawers. If you can pull one drawer all the way out and see the stuff in the drawer underneath it, then the manufacturer hasn't

bothered with this inexpensive, but very practical, sign of quality.

## CHECK THAT LABEL TWICE

**F**urniture makers didn't just fall off the turnip truck! They can be pretty tricky in the wording of their labels—if you don't read them carefully, you may find yourself paying more for a new piece of furniture than it's worth. Here's what a few of the most frequently printed descriptions (using walnut as an example) mean in plain old English instead of that city slicker furniture-speak:

**"Walnut veneer."** The piece has a layer of walnut on the outside or top. If there's no

---

### FINISH IT YOURSELF!

If you want to save up to 40 percent on new furniture and don't mind getting out your gloves and old paint shirt to do it, unfinished furniture can be a real deal. Check for the same quality construction you look for in finished furniture, and find out what kind of wood you're buying. Dealers sometimes sell unfinished furniture made of inferior woods such as poplar or fir at prices that'd be better suited to unfinished oak or maple. And that, of course, is no bargain.

other wood name on the label, then the inside should be walnut, too. If another wood is included, the label should say something along the lines of "walnut veneer with beech (or another wood) solids."

**"Solid walnut."** All the exposed surfaces of the piece are made of walnut.

**"Walnut finish."** The product is the color of walnut. It may not be made of walnut, or for that matter, may not even be made of wood!

**No label at all.** Heads up, there's no worse sign than that! Any retailer who removes labels

**$ BARGAIN ALERT!**

"Wanted: part-time sales clerk. Benefits include furniture at cost." Okay, okay, the ad might not read exactly like that, but often, if you work as little as 10 to 15 hours a week at a furniture store, you enjoy great discounts on top-of-the-line items—sometimes at cost or at a fraction of the retail price. It's like I always say, if you can't beat 'em, join 'em! And remember, you can always quit once you've furnished your home, and your kids' homes, and your friends' homes.... Come to think of it, you may not want to plan an early retirement after all!

from furniture for sale is probably hiding something about his wares. By all means, shop somewhere else.

# Understanding Upholstery

When you look at a piece of wood furniture, everything you need to know is right there in front of you, plain as the nose on your face. You can tell how it's made, what it's made of—and make a very good guess as to how well it'll hold up to daily wear and tear. But with upholstered furniture, all that info is hidden under layers and layers of fabric and padding. Getting to the bottom of quality upholstered goods is a little like solving a mystery. But if you follow these clues, you'll soon know whether you're looking at high-quality

chairs and sofas or cheap knock-offs that should be priced accordingly.

# TAKE THE FABRIC TEST

If your house is anything like mine, there's no item that has a harder life than the sofa—except maybe the easy chair. For these pieces of furniture, be sure you're getting a quality fabric that will stand all of the sitting, rocking, climbing, sleeping, and snoring it's going to endure from your family. Here's how:

**Scratch and sniff.** Scratch the upholstery—gently—on new furniture with your fingernail to make sure the fabric doesn't have a tendency to pull apart. If it's used, also make sure it doesn't have one of those enduring (but not endearing) odors that will probably never come out.

**Wanting a washing.** I never, ever buy fabrics that can't be washed. I've had enough "Oh shoots!" with the salsa to know better. Whether your nemesis is salsa, mustard, or chocolate ice cream, sooner or later, you'll have to get it out of your new couch. You'll sleep better knowing that the fabric can hold up to soap and water.

**Color coordinate.** Don't laugh, because you'll thank me later if you follow this advice. If you have a white pet, get light-colored fabric on your furniture. If your pets are dark, buy dark upholstery, instead. Now I'm not suggesting you give up cleaning the "matching" couch. I just know from experience that if "your" white couch is really owned by a black cat, you're going to spend a lot of time trying to keep your couch from looking like it was upholstered in black fur!

**Perfect prints.** A good print can hide a multitude of sins, and that means a longer life for your furniture. It can hide so many, though, that it deserves extra inspection before you buy it. Make sure the print pattern matches up throughout the piece, and carefully check the fabric for flaws before you make any kind of commitment.

**Love leather.** If you're really looking for something that will last forever (or close to it), consider leather. It outlasts

$ BARGAIN ALERT!

Want expensive furniture at bargain-basement prices? Just let your fingers do the walking (or the pointing and clicking). Look up "Hotel liquidators" in the Yellow Pages or on the Web. These "too good to be true" businesses sell premium, slightly used hotel furniture for pennies on the dollar. (You can get an entire bedroom set for less than $500!) Now your champagne tastes and caviar dreams can become reality!

even the sturdiest furniture fabrics, and the simple styles of most leather furniture almost always stay in fashion longer, too. Change the pillows and throw blankets on your leather couch to change the look every couple of years, and it'll last you a lifetime. One word of warning: If you are a pet owner, keep in mind that cat claws and dog nails can do a real number on leather.

# CHECK THE CUSHIONS

Cushions hold the best clues about the quality of new upholstered furniture. If they're well made, then chances are good that the rest of the sofa or chair is, too. Here's how to tell what you're looking at, in three easy steps:

1. **Sit on it.** Now stand up. If there's still an indentation where your behind was by the time you turn around to look at it, then the insides of that cushion aren't up to snuff. That tiny depression in the fabric will soon lead to a permanent sag.

2. **Read the tag.** The best cushions are made with springs wrapped in layers of padding. If that's the case with the cushions you're inspecting, then you can be sure that the manufacturer is bragging about it on the paperwork.

3. **Zip it up.** While not all cushions with zippers are of good quality,  most without zippers are of poor quality. Zippers make it possible for a manufacturer to get the best fit on their cushions, and their presence

usually means you're looking at a better cushion. Look for zippers with material plackets, too. (That's the fabric "lip" that folds over the zipper so it isn't exposed.) Most manufacturers who make an effort to make their zippers look good and to protect the body of the furniture piece from wear by rubbing against the zipper pay close attention to other details of construction, as well.

## WHEN SECOND BEST IS GOOD ENOUGH

* * * * *

How well do you know your own style? A guy like me is happy to sit on the very same sofa for 10 years or more and hope it lasts another 10 years, too. Not everyone, however, is so happy with last year's furnishings. If you know you're going to get tired of that new couch after 3 years—just like the last one and the one before that—don't bother shopping for the top-of-the-line stuff. Choose a low-price model that'll hold up for as long as you'll want to look at it, and save yourself some money to put toward the next one!

## DON'T FORGET THE FRAME!

Take a minute to squeeze the armrests of upholstered chairs and sofas. If you can feel the frame underneath, sooner or later (and with my luck, definitely sooner!), it'll wear through the fabric. Then lift one side of the sofa. If it's not heavy enough to cause you to strain, then it's probably not strong enough to support Uncle Al's crash-landing sitting style or a furniture-jumping child, either.

# Spotting the Signs of Quality Construction

Sometimes a sign of poor construction stands out like a sore thumb: the floor model entertainment center with doors that close at uneven angles, the dresser drawer that will only come out with a mighty tug—or the one that falls out altogether. But there are lots of in-betweens in furniture quality. Here are some of the best indicators of well-made goods.

## WHAT'S HOLDING IT ALL TOGETHER?

Think of all the ways you could get two pieces of wood to attach and stay together. Chances are, anything you come up with, the furniture industry has already tried. There are methods of putting furniture together that are quick and cheap, methods that are costly and time-consuming, and a few that are in between.

Interlocking pieces of wood and dowel joints are signs of top-flight work. At the other end of the spectrum are two decidedly more modern joining tools: glue and staples. Call me old-fashioned, but over the years, I've used both of the latter to join two sheets of paper and have had mixed results, so I certainly don't want them holding my furniture together!

## LEAN INTO IT

Now, I don't go around banging on unbought furniture as a habit. However, I'm not above applying a little "strategic pressure" before I buy. Lean on the piece of furniture from the side and the top to see how it responds. Anything (other than a rocking chair) that shudders or bends is better left for somebody else.

## SWEAT THE SMALL STUFF

To be sure, I can change or repair a drawer pull in a few minutes, and I'd be happy

### Pennypincher's Hall of Fame

Make no mistake—J. P. Johnson of Ann Arbor, Michigan, loves to recycle, but he's no environmentalist. He's a capitalist who spends his weekends driving around town collecting discarded aluminum cans. Although I totally agree with J. P.'s thriftiness, I draw the line at scrounging for aluminum cans. But, to each his own. And believe it or not, J.P. managed to purchase a $1,100 living room set (bought on sale, of course) with the money he earned turning in those recyclable cans! Now I hear he has his eye on a nifty new bedroom set. Maybe I should rethink my moneysaving strategy!

to do it for a used or deeply discounted piece of furniture in need of some TLC. But if those pulls are sloppily placed or shoddily attached to new merchandise, then I have to think the manufacturer didn't put enough care into the entire piece for it to live up to my expectations.

Test all of the hardware on any furniture you're considering. Hinges, knobs, and drawer pulls should be snugly attached and evenly placed. Then cast a critical eye over the entire piece. Try everything, and if the drawers don't slide easily, the doors don't close squarely, or the sofa bed or futon doesn't fold up with ease, move on to the next model.

# Carpe Dealem: Seize the Deal

As far as I'm concerned, purchasing furniture has both the best and the worst that the world of buying has to offer. There are few retail purchases that have higher markups or as wide a range of quality. But there is no other category of goods that has so many cheap and even cheaper options for meeting your needs, either.

Read on for my game plan for hunting down just the right furniture at just the right price.

## Planning Ahead

Don't search for furniture without knowing what you want and what you're willing to pay for it. Decide the details *before* you hit the stores, to save time and trouble.

## DON'T BREAK THE BUDGET!

My Grandma Putt used to say that it's better to sleep soundly on an old mattress than to toss and turn on a new one you can't afford, and boy, was she ever right about that! So

## 'TIS THE SEASON

* * * * *

The best times to look for furniture sales are in January, February, July, and August. These are big clearance months for just about any retail industry, but they're especially good for furniture. That's because new furniture lines, which debut at the industry's annual trade shows in October and April, are starting to arrive in stores at those times, and the stores have to move the older merchandise to make room for the latest and greatest designs.

*Closeout!*

vendors to fine furniture sales staff knows that the best customer is one who wants to stock up and save. As a rule, I ask for a discount of 10 percent if I'm buying one item, 15 for two, 20 for three, and so on. You'll be surprised at how low some salesmen will go when they see a multi-item sales ticket at the end of the tunnel. If you don't ask, you'll never know.

before you spend a dime on any kind or quantity of furniture, set a budget and be determined to stick with it. And no one says you can't mix and match quality (and price) levels of furniture in one room. If you spend a bundle on that new armchair, look harder for flea market end tables to compensate. Or go for the high-quality sofa bed and spend less on the chairs.

## DON'T STOP AT ONE

No matter where you buy your new furniture, your Number 1 bargaining chip is buying more than one piece at a time. Everyone from flea market

## CASH-FREE CREDIT

Let's pretend for a minute that we haven't got any extra money just lying around, waiting to be spent on a roomful of furniture. (I know, this doesn't take much imagination, huh?) You may be able to manage a small payment and be thinking about renting instead of buying. Don't do it! Ask your furniture dealer if they offer same-as-cash credit lines. You can make payments—without costly interest charges—and have every dime go toward your purchase price. As long as you pay it off before the preset deadline, it's like a layaway you can take home—and how can you beat that?

## LET'S MAKE A DEAL

O nce you find what you want, it's time to put on a poker face and see what kind of deal you can make. Furniture prices are almost always open to negotiation. Personally, I always ask for a good discount, plus free delivery and setup. More than half the time, the response I get is, "Okay, Mr. Baker," a handshake, and a pat on the back. Now I hope your salesman won't call you Mr. Baker, but I don't doubt for a minute that you, too, can cut a great deal.

## Shopping for New Furniture

**Here's a furniture-industry secret to keep in mind as you decide where to shop for your furnishings. As a rule, each handler of the furniture marks it up 100 percent. And when it comes to small items like lamps, framed artwork, and decorations, the markup is usually more. So keep the middlemen to a minimum, and you'll save big.**

## FINE FURNITURE FINDS

F ine furniture stores are the places you'll pay the absolute most for new furniture, something I don't recommend. But even with their steep prices, furniture galleries have deals to offer for folks who know how to find them. Here's the lowdown:

SWIVEL

**Hidden bargains.** Every store accumulates returned, slightly damaged, and just-one-left items, but many upscale stores keep them hidden away unless someone asks for them. If there are several outlets of one furniture chain in your area, those goods may all go to one central clearing-house location. Ask the salesperson about a clearance room, and you may be surprised to find yourself in a treasure trove of bargains that weren't even on display!

**Floor finds.** Many furniture stores have occasional floor-sample sales to make room for new display models. (After all, furniture fads change just a hair slower than clothing styles do.) Ask a salesperson or manager when the next sale is coming up, and then make sure you're the first in line to reap the rewards!

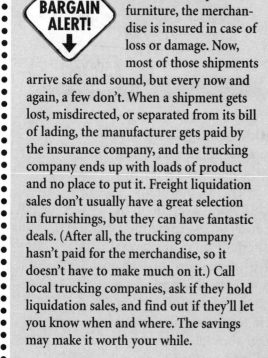

Any time a manufacturer sends out a shipment of furniture, the merchandise is insured in case of loss or damage. Now, most of those shipments arrive safe and sound, but every now and again, a few don't. When a shipment gets lost, misdirected, or separated from its bill of lading, the manufacturer gets paid by the insurance company, and the trucking company ends up with loads of product and no place to put it. Freight liquidation sales don't usually have a great selection in furnishings, but they can have fantastic deals. (After all, the trucking company hasn't paid for the merchandise, so it doesn't have to make much on it.) Call local trucking companies, ask if they hold liquidation sales, and find out if they'll let you know when and where. The savings may make it worth your while.

## DISCOVER THE DISCOUNTS

**M**ost of the true furniture factory outlets in the United States are in North Carolina, but there are a few sprinkled around the rest of the country. Check in the Yellow Pages under "Furniture" to see if there are any near you.

Other good outlet prospects are big catalog operations like JCPenney, Sears, and Spiegel. They can't reship returned items as new merchandise, so they often end up with lots of flawless pieces of furniture for sale at deep-discount prices. Be sure to check them out.

## PHONE IT IN

**H**ere's a little-known way to save a lot of money on new furnishings. Write down the exact name and a detailed description of the pieces you want, then call the manufacturer to see if they can put you in touch with an outlet store. Many companies will sell their wares through their own outlets or preferred discounters at big discount prices—savings that

## FURNITURE CENTRAL, U.S.A.

\* \* \* \* \*

Now, if you're not from the southeast, you may think I'm nuts to suggest that you get your bod to North Carolina to buy your new furniture. The fact is, though, it may be worth your trouble. More than half of the furniture sold in the United States is manufactured in North Carolina—most in the Greensboro/High Point/Winston-Salem area. And that means that the majority of the true factory outlets, including Century, Drexel-Heritage, and Thomasville, are located there, as well. If you can go, don't miss the Hickory Furniture Mart in Hickory, North Carolina, with dozens of discount furniture outlets, or the nearby Lenoir Mall, with furniture outlets, too. The savings you'll find there can range from 30 to 70 percent or more on discontinued items and samples.

If you do decide to go to North Carolina to buy furniture, be sure to ask whether the outlets reimburse travel costs for people who buy. Under some circumstances, several outlets do. And unless you're hauling the furniture yourself, be sure to factor in shipping charges before you buy.

---

can add up to 30 to 50 percent. You'll have to pay for shipping, but depending on your state, you may *not* have to pay sales tax! You may have to wait a few weeks for your furniture, but the savings is worth waiting for.

## BUY FROM THE BUILDER

Another great way to get a good deal on your furniture is to buy directly from craftsmen. I've seen plenty of mighty fine tables, chairs, and other goods for sale at a fraction of their furniture-store value in the workshops of Amish and Mennonite craftsmen and even folks who make furniture as a side business. You'll take away a piece of hand-crafted furniture at a modest price and with a personal touch no furniture store can provide.

## KNOW YOUR PRICES

The Number 1 rule of furniture outlet shopping (or

any other kind of shopping!) is to know what the furniture is worth when you see it. Don't be fooled by those tags that tell you the manufacturer's suggested retail price (MSRP) is thousands of dollars more than the sale price. Chances are, not even the fanciest furniture store is charging the MSRP, so your "discount" may be a lot less than it appears to be.

# Getting Great Deals on Used Furniture

**Sometimes, the best deal for your dollar isn't at a furniture store at all. For the price of a couple of nice lamps at the local fine furnishings store, you might just find a full dining set at a good garage or estate sale.**

## SOLD!

**S**ome of the best furniture deals around are waiting for you at auctions. But if you're going to invest your valuable time at an auction, be sure it's worth your trouble. Events

advertised as "absolute" or in terms that specifically state that there will be no minimums are the way to go. That way, if only a handful of tightwad bidders show up wanting furniture, there's no end to the possibilities for a low-price sale.

# BARGAINS TIMES TWO

**I**f you want to get the very best deals on secondhand furniture, you'll need two powerful tools of persuasion: cash and a truck. Most secondhand dealers will tell you they'd sooner take 20 percent (or

## NO STRINGS ATTACHED

The offer you made to purchase a house was accepted. Now you've got your eye on the sectional sofa in the den of that very same house. What do you do? Get ready to negotiate. Offer to take it off the owners' hands to save them moving costs. Point out that their old furniture might not fit their new decor. Oftentimes, you can secure rooms full of used furniture for free or almost free, especially when the house seller is moving far away and will incur high moving costs.

**BARGAIN ALERT!**

You might think I'd be the last guy to send you to a rental shop—after all, unless you need furniture for only a few months, there's no sense investing your hard-earned dough in stuff that's going to be loaded on a truck and taken back when you stop paying for it. But you can get a great deal at a rental shop by asking about their furniture sales. Plenty of rental stores sell previously rented furnishings at a discount. And since most folks who are in the market to buy furniture don't stop at rental places, those discounts get deeper all the time.

more!) off their asking price and get cash than take a check for the full amount. (Seems they've been bounced around by a rubber check or two.) As for the truck, many of these deals are only for folks who are willing to cart their purchases away themselves. Don't miss out on a great opportunity just because it won't fit in the hatchback! Shop prepared.

# FLEA MARKET FINDS

Flea markets are one of the true treasure troves for furniture shoppers. First, there are the standard flea market jewels waiting to be found—"mature" and "slightly worn" furnishings that need a little TLC to be returned to their former shine. But there are other kinds of flea market deals, as well.

Furniture craftsmen, small manufacturers, and the like rarely have the budgets to establish their own stores to market their wares. They stand to make the most profit from their pieces if they sell them directly to consumers. With their flat fee systems and occasional nature, flea markets are the perfect places for these folks to sell their wares—and great places for you to make a deal!

# BARGAINS BY THE YARD

There are two secrets to getting the best deals at yard sales: time and place. Nowhere is the expression about the early bird getting the worm more true than here. Any decent piece of furniture laid out in a neighborhood driveway sale will be picked up before most of the world sits down to breakfast, so be sure that you're the first one to spot it. Now, if it's overpriced and the seller won't deal, walk away and hope that no suckers come along. Then go back at the end of the day to repeat your best offer.

If you're going to hit the yard sales, my philosophy is that you might as well hit the best ones. Neighborhoods where folks can afford to toss out their old goods because they've become allergic to the color (and not because the furniture is falling to pieces) are the places to go. Beverly Hills 90210, here I come!

# CHARITY BEGINS AT HOME

Or, what I should say is, charity can furnish your home! When it comes to making charitable contributions, folks don't donate only clothing and small household goods. They often donate furniture, too. So charitable organizations that provide pickup service may have great furniture finds. Check out your nearby Salvation Army and Goodwill stores when you start furniture shopping—you may be surprised to find some decent used furniture there.

# CHAPTER 5

# Outdoor Living for Less

Remember back in Chapter 2, when I said you can tell a lot about people just from the way they dress? Well, the same goes for the way they "dress" their homes. Just one look at the outside of a house can tell you volumes about the folks who live inside. And I don't just mean the way they keep it up, either. I'm talking about the things people have outside their four walls—decks, patios, ship-shape lawns, and so forth.

Now, in this chapter, I'm not going to talk about planting and tending lawns and gardens—as you well know, I've written plenty on those subjects in other books. Instead, in the pages coming up, I'm going to give you some tips on controlling costs in the *nonliving* parts of your outdoor scene.

# Out and About

**W**hether you have sprawling acres to call your own or a yard that stops 20 feet from your front door, tending that space can swallow up a whole lot of the old paycheck if you're not careful. But I'll show you how to start spending less on that chunk of the great outdoors, while actually enjoying it more. The process starts with one simple question: What exactly do you want to *do* out there?

## The Old Thinking Cap

If you want to sink more of your cash in the bank and less into the view outside your windows (and who doesn't, really?), take some time to do some ponderin', as Grandma Putt used to call it. It costs nothing, and I guarantee it'll save you a bundle! Here are a few things to consider before you build a deck, order a load of topsoil, or start shopping for patio furniture.

## TEST TIME

**T**he first step in trimming outdoor-living costs is to take my "What's So Great About It?" test. The answers will help you decide how and where you want to spend your money in that green scene of yours. After all, why splurge on a big, fancy deck, when all you really want is a quiet corner that'll hold a lawn chair or two? Just check off all the statements that apply to you, and keep them in mind when it comes time to make changes in your landscape. And remember: There are no wrong answers to this test—it's *your* homestead and *your* cash!

I want my backyard to be:

☐ Perfect for hosting big get-togethers for family and friends.

☐ A place to sit back, put my feet up, and watch the world go by.

☐ Somewhere I can romp with my dog and grandkids.

☐ Spacious enough to play games such as croquet, horseshoes, or badminton.

☐ The place I go to relax by tinkering with and tending to my lawn.

☐ Natural enough to attract birds and butterflies.

☐ Home to a really beautiful or productive flower or vegetable garden.

☐ Attractive to potential future homebuyers.

# MOVIN' ON

**I**f you checked the last box above, and you're planning on selling your home within the next year or two, the best thing

**NO STRINGS ATTACHED**

If you're thinking of selling your house—and even if you're not ready to list it yet—get together with a real estate agent who knows your neighborhood and the current market. He or she can clue you in on which outdoor projects are likely to get you bigger bucks for your house and which ones would be like throwing your money right down the drain.

you can do to your property just might be nothing at all. It's true that attractive landscaping increases what real estate agents call "curb appeal," but if your yard is neat, clean, and fairly in sync with the rest of the neighborhood, think twice before you invest in anything beyond basic maintenance. Sure, adding a deck, patio, or new driveway could increase the selling price of your house—but probably not by enough to offset all the cash you'd have to shell out on the project.

## BACK IN YOUR OWN BACKYARD

What's more American than apple pie? A big ol' yard with a large, expansive lawn, that's what— and for a whole lot of good reasons. After all, who doesn't get a kick out of wigglin' his toes in soft, green grass, or at least watching the grandkids do it? And I don't know about you, but there's nothing I enjoy more at a barbecue than a rousing game of croquet—and I can't imagine whacking my best shot across a bed of pachysandra!

Unfortunately, though, an *expansive* lawn is also an *expensive* lawn, and the price tag we're talking about is a big one. In fact—are you ready for this?—lawn care in the United States is a $25 billion-a-year industry! Now, as you know, I'm a lawn guy from way back, but I'm also a big-time penny-pincher, and my best frugal advice is this: Cut back that turf to the smallest chunk that'll keep you happy.

How much is enough? Only

you can decide that— which is why I advised you to take my "What's So Great About It?" test. (See "Test Time" on page 96.) Once you've zeroed in on what you want to do in your yard, it's easy to figure out how much of that space needs to be a high-maintenance lawn. For instance, if you checked the "play games" box, lay out a space that's big enough to host your favorite contests in comfort. Then turn the remaining territory over to something that's less costly to maintain than turf grass, such as:

★ Hardy groundcovers

★ Ornamental grasses

★ Low-maintenance perennial flowers

★ Trees, shrubs, or wildflowers that are native to your growing area

★ Gravel, shredded-bark, or other mulch

★ Porches, decks, or patios

As for taking care of whatever lawn you want to keep, you can get the full lowdown in my book *Green Grass Magic,* available at **www.jerrybaker.com**.

# Sittin' and Sippin'

It seems that every time you pick up a slick magazine these days, you see a big article on "outdoor rooms." Why, the way those home-and-garden writers carry on, you'd think that just last week they had *invented* the whole idea of relaxing in comfort in the great outdoors! Well, I have some news for them: Since long before Grandma Putt was a pup, folks have been kickin' up their heels or just sittin' and rockin' on porches, patios, balconies, verandas, terraces, decks, and courtyards all over the world. And a space like that doesn't have to cost a bundle of money, either.

## Decisions, Decisions...

Is lounging on a wide-open deck your idea of the good life? Or would you rather hang out on an old-fashioned porch like Grandma Putt's? Or maybe you enjoy getting the gang together on a brick patio with a matching, built-in barbecue? Whatever your pleasure, here are some things to keep in mind as you ponder your decision.

## WOODEN IT BE LOVERLY?

Unless you're already a real construction whiz, you'll probably want to hire an experienced builder to put together a wooden structure like a porch or a raised deck—and this is a definite must if the area you're building on is steep or unstable. On the other hand, concrete, stone, and brick are a completely different kettle of fish. With a good set of instructions, a little time, and a few tools, any able-bodied do-it-yourselfer can make a first-class patio, walkway, or even a low wall. And it's fun, too!

## KEEP IT UP

**R**emember: Whatever you build, you'll have to maintain, and wooden structures will cost you more to keep up, in terms of both time and money, than their hard-surfaced counterparts. That's particularly true if you live in the muggy South or in a rainy territory like the Pacific Northwest. In any part of the country, though, uncovered decks win the high-maintenance prize, hands-down, because they need regular cleaning and sealing to stave off Ma Nature's elements. (In Chapter 13, you'll find tips for trimming those costs, but sadly, there's no way to kiss them goodbye entirely.)

## THE BIG COVER-UP

**T**here's no question about it: A covered, enclosed porch is a big investment. Is it worth it? It could be, if:

☞ you and a lot of hungry insects want to enjoy the same chunk of the great outdoors at the same time;

☞ you want to use the space year-round, and you don't live in a balmy place like Florida, Arizona, or southern California;

☞ you could use extra sleeping space for visiting family or friends;

☞ the structure won't block a knock-your-socks-off, beautiful view.

**BARGAIN ALERT!**

When you're thinking about an outdoor project of any kind, a home and garden show is a gold mine of ideas and know-how. Usually, you have to pay an admission charge, but once you get in, you'll find freebies galore, including fact-filled brochures, videos, building plans, and even workshops and how-to demonstrations by construction pros. You can also bet that manufacturers' reps will be on hand with plenty of free samples. Prime home-show time in most parts of the country is February and March. Keep an eye on your local newspaper for dates and times, as well as discount admission coupons.

# EASE ON OUT

**W**hile you're still in the thinking stages, haul out the property survey that you got at your house closing, and note where the easements are. Then make sure that whatever you build doesn't cover them. (Easements, if you're unfamiliar with the term, are places where the community retains the right to run power lines, put in sewers, or even build new roads—and if it comes to a contest between City Hall and your new deck, you *know* who's going to win!)

## BY THE BOOK

* * * * *

If you're anything like me, when you start thinking about changes to your outdoor scene, you soon find yourself with a mountain of pictures, plans, supply lists, and how-to clippings from newspapers and magazines. All that paper can get out of hand pretty quickly if you don't corral it, which is why I keep my collection in photo albums that I pick up at the thrift store for next to nothing. That way, when I'm ready to try out an idea, I know right where to find the instructions. And, if I decide the project isn't so great after all, I just lift the plastic page cover, toss the clipping into the recycling bin, and make room for a better one!

# Bringing in the Hired Guns

**Even when you have some building experience under your belt, joining forces with a contractor is nothing to take lightly—even for a small project, there's a lot of money riding on your decision. But when you're brand-new to the hiring game, the process can be downright terrifying. It doesn't have to be, though. Read on for tips on getting work that you'll be proud to show off, at a price that won't break the bank!**

## READ FIRST, TALK LATER

**B**efore you start looking for a contractor, invest in a good manual on building whatever it is that you have in mind, then read that book from cover to cover. Even if you have no intention of so much as lifting a hammer, having some knowledge under your belt will give you more power at negotiating time. You'll also know what to look for as you conduct your work-in-progress inspections.

## WORD GETS AROUND

**F**or my money, the best way to find help with any job is by good old word of mouth, and landing a top-rate contractor is no exception. Your obvious first contact is a friend or neighbor who's had outdoor building work done in the last year or so, but don't stop there. Visit a few building-supply companies, explain the nature of your project, and ask the staff for recommendations. These folks work with contractors on a daily basis, so they know firsthand who's got the right stuff for your job. Another likely source of names is the staff of a big garden center. Many of them work closely with landscape architects (some even have garden designers on staff), and

they can almost certainly point you toward some good, reputable outdoor contractors.

And don't stop at just one recommendation—the bigger your project is, the more important it is that you talk to several contractors. Have each one come out to your place, look over the territory, and give you a bid.

## DO THE 3-STEP

**W**hen you start calling contractors, always ask to contact clients of their last *three* projects. (Anyone can corral *one* good reference.) When you call, have your pen and notepad ready—you don't want to forget any details that could make or break your budget. Of course, you want to hear that all these folks are pleased as punch with their new decks, gazebos, whatever. But don't expect to hear that everything was hunky-dory, down to the last finishing nail—at least, not if the project was a big one. (As Grandma Putt would say, if you're lookin' for perfection this side of the Great Divide, you're shootin' for the moon.) Instead, focus on the things that really matter. What you want to know is this:

☐ Did the crew stick to a reasonable schedule?

☐ Did they answer questions and explain procedures in easy-to-understand terms?

☐ Were they mature, courteous, and respectful of the homeowners' property?

☐ Were they aware and careful if children or pets wandered close to the scene? (Of course, it's *your* job to keep little feet and paws at a safe distance, but we all know what can happen if you turn your back for even a second or two!)

☐ Last, but for-darn-sure not least, did they manage finances honestly and responsibly?

## COVER YOUR BASES

Now, this isn't the place for a class in Contract Negotiation 101, but I can offer you a few pointers on what you should bear in mind when you're ready to hire a contractor:

1. Never pay the whole price up front, but do expect to make

**If you want to provide your builder with detailed** plans, take a quick tour of the Internet—you'll get more construction drawings than you can shake a hammer at. Check out online garden and home-improvement sites for free instructions on whipping up simple projects such as trellises, fences, and benches. (You might even want to tackle some of those projects yourself.) More hard-core building Web sites offer professional-level plans for decks, porches, patios, and other structures at prices to please even an old penny-pincher like me. To jump-start your shopping spree, go to your favorite search engine, and type in the name of your structure, plus "building plans". (For instance, search for "porch building plans" or "deck building plans.") Whatever you do, don't search for just "building plans," or you'll be treated to screen after screen of progress reports on school, church, and municipal construction projects!

some sort of down payment. Usually 10 to 15 percent is a good rule of thumb.

2. Don't start even a small project until you have a contract that's signed by both you and the contractor.

3. Make sure that all the necessary permits are in order before any work begins. Otherwise, you could be in for an expensive visit from a zoning inspector.

## PITCHIN' IN FOR DOLLARS

Even if a contractor's crew is building your project, you could save big bucks by doing a few basic tasks yourself. When you're negotiating the price, ask for a discount if you:

✦ **Do the legwork at City Hall.** Some contractors will tack on a substantial fee for getting the building permit and doing any other necessary paperwork. If you handle that chore, you'll get whatever permits and licenses you need for exactly the price that your town charges.

✦ **Take care of some after-work cleanup.** Simply by sweeping sawdust and bent nails or gathering up stone or lumber scraps, you could save yourself hundreds of dollars. (And hang on to those scraps—at least the bigger ones. They could be very useful for all kinds of projects later on.)

✦ **Tackle preconstruction demolition.** This is along the lines of tearing down a small, old porch to make way for the new one, or pulling up old paving stones. It rarely takes any great skill or fancy equipment to pull something apart, and if you've got the time, you can save a bundle.

## BE NEIGHBORLY

Talk to your neighbors and see if they're interested in doing similar outdoor projects on their own homes. Say, for example, you and some other folks on your street are all thinking about adding patios. Why not get together and divvy up the phone-call duties (see "Do the 3-Step," on page 102), and then compare notes? And be sure to tell potential contractors that there are several projects awaiting them at roughly the same time and location. This saves the contractor travel time (which means less cost passed on to you!), and if the contractor can buy materials in quantity for several projects at a time, you and your neighbors can all enjoy the savings.

## LET'S TRADE!

If you lack the time, inclination, or know-how to tackle a building project yourself, but paying a pro would drain your bank account, here's another option: barter. Call a friend who's an amateur carpenter or a pro who's between projects, and offer to make a trade. For example, if he'll build your deck, porch, or fence, you'll prepare his taxes, sew curtains for his house, baby-sit his kids, tend his garden, paint his living room, or produce a marketing brochure for his business. Here's how to get into a win-win situation:

1. Establish the price for the builder's labor.

2. Decide on an hourly rate for your work.

3. Agree on a job—or jobs— that you can do to equal the builder's fee, along with a time frame for completion. Presto! You're in business!

## AN OLD DOG <u>CAN</u> LEARN NEW TRICKS

Every time you see a carpenter hammerin' away or making fancy cuts with a jigsaw, do you sigh and say, "Gee, I wish I could do that"? Well, stop sighing, and sign up for an adult-ed woodshop class at a local vocational school or community college. After all, it's never too late to learn something new—especially when what you're learning will save you big bucks around the homestead!

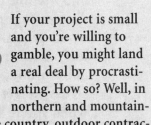

**BARGAIN ALERT!**

If your project is small and you're willing to gamble, you might land a real deal by procrastinating. How so? Well, in northern and mountainous parts of the country, outdoor contractors need to have major jobs wrapped up before the snow flies. At the end of the season, look for a contractor with some time on his hands—but not enough time to tackle anything big—and he might just lower his price a tad in the interest of keeping busy until the end of the season.

# A-Shopping We Will Go

Shopping for building materials and tools is not quite the same as shopping for clothes and groceries, but there is one *big* similarity: There are a lot of businesses out there clambering for your hard-earned bucks. So how do you hang on to as much of your cash as possible? Simple: Know as much as you can about the products you want and the sales tactics you'll encounter *before* you head off to the hardware store, lumberyard, or home-improvement megastore.

## Into the Woods

Most decks, fences, trellises, and a whole lot of other outdoor structures are made of wood. It could take years to learn all there is to know about wood, which is why it's so easy to get shortchanged when you're shopping for it. So before you head off

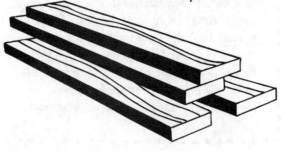

to the local lumberyard, take some time to peruse my short course in lumber lingo.

## THAT'S NOT SO HARD!

Lumber is divided into two basic categories: hardwood and softwood. Like a whole lot of other wood lore, this distinction can get a tad confusing, because some softwoods are actually harder than some hardwoods. For instance, Southern yellow pine—the most popular wood for outdoor projects—is harder than both cherry and elm—two classic hardwoods. Here's the distinction in a nutshell:

**Softwood** comes from evergreen trees, such as pine, fir, cypress, cedar, and redwood. Generally speaking, it's easier to work with, easier to come by, and less expensive than hardwood. Most of the lumber used outdoors—for both construction projects and outdoor furniture—is softwood.

**Hardwood** comes from deciduous trees, such as oak, maple, cherry, and walnut. It can be very tricky to work with, especially for a beginner, and it's used mostly for indoor furniture and other fine woodworking inside the house.

# IT'S WHAT'S INSIDE THAT COUNTS

Cedar and redwood naturally fend off decay—but that's true only of the dark wood at the core of the tree, known as heartwood. The outer layer of wood, called sapwood, can fall prey to rot just as quickly as any other wood, which is why it costs a lot less than heartwood!

All trees have both heartwood and sapwood, but for outdoor building purposes, you only need be concerned with redwood and cedar. In the cases of other tree species, insects and decay will attack *both* heartwood and sapwood.

# UNDER PRESSURE

One glance at those price tags on heartwood sends most folks running to the racks where they keep the pressure-treated pine! In fact, Southern yellow pine is the lumber most often used for decks and other outdoor structures. It's easy to work with, easy to come by, and it's been treated with a chemical compound that makes the wood resistant to decay and insects.

That was the good news. The bad news is that the compound most often used to treat wood is chromated copper arsenate, and it's toxic. So, any time you're working with pressure-treated wood, keep these guidelines in mind:

★ Don't use it where you're growing vegetables or cooking herbs—the plants can absorb the chemicals from the soil. The experts disagree on just *how much* of these substances wind up in the edible parts of the plants, but I don't take any chances. The way I see it, I don't want to chow down on *any* chromium, copper, or arsenic!

★ Don't use pressure-treated wood where anyone's skin will come into contact with it, such as in a picnic table or a child's play gym.

★ When you handle treated wood, wear long sleeves, a mask, and gloves.

★ Never burn this stuff! The fumes'll make you sick faster than you can say, "Oh, my achin' tummy!"

**If you do decide** to work with redwood, you can learn plenty from the California Redwood Association. Their Web site will tell you all you want to know about buying and building with redwood. You can even download free plans for building everything from benches to decks of all shapes and sizes. Visit their site at **www.calredwood.org**.

# THE HEART OF THE MATTER

**Y**ou won't find a nicer-looking or longer-lasting deck than one made from redwood or cedar heartwood. But that deck will easily cost twice as much as one built from pressure-treated pine. Why? Because it's only the *heartwood* of these two woods that's rot- and insect-resistant; the sapwood is not. And even the hardware will cost more because you have to use stainless steel nails and bolts—both cedar and redwood contain chemicals that break down nonstainless steel.

# THE GREAT PRETENDERS

**E**ven woods at the top of the quality heap need regular care to fend off cracking, splitting, and warping, not to mention mold and mildew. If you fall behind in your cleaning and sealing routine—or try to economize by using cheap sealer—you could be in for some nasty and expensive surprises. So what do you do? Well, friends, you have two choices: You can give your deck the TLC that I'll tell you about in Chapter 13, or you can build with either composite lumber or recycled plastic lumber. These wood look-alikes get better all the time, and I've become one of their biggest fans. Here's why:

**Durability.** These pseudo-woods last much longer than pressure-treated pine.

**Low maintenance.** The fact is, they need almost none.

**Economy.** The upfront cost is a little more than you'd pay for treated yellow pine, but your investment pays for itself in a couple of years through avoided maintenance costs.

**Easy working.** Both types cut, handle, and take a nail just like regular lumber.

**Good looks.** Both types can look exactly like high-grade lumber. Some even fade to a rustic, weathered gray. But if you'd like something a little jazzier, you can also get plenty of colors and patterns.

**Comfort and safety.** These alternative woods don't splinter—which is great news if you kick off your shoes as often as I do! Furthermore, they're slip-resistant when wet, so you're less likely to fall.

---

## WHEN **NOT** TO PINCH PENNIES

\* \* \* \* \*

In many places, building codes specify the minimum grade of lumber you can use for structural supports. But codes aside, my rule of thumb is this: When you're building anything you plan to sit on or stand on, fork over the cash for top-grade wood. After all, you don't want to risk falling through your deck—or having someone else fall through and get injured!

---

# GRADE SCHOOL

The business of grading lumber sounds complicated, but it's really pretty simple, and once you know the basics, you can save big bucks. Each board you see at a lumber-yard has a stamp that shows its grade, species, and  moisture content. It also shows the mill that produced the board and the agency that graded it according to these factors:

☞ Natural growth features, such as knots.

☞ Defects resulting from any mistakes in cutting or milling.

☞ Strength, durability, and appearance.

## TERM TIME

In general, the higher the grade, the more a board will cost. The simple secret to saving money on lumber is knowing when to cut corners—because there are plenty of times when you don't need, or even want, the highest grade. For instance, for deck floor supports, you want maximum-strength boards, but for railings, a slightly lower strength grade will do just fine. Here's a rundown on grading terms. (These will come in handy when you're talkin' shop with the fellas at the lumberyard.)

**Structural lumber** is rated for strength. For pine, the most common system uses the terms Select Structural (the strongest), No. 1, No. 2, and No. 3. You won't always see every one of those numbers on the sales floor, though. A lot of lumberyards don't bother with No. 3, but sell a mix of grades called "No. 2 and Better." On the other hand, the home-improvement megastores sometimes sell *only* No. 3 (which means the slightly cheaper price might not be the bargain it seems).

**2 x 4s** have a slightly different grading system. They're usually graded as either Construction, Standard, or Utility, and are often sold as "Standard and Better."

## NEVER A DULL MOMENT

Just to spice up the action, some lumber retailers have invented their own grading systems, such as Select, Middle, and Economy. At the other end of the spectrum, some retailers don't bother to inform you of *any* grade. If you should stumble into a place like that, turn right around and take your business elsewhere—you're not likely to get any bargains if you don't even know what you're buying!

# MEGASTORE MIRAGES

* * * * *

The folks who put up those giant-size, home-improvement stores have made fortunes for themselves by convincing you that they're saving you money. But are they? Not necessarily, judging from what I've seen! Before you head off on your next trip down those long, long aisles, ponder these megastore come-ons:

**The lure of the low-price drill.** The companies that manufacture top-of-the-line tools and fixtures also make lower-price lines just for the mammoth stores. Those are the things you see in full-color ads in the Sunday supplements. And, why do you suppose that gear (a drill, let's say, or a fancy hot tub) costs less than you might pay elsewhere? You got it—it's lower quality. When the big store does happen to carry a better-quality drill or hot tub, it will probably cost about the same as you'd pay at your local lumberyard or hardware store.

**We'll show you how!** Want to learn how to build a fence, or maybe put an addition onto your deck? Well, head on down for a free, in-store workshop. Of course, while you're there, you'll buy all the materials you need for the project—and probably a lot of stuff you don't. Heck, you might even decide on the spur of the moment to make an "essential" home improvement you've never even thought of till now!

**Buying in bulk means we sell it to you for less.** Don't count on it. In many cases, that may be true, but I can give you plenty of examples, from picture hooks to pipe fittings, where the closest megastore actually charges more than my local hardware store. (Plus, when you consider the distance you may have to drive to get to the big store, you really haven't bagged a bargain!)

**Service with a smile.** All the folks I've dealt with at the megastores have been cheerful and friendly as could be. But I have yet to find the kind of knowledge, experience, and bend-over-backwards help that I get in a good local lumberyard or hardware store—and that kind of service is worth a lot more than the few bucks I might save on materials. I know for a fact that the savvy folks where I shop have saved me from some mighty expensive mistakes! (I'd also like to add that they've actually talked me out of buying plenty of gadgets that I was convinced I needed to do a job. How many times has that happened to you at a megastore?)

**$ BARGAIN ALERT!**

Here's one of the niftiest places I've come across in a month of Sundays: Habitat ReStores. These are places that sell both new and salvaged lumber and other building materials, for indoor and outdoor use. The goods are donated by construction companies, demolition outfits, and general good Samaritans. The prices are bargain-basement level, the quality is top-rate, and all the proceeds go toward building Habitat for Humanity houses in the community. There are lots of ReStores across the United States and Canada, with more opening all the time. To find one near you, log onto their Web site, **www.habitat.org**, or call your closest Habitat for Humanity office.

If there's not a ReStore near you, look around for commercial recycling stores. You'll find great bargains on used and surplus building materials of all kinds. Many places even have wish lists for things that they don't have in stock right now. Look in your yellow pages under "Building Supplies, Used."

## YA GOTTA HAVE HEART

When folks buy redwood, they're looking for two things: good looks and rot-resistance. That's why you'll see redwood graded by both appearance and its ratio of heartwood to sapwood. The top four grades are pure heartwood. Clear All Heart is the superstar, with a price tag to match. Next—from most to least expensive—come B Heart, Construction Heart, and Merchantable Heart. Lower on the ladder are the heartwood/sapwood combos and the sapwoods, usually with a fair number of flaws.

## YOU CAN TELL BY LOOKIN'

Cedar graders don't bother to mention heartwood. Their terms focus on appearance alone. Starting with the top of the line, they are Architect Clear, Custom Clear, Architect Knotty, and Custom Knotty.

## MEASURE UP

When you're used to shopping for quantities like ten pounds of potatoes, a half-gallon of milk, or three pairs of socks, lumber measurements can seem a little odd at first. It's a pretty simple system, though. Here are the highlights:

**Linear foot.** When you walk into a lumberyard to buy just a few boards, they'll charge you simply by length. For instance, if you ask for "three 1 x 12-inch boards, 6 feet long," you'll pay for 18 linear feet of wood.

**Board foot.** This is the standard measurement for lumber when you order it in a large quantity, as you would if you were building a deck, for instance. A board foot is a piece of wood that is 1 inch thick, 1 foot wide, and 1 foot long. To do the math, just multiply thickness (in inches) by width (in feet) by length (in feet). So, for example, a plank that's 1 inch thick, 1 foot wide, and 10 feet long measures 10 board feet. So does one that's 2 inches thick, $\frac{1}{2}$ foot (6 inches) wide, and 10 feet long.

**Nominal sizes.** This concept baffles most beginning lumber buyers. (It sure confused me the first time I went wood shopping years ago.) It simply means that lumber is not quite as thick or as wide as the size that's marked on the rack at the lumberyard. For instance, what's known in the trade as a 1 x 12—that is, a board that's 1 inch thick and 12 inches wide—actually measures $\frac{25}{32}$ inch thick and $11\frac{1}{2}$ inches wide. Now, this isn't a case of marketing hanky-panky. That

piece of wood was full size when it was sawed from the log, but the planing process shaved off a little of the surface. Then, as the board dried out in the seasoning shed, it shrank a little more.

## ASK AND YE SHALL RECEIVE

**A**ll the building plans I've ever seen are based on nominal sizes, so chances are you'll never actually *need* boards that are a full 1 inch thick. If you *want* 'em, though, you can get 'em. Just be prepared to place a special order—and to pay more.

# Let's Rock and Roll!

**There's no doubt about it: Hefting stone, brick, or concrete pavers will give you a first-class workout—but I'd be hard pressed to think of simpler materials to work with. Just get yourself a good book on building patios, walkways, walls, or whatever project you have in mind, and go at it. Even if you're brand new to the**

do-it-yourself game, you'll feel like a pro in no time. Here are some ideas for projects that won't break your back or your budget. I'll also clue you in on where to find low-cost—or even free—materials.

# YOU'VE GOT IT MADE!

**W**ell-made, good-looking patio pavers can put a real crimp in the budget, but it's a snap to make your own. All you need is a sack of ready-mix concrete and a mold to pour it into. For $30 or so, building-supply stores sell special plastic molds that are made to look like a cluster of bricks or cobblestones. But why pay 30 bucks? At thrift shops, tag sales, and discount restaurant- or office-supply stores, you'll find terrific molds by the dozen, in all sizes and even fancy shapes—all for next to nothing. Here's a starter list:

✦ Metal pie or cake pans

✦ Plastic storage boxes or shoeboxes

✦ Large plastic plant saucers

✦ Cardboard gift or pizza boxes (line with aluminum foil and reinforce with duct tape before use)

Don't forget: The bigger your molds are, the heavier your pavers will be. Stick to a size that you can lift and

---

## PARSIMONIOUS PAVERS

One of the best-looking patios I've ever seen belonged to my frugal friend Susan, who got her pavers absolutely free. As she was walking her dog one day, she spied a concrete driveway being broken up. She asked the fella wielding the jackhammer if she could have the rubble, and he said, "Sure thing—it'll save us from having to cart the stuff away."

Well, Susan borrowed a pickup truck, enlisted a couple of pals, hauled the pieces back to her place, and installed them in her yard. In the gaps between the crazy-shaped chunks, she planted creeping thyme, Corsican mint, and other low-growing, great-smelling herbs. The result: a neighborhood showplace that's a favorite stop on fancy garden tours. The moral of this story? Walk your dog, and talk to strangers!

maneuver comfortably, and take plenty of rest breaks. After all: No patio is more expensive than the one with an achin' back for a price tag!

# 5 FOR THE PRICE OF 1

If you've got a round, 5-gallon plastic bucket in the garage, you've already got five molds, ready and rarin' to go. Just measure the height of the bucket, divide that number by 5, and mark the intervals on the side of the bucket. Then cut or saw crosswise through the plastic at each of your marks, and bingo! You've got five circular molds, each about 3 inches deep.

# SLIPPERY STONES

Whatever you make your molds from, spray them with nonstick cooking spray before you pour in the concrete. That way, your stones will slip right out, and they won't leave pieces clinging to the bottom and sides.

# ALL BRICKED UP

Got a traditional-style house that's just cryin' out for a brick patio or even a walled courtyard—but the thought of paying the price makes *you* want to cry? Well, don't. At least not before you investigate one of these budget-pleasing options:

**Ride the range.** Tell the folks at the building-supply store that you'd like to poke through their stock of "range" bricks. They're called that because they haven't been sorted by color, and they range anywhere from light red to black. If you're happy with variations in tone, you can just gather up as many bricks as you need to do the job. Or, if you're hankering for a particular color, you can spend time poking through the piles and—unless you've got a real monster of a project—probably come up with a full slate of a shade that suits you to a T. Either way, you'll pay a *lot* less than they're asking for the all-medium-red stack just around the corner.

**Run over.** After they've finished big commercial jobs, brick and paver suppliers usually have over-runs. But, because there aren't enough to use on another major project, they sell the left-overs at serious discounts. With a little calling around, you should be able to get all the top-quality bricks you need for about a third of what you'd pay at a home center. (The same applies to flagstone, cobble-stone, and other kinds of pavers and wall-makings.)

**Pick up the pieces.** Unfortunately, perfectly good build-ings get torn down every day. (Grandma Putt used to have a fit about this, and I still do.) But all that history could live on—at no cost to you—in your patio or courtyard walls. Call con-tractors in your area and ask if they've got any demolition proj-ects scheduled. Then, after the wrecking ball has done its dirty work, charge in and pick up the pieces.

## A BIT OF THE BUBBLY

Before you cart off any load of bricks that you plan to use outdoors, make sure they're well-fired and sealed. If they aren't, they'll absorb moisture and, come winter, that water will freeze and the bricks will break. Of course, if you're buy-ing your supply, all you have to do is ask whether they're suitable for use as exterior walls or flooring. But if yours is a scavenged load, put it to this test: Simply place a brick in a bucket of water. If you see bubbles, it means that the water is penetrating the brick and you should say, "Thanks, but no thanks."

## FLY THE FLAG(STONE)

Flagstone is a catch-all name for any kind of stone that's split into flat slabs that measure at least 1½ inches thick. Like brick, it has a classy appear-ance—with a price tag to match. Of course, you can lower that price by following the bargain-hunting tips above. But here's another way to trim the cost of a flagstone patio: Just make it a curvy shape, rather than a straight-sided rectangle. Why? Because that way, you'll be able to use irregular shapes and sizes, which are priced lower than stones that have been cut with flat sides and specific dimensions. ("Crazies" are also far more likely to crop up in contractors' scrap piles.)

# Getting the Goods

Whether you've got a big, old yard or a teeny, tiny balcony, you need a certain amount of gear to keep that space looking its best—and to enjoy it to the hilt. Of course, all those sales folks in retail-land want you to believe that you need a whole lot of very expensive gear. Well, my friends, I'm here to tell you that it just ain't so. Step right this way, and take a gander at my sure-fire strategies for outfittin' the outdoors without bustin' the ol' budget.

## Tooling Along

Remember the first bit of advice I gave you in Chapter 3, about shopping for appliances and electronics? Well, the same applies to tools: Before you set one foot out the door, ask yourself why you need this gadget and exactly what you intend to do with it. For instance, if you've got any lawn at all, you need a mower. But if you've got a rolling half-acre or so, you need one kind of machine. If your lawn is a flat-as-a-pancake rectangle the size of a couple of tennis courts, a smaller, simpler model will do the job just fine, thank you. And believe you me, the difference in price between those two mowers can buy a whole lot of burgers for the ol' barbecue grill! Read on for more of my money-saving tool savvy.

## TOOL POOL

We all know commuters who save big bucks by forming carpools. So, why not form a tool pool? Before you shell out cash for a major piece of equipment—say, a mower or a snowplow—consider joining forces with a neighbor or two. If you can work out a user-time arrangement that suits everyone, you'll save a bundle on both purchase and maintenance costs.

## LET'S MAKE A DEAL

There's no doubt about it: You can get some great bargains on big-ticket power tools at garage and moving sales. But, unless the price is so low that you can afford to toss the gizmo out if it breaks down, think twice. Usually, the best place to buy major outdoor equipment—new or used—is the same place you'd buy a car: from an honest, reliable dealer. You'll get a warranty, and when you need parts and service, you'll know right where to go.

Whatever kind of equipment you're shopping for, you'll find the biggest reductions at end-of-season sales. In most parts of the country, that means late August through September for lawn and garden gear, and late February through March for snow-removal tools (automated and otherwise). When it gets *really* late in the season—say it's April, and that walk-behind snow blower you've been eyeing for months is still on the floor—make an offer. Chances are, the dealer would like to get the thing off his showroom floor as much as you'd like to get it into your garage.

# Put Your Feet Up

**With outdoor rooms all the craze these days, you could pay a fortune to give yourself and your guests a place to sit and relax. But you don't have to. Here's the lowdown on finding outdoor furniture that you'll have plenty of time to use because you won't have to work day and night to pay for it!**

## THE SEARCH IS ON

Most of the places that sell indoor furniture also stock the outdoor stuff, so before you start shopping, give Chapter 4 a look-see. But, what if you've blown your whole budget on building your deck or porch, and there's not a dime left to furnish it? Will your friends have to sit on the floor and eat off cardboard boxes?

Not if you try a few of these extra-frugal ideas:

**Scavenge.** I have a friend who's furnished almost his entire house—inside and out— with pieces he's found dumped at the local landfill, set out with the weekly trash, or just abandoned on city streets. Keep your eyes open: Someone else's trash could be your treasure.

**Adopt.** From Mother Nature, that is. Just haul in some big boulders and tree stumps, top 'em with borrowed cushions from indoors, and you've got instant chairs! Lay some leftover boards between them, and you've got tables and benches.

**Swap.** I'll bet you dollars to donuts that at least a few of your friends have outdoor furniture stowed away and forgotten about in their attics or garages. And I'm just as sure that somewhere you've got a stash of things that you haven't even looked at since 1979! So hold a swap meet. (It could even be the christening event for your new outdoor room!)

**Ask nicely.** Outdoor furniture isn't the first gift idea that pops into most folks' heads, especially if they live far away.

## Pennypincher's Hall of Fame

Teak garden furniture might wear fancy price tags now, but the first crop came from a scavenger's brainstorm. At the end of World War I, the British Navy started breaking down its battleships, and some enlightened soul—a kindred spirit of Grandma Putt's—shouted, "Save those decks!" Well, the Navy listened. The wood was so drop-dead gorgeous that people started making garden benches from it—and it was so sturdy that, in gardens all over England, those benches are still being sat on today!

So, if you've got a birthday, anniversary, or gift-giving holiday coming up (say, Mother's Day or Father's Day), call your nearest and dearest, and casually mention that you've got a new outdoor living room that could use a few things. Who knows? Maybe you'll get a gift certificate for one of those glossy catalogs!

Upscale stores and catalogs sell rustic, bent-twig furniture for pretty fancy prices—but you can make your own for free, or close to it. There are plenty of books and magazines that show you how to turn a pile of flexible branches into tables, chairs, benches, and trellises. But if you'd like more hands-on help with your initial efforts—and some inexpensive fun, besides—call the closest botanical garden, arboretum, or nature center. These places often have low-cost classes and workshops on all kinds of outdoor topics, and in recent years, making bent-twig furniture has been one of the hottest topics all over the country. It's no wonder—for the price of a hike in the woods or an afternoon of pruning your shrubs, you can furnish a whole outdoor room!

## THE KING OF 'EM ALL

If you're looking for furniture that you can pass on to your children—and their children's children— teak is the biggest bargain you could find in a month of Sundays. If it's well-crafted and given proper care—which in this case means simple, periodic cleaning—this stuff will last for centuries. If buying it new is out of the question, look for bargains at auctions and estate sales (especially those in high-end neighborhoods). Believe me, the search will be well worth the effort!

## IT'LL WEAR LIKE IRON

In Grandma Putt's day, most outdoor furniture was made of one of two materials: wicker or cast iron. Wicker took (and still takes) some babying, but cast iron could take a lickin' and keep on tickin'. It still can, of course, though now, as then, you need to keep an eye out for rust (see Chapter 13 for more about that). Cast iron's cousin, wrought iron, is mighty durable, too, and often less expensive, but it's also much lighter in weight. That means it's easy to move around, but it also means that high winds can send it sailin'. The iron look-alike—cast aluminum—is less expensive, but lighter still. So beware: If your home sweet home is in Tornado Alley or Hurricane Heaven, you'll have to keep your metal bargains well anchored to good old terra firma!

# PLASTIC, BUT...

**I**f you think of plastic lawn furniture as those flimsy tables and chairs that you can pick up for a couple of bucks apiece at the discount store, think again. Nowadays, there's another kind of plastic furniture that's made from recycled resins and designed to look just like upscale wooden pieces. It's so good-looking—and so sturdy—that it's even cropping up in city parks and public buildings all over the country. Of course, you'll pay more for the new, improved plastic than you will for its throw-away counterpart, but you'll get a whole lot more for your money!

# RED ALERT

**S**ome folks call redwood "the poor man's teak." That's because, like teak, it's attractive, rarely rots or warps, and is seldom munched on by insects. But it's not perfect: It can split, and if you want it to stay that rusty-red color, you'll have to give it a coat of sealer; otherwise, it'll turn gray in a year or so.

# GIVE YOURSELF A HAND

**H**ere's a tip for all you bargain-hunters out there: Measure the length of your feet and the width of your hands, and commit those figures to

**A number of home-and-garden Web** sites use product testers to try out new gear of all kinds—including grills, barbecue tools, and outdoor cleanup gadgets. If you're game to gamble, you can sign up at the site. If your name is chosen, you get the products for free. All you need to do is use them and fill out forms evaluating their performance. One major site is **www.domus.com;** to find others, search under "product testing." (There is one catch, though: Your name will be added to the company's e-mail list, and probably sold to others.)

memory. That way, any time you come upon a great furniture find—whether it's at a tag sale, a flea market, or the local dump—you'll be able to gauge its size, even if you don't have a measuring tape on hand. After all, even if it's free for the taking, a bench, table, or porch swing won't do you much good if you can't squeeze it into the space you've got!

this, though: If you're looking for one of the high-end gas models, do the same legwork that you'd do when you're shopping for any major appliance (see Chapter 3 for the lowdown on that). Be sure to check consumer publications for the latest ratings, because new, "improved" grills come on the market every year.

## GRILLIN' TIME

**L**ike furniture, grills come in so many shapes, sizes, and prices that I won't even try to advise you what to buy! They'll all cook your kebabs and burgers just fine. I will say

## WHAT A RACKET!

**T**he next time you're at the local landfill, look for old refrigerators with the shelf racks still in them. As long as the metal is not vinyl-coated, these grates are great for cooking over a charcoal fire or to use as holding racks for burgers and hotdogs on the grill.

# CHAPTER 6

# The Frugal Traveler

Every time I leave on a trip or drop friends off at the airport, I wonder what Grandma Putt would make of all the gallivanting most of us do these days. In her time, folks sure believed in the old adage "Travel broadens the mind," but not many of them got to put that belief to the test very often.

Like a lot of other old-time luxuries, travel has turned into a necessity for a lot of us and a commonplace pleasure for nearly all of us. But it sure hasn't turned into cheap fun! Roamin' from home still broadens the mind, all right, but it can flatten the pocketbook faster than you can say "Rand McNally." Well, folks, this chapter will show you some tricks for keepin' that billfold pleasantly plump as you trot the globe.

# Getting from Point A to Point B

Whether you're traveling by train, plane, or automobile, the cost of transportation usually eats up the biggest chunk of your travel budget—even when it's not a major part of the fun. Here's how to keep those costs in line.

## Come Fly with Me

When Grandma Putt was a lass, most folks had never even laid eyes on an airplane (except in the newsreels), much less gone up in one. Nowadays, though, traveling any great distance in a vehicle *other than* an airplane is a luxury most of us can't afford very often—not if we want to keep our day jobs, that is. Well, friends, whether you're flying for the thrill of it or simply because you need to get someplace pronto, come with me: I'll tell you how to drop as few bucks as possible along the way.

## PLAN AHEAD, BUT...

We all know the airline mantra: Book at least two weeks ahead of time, begin your trip in the middle of the week, and stay over a Saturday night. If you can make your reservations 21 days or more in advance, most airlines will give you even deeper discounts. What the airline ads don't tell you is that you can sometimes get the cheapest fares at the very last minute. That's because an airline likes every plane to take off with a full load of passengers. When it gets close to taxi-out time and there are still empty seats, you might just get one for a song.

**Often the very cheapest fares are only available** online, through individual airline Web sites. Many of the major carriers let you sign up for weekly e-mail alerts that give you the latest low-price offers. Of course, there's no guarantee that any of the available flights are going where you want to go—and they're last-minute deals, so you'll have to be ready to go on the spur of the moment. If you're looking for bargain fares to a specific city, sign up for a free, personalized fare tracker at a travel site such as **www.expedia.com.** You fill out an on-screen form telling what airport you'll be flying from and where you want to go. Then every week (sometimes more often), you'll get an e-mail advising you of the lowest current ticket prices.

# CHECK 'EM OUT

These days, the Internet is usually the surest road to lower airfares. It's not a quick fix, though, so be prepared to spend some time cruising. Check individual airlines, as well as the big one-stop-shopping sites such as **www.expedia.com** and **www.onetravel.com** (or other sites that you find via your favorite search engine). And don't just peruse the standard fare listings—let the old creative juices flow. Here are some possibilities:

✔ **Do the two-step.** Instead of a single flight to and from

your destination, check the cost of two roundtrip flights. Let's say you want to go from Boston to Seattle and back again. You might pay a lot less for two separate roundtrip tickets: one Boston-Chicago-Boston and one Chicago-Seattle-Chicago. Just make sure the money you'll save will be worth the extra hassle of changing planes in Chicago.

✔ **Broaden your territory.** Investigate flights to all the cities that are near your destination. For instance, if you're heading off to Cape Cod on vacation, don't limit your search to Boston. You might find a lower fare to

Providence, and the driving distance is about the same.

✔ **Pack it up.** Often you can save big bucks by booking your plane tickets, hotel room, and rental car as a package deal.

✔ **Check the roster.** Nearly all airlines have partnership agreements with particular hotel chains, rental car agencies, cruise ship lines, and resorts. Even if the Web site doesn't offer you a package option, the partner companies will reward you with frequent-flyer miles, discount prices, or other special offers when you use their services during your trip. Usually, you'll find these outfits listed in a special travel partners section of the site.

## ADVICE FROM UNCLE SAM

**N**o matter how little you pay for a plane ticket, it's not a bargain if your flight gets in hours late, you're treated rudely, or your luggage arrives in shreds (or not at all). To set your mind at ease, before you book your flight, log onto the U.S. Department of

Transportation's Air Travel Consumer Report Web page at **www.dot.gov/airconsumer/ index1.htm.** It'll give you the lowdown on flight delays, oversales and overbooking of flights, damaged or lost baggage, treatment of passengers with disabilities, and all manner of consumer complaints for the major U.S. airlines.

## JOIN THE CLUB

**E**ven if you don't fly very often, it pays to join a few frequent flyer clubs. It'll cost you nothing, yet you'll get regular mailings telling you about special sales and programs, including moneysaving deals on things like cruises, hotels, and rental cars. Plus, if you ever run into a problem with an airline's customer service department, your membership will give you at least a little more leverage.

## SURE THING

**N**o matter where you shop for your tickets, here are two sure-fire ways to save money on your fare:

1. **Bend a little.** The more flexible you can be about the day of the week and the time

of day you travel, the more money you're likely to save. For instance, early-morning and late-evening flights often cost less than those at more, um, civilized hours.

2. **Travel off-season.** Like every kind of business, an airline charges as much as the market will bear. So it only stands to reason that when everybody and his uncle is hankerin' to be in a particular place, it's going to cost a pretty penny to get there. But, you can get some big bargains if you head to your destination when most folks are going someplace else.

# THE HUMAN TOUCH

There's no doubt about it: You can find some real bargain-basement prices on the Internet. Sometimes, though, there's nothing like a real, live travel agent. You can just pick up the phone and say, for

When next Sunday's newspaper hits the doorstep, pull out the travel section and look for the tiny ads boasting super cut-rate airfares. If you've overlooked them in the past—or passed them by because they seemed, well, maybe not entirely on the up-and-up— here's good news: These ads are placed by ticket consolidators. Consolidators work like travel agents, except that instead of making their money on commissions from the airlines, consolidators buy large blocks of tickets at wholesale rates. Then they sell them to you at bargain prices. Usually, you can count on saving at least 20 percent and sometimes as much as 40 percent on the airlines' cheapest coach fares. So, why hasn't your friendly neighborhood travel agent told you about these guys? Because they're direct competitors, that's why!

Of course, a consolidator can't offer you a seat on every flight on every airline. But if they have what you want—or you can bend your schedule to suit their inventory—you can save bucks with a capital B.

instance, "I want to go to New York sometime during the first week in July and return about two weeks later. I don't care which airport I fly into, or what time of day I travel; just please find me the cheapest ticket." Try typing that into a search engine and see what happens!

# THE CHAMPS OF CHEAP

**\* \* \* \* \***

What would you say if I told you that you could fly to Paris, London, Hong Kong, and dozens of other high-toned places for less than you probably spent at the grocery store last week? Or even for free? You'd probably say ol' Jer has lost his marbles! I agree, it does sound too good to be true and, yes, there is a catch, but it's a small one: You need to be an air courier. It's not a real day job, though—just a temporary and perfectly legitimate arrangement. Here's how it works.

Most overnight letters and packages get to overseas destinations the same way you and I do: on regular, commercial flights. The air cargo companies simply check the goods as excess passenger baggage. But, of course, passenger baggage must have a passenger to go with it. Enter the air courier. In essence, he or she trades baggage allowance for an el cheapo—or even free—plane ticket. So how do you get in on the fun? It's simple:

**1. Sign up with a courier clearinghouse.** These outfits coordinate flights for many different courier companies, and, for a modest fee, you'll get access to their flight listings for a year. Two of the major outfits are the Air Courier Association (**www.aircourier.org**) and the International Association of Air Travel Couriers (**www.courier.org**).

**2. When you're ready to ramble, log on to the clearinghouse Web site or call its toll-free number.** Then choose your destination and book your flight. Fares are discounted by as much as 85 percent—and almost always, you'll find at least a few free flights to some pretty exciting places.

**3. On the day of your flight, arrive at the airport two to four hours earlier than you normally would.** A representative from the cargo company will meet you, and give you your ticket and receipts for bags that he or she has already checked (in the company's name, not yours).

**4. Board the plane as usual, take your seat in the coach section, then sit back, relax, and enjoy the flight.**

**5. When the plane lands, pass through immigration as usual, and show the paperwork for the baggage.** A representative from the cargo company will meet you, collect the documents, and wave you on your way. You probably won't even see the shipment—and you'll never have to carry it through customs. The company folks and customs officials handle all the heavy lifting—and the niceties like inspecting and x-raying the goods *before* the plane takes off. (So if a little voice in your head is saying, "Could I get in trouble—or worse?" the answer is "No way!" This is an accepted business practice that's been going on for years. It's completely aboveboard, legal—and safe.)

## The Trade-Offs

When you fly as a courier, you have to weigh the ultra-cheap prices against a few facts of business life—after all, technically speaking, you are a temporary worker, and that bargain-basement ticket is your paycheck. Here's what to expect:

+ Usually, you'll only be able to take carry-on luggage, so you'll have to pack light. (Remember: The cargo is taking up your allotted space in the baggage compartment.)

+ Your choices of dates and times might be limited. If you want to fly a busy route—say, New York to Paris, or San Francisco to Tokyo—you'll have a whole roster of flights to pick from. But if you're hankerin' to get from Des Moines to Amsterdam, you might have to wait a while.

+ Your stay could be short. Often, the deal requires you to ferry more cargo back to the States on a certain date. That date could be far enough away to give you all the time you want, or it could mean that you get to enjoy dinner and an evening on the town, then fly right out again.

+ You could face delays or last-minute cancellations. It rarely happens—especially on the major commercial routes—but if details go awry with the shipment, you could wind up cooling your heels while the cargo folks straighten things out. The shipment could even be cancelled, leaving you to find another flight or stay on good old terra firma.

The moral of the story: If you're flexible about where you go or you're not under tight time constraints, flying as a courier is a terrific way to do some low-cost jet-setting. On the other hand, if you have your heart set on two weeks in the Bahamas in January, or you need to get to Paris in time for your daughter's wedding, this is not your best bet.

# CHARGE!

**W**ell, maybe. Those credit cards that offer frequent flyer miles for every dollar you charge can be mighty tempting. So can the ones that give you big discounts when you charge your plane fare to the card. But think twice before you sign up. That card can land you some genuine bargains if you pay your bill in full every month. But if you routinely carry even a small balance, you'll probably wind up paying more in interest charges than you'll ever save on airfare.

# SPEAK UP!

**A**irlines have all kinds of special deals going—in fact, if you're not eligible for a lower-than-normal fare for at least one reason, I'd be very surprised. But your travel agent or the airline reservation clerk may not volunteer the information, at least in any detail. Don't take chances—ask about discounts in very specific terms. Here are some ways you might qualify:

**Membership in a club or association.** The obvious ones are travel-related or age-based groups such as AAA and AARP, but the list goes beyond that. Some airlines have special deals with fraternal and professional organizations, and even college alumni clubs.

**Membership in clubs sponsored by hotel chains.** These often carry airline-discount status.

**Being of a certain age.** Both children and seniors usually qualify for lower-than-standard prices.

**Cracking the books.** Full-time students, regardless of age, are sometimes eligible for airfare discounts.

**Traveling with a large group.** What "large" means and how official the group has to be can vary from airline to airline, but take it from me, it never hurts to ask!

**Serving your country.** Discounts are often available for active military personnel, as well as veterans.

**Doing your job.** Government agencies and many corporations have special deals with major airlines, and some airlines extend those discounts to employees' leisure travel.

# Well-Grounded Advice

So, you got yourself a bargain ticket, and the plane has just landed at the airport. Now you need to cover ground *on* the ground—and if you're not careful, you can still drop a lot more dough than you need to. In this section, I'll show you how to hang on to those greenbacks. Oh, and if you're taking your whole trip on the ground, there's help here for you, too.

## OH, TAXI!

When you rent a car at most airports, you're shelling out an extra fee of 10 to 20 percent of your total bill just for the convenience of getting the car at the airport. Even for a weekend jaunt, that translates into a pretty penny. For a one- or two-week vacation, it's a first-class budget breaker! So how do you avoid that surcharge? Simple: When you reserve your vehicle, ask where the closest off-premises office is, and arrange to pick up the car there. Then,

### Pennypincher's Hall of Fame

Here's something interesting that I read in a book called *The Penny-Pinching Hedonist* by Shel Horowitz. He writes about a woman he met in 1981 named Wing Red Cloud, who didn't pinch pennies. Fact is, she refused to even touch them—or any other kind of money. Instead, she traveled the states with her two horses and two dogs, bartering all the way. In exchange for lodging, grub, or whatever else she needed, Ms. Red Cloud taught classes in herbal lore and Indian tradition, cooked, cleaned houses, and looked after people's animals. If that's not travelin' cheap, I don't know what is!

when the plane lands, hop a taxi or—cheaper yet—a shuttle or city bus, and go claim your wheels. (Just make sure the office is close enough that getting there won't cost more than the airport pick-up fee or be more hassle than it's worth.)

## NO THANKS, I'LL PASS

J ust like the rest of us, rental car companies have to make money—and they make a bundle on the insurance they sell to folks who just want to make *sure* they're covered if anything happens. Well, the fact is, you probably have all the insurance you need, courtesy of your own auto insurance policy or your credit card. Check before your trip, then politely decline the insurance coverage at the rental desk.

## ASK FIRST

B efore you confirm your car reservation, ask about the company's cancellation policy. Some rental agencies will charge you a fee if you cancel on the day that you're due to arrive. If that's the case, you might want to set your mind at ease by taking your business elsewhere.

## ALL ABOARD

W hen your time is limited, it might seem that flying is your only option, but, as Mr.

---

### $ BARGAIN ALERT!

If you're hankerin' to see the U.S.A. at ground level, rather than from 20,000 feet in the air—or if you just need to get somewhere and you'd rather eat worms than go up in an airplane—here's a terrific deal: Drive somebody else's car. Lots of folks need to have vehicles transported from one part of the country to another, and for whatever reasons, they don't want to do the driving themselves. Rather than towing the car behind a truck or having it shipped, they hire an agency to find a driver. Enter *you!*

Chances are, you won't have much time to dawdle along the way, but you'll sure as shootin' get cheap transportation—and it might be a lot spiffier than the kind you're used to. To put yourself behind the wheel, check the yellow pages or your favorite Internet search engine for "drive-away companies" or "automobile transporters." Before you step on the gas, though, find out who'll pay the expenses if the car breaks down or you have an accident that's not your fault. Otherwise, you could wind up spending a lot more than you'd have paid for a plane ticket!

Gershwin said, "It ain't necessarily so." Taking a train actually might be faster than flying—especially when you're traveling between cities that are only a few hundred miles apart. And it can be a whole lot cheaper, to boot! Consider this:

☞ New high-speed trains zip along at 125 to 150 miles an hour.

☞ You can start off and end up in a big city, a small town, or a teeny suburban station—instead of an airport that might be a *long* way from your destination.

☞ You can arrive at the station just in time to catch the train; you don't have to show up hours in advance, go through elaborate check-in procedures, and then sit around cooling your heels (or spending money at all those overpriced airport shops and snack bars).

# CLICK AND GO

If the sound of a lonesome whistle and the clickety-clack down the track makes you want to pack your bags and grab your traveling hat, boy, do I have a deal for you! Or I should say,

Amtrak has. Log on to **www.amtrak.com** and click on "Rail Sale." You'll find discounts of up to 70 percent off regular coach fares to dozens of cities. These tickets are only available online, on a first-come, first-served basis, so you need to act fast. So what are you waiting for? If you're itchin' to ride the rails, start clickin' that mouse!

If the Rail Sale tickets to your destination are all sold out, you'll have plenty of other bargain fares to choose from. For instance:

★ Discounts for seniors, students, and veterans.

★ A North American Rail Pass that's good for 30 days of unlimited travel in the United States and Canada—for a price that's so low it'll boggle your brain!

★ Regional rail passes with even cheaper rates.

★ Air/Rail combos that let you take the train one way and fly the other.

## NO, SUR(CHARGE)!

**H**ere's another way that train travel might save you big bucks: When you ride the rails, you can wind up within easy strolling or cabbing distance of a rental car office. Sometimes, there's even one in the station. That means you can get off the train and slide right into a car—without being nicked for the airport-pickup fee.

# Safe and Sound

Just about anyone who's taken more than a couple of trips—whether by plane, train, car, or boat—has at least one tale to tell about luggage that's gone astray. At best, parting company with your bags will put a damper on your trip. At worst, it can put a big hole in your travel budget. You'll get an even more unpleasant surprise if an uninvited visitor steps into your empty house (courtesy of the luggage tags on your bags), and helps himself to the

contents. I've learned this stuff the hard way, folks! That's why I've come up with some strategies for safeguarding my travelin' bags—and the house I've left behind.

## LEAVE HOME WITHOUT IT

**E**ven in Grandma Putt's day, things got lost on the road. Whenever she packed her suitcase, she followed her Rule for Fret-Free Traveling: If losing a particular object would break your heart or your budget, leave it at home. What that means is different for everybody. In my case, it means, for instance, that the cuff links my grandchildren saved up to buy me for Christmas last year go into my dresser drawer, and I take along a set that I won't miss if my bag takes off for never-never land. For you, it might mean leaving your favorite designer dress in the closet and taking a less treasured, and less expensive, stand-in.

## TAKE IT ON

**A**ll rules need to bend, even Grandma Putt's. We all have to travel with a few things that would be hard, expensive, or impossible to replace. For the sake of your peace of mind and your budget, never check things like prescription medicines, eyeglasses, used camera film, your address book, or any country's cash. Pack them in your carry-on bag or your pocketbook.

## PUT IT IN YOUR POCKET

It's not just checked baggage that can go astray. Though the chances are slim (as long as you're careful), your carry-on bag could be stolen—and if you have to evacuate the plane for any reason, you'll have to leave the bag, and (yes, ladies) probably your pocketbook, behind. So don't take chances. Carry the following papers in your pocket, and leave a duplicate set at home with a trustworthy friend:

✦ A list of the contents and approximate value of your carry-on and checked bags.

✦ The numbers and denominations of your traveler's checks.

✦ Photocopies of your tickets, passport, visas, driver's license, and any essential prescriptions.

✦ Credit card numbers or, if you've registered them, the

### DON'T GO ON TRIAL

* * * * *

When you're shopping for travelin' supplies, walk right on by the trial-size cosmetic section. Those tiny bottles of shampoo, mouthwash, and so on seem tailor-made for suitcases, and at less than a dollar a pop, they sure do look like bargains. Ounce for ounce, though, they cost a fortune! Instead, buy the giant, economy size of whatever you need, and pour it into smaller bottles. Make sure the bottles have screw-on lids, though, and not pop-tops—at high altitudes, or under the weight of a pile of luggage, those things tend to pop open—and then, splat! You'll have a mess on your hands, and maybe even some ruined clothes (plus, cleaning or shopping bills that you hadn't planned on).

phone number of the registration service.

✦ Any phone numbers that you'll need on the road and may not be able to track down easily.

## COLOR IT SAFE

I have an old friend who spent years traveling the world for a big corporation. She all but *lived* on the road. And you know what? Her luggage got

sent to the wrong destination only a couple of times, and she never once had a bag stolen or accidentally carried off by another traveler. Her secret, she says, was this: She always carried moderately priced and very brightly colored luggage, and this ploy worked for two reasons:

1. Because those bags were so eye-catching, no one could grab them by accident, no thief in his right mind would want to risk taking off with them, and the baggage handlers couldn't miss them.

2. Bright color aside, serious snatchers didn't bother with these bags for another reason: Though they were sturdy and good-looking, they were obviously not top-of-the-line models. To a thief's way of thinking, a fancy case with a big-name designer's initials all over it is bound to be full of expensive goodies. Even if you got designer luggage for five bucks at a tag sale, it all but jumps up and shouts "Take me!"

## THE CASE FOR ART

If you can't find luggage in a knock-their-socks-off color (my friend's bags were brilliant magenta), you can still have goof-proof and thief-resistant cases. How? Turn your plain old black, gray, or green bags into works of art. Just get yourself some brushes and paint—the brighter the better—and have at it. The kind of paint you need will depend on what your luggage is made of, so ask the folks at an art-supply store what they'd recommend. If you don't feel comfortable doing your own freehand designs, use stencils. You can bet that nobody in the airport (or on the cruise ship) will have anything like it!

---

### PICTURE THIS

\* \* \* \* \*

Before you leave home, take a picture of your travelin' bags. That way, if you and they part company along the way and you need to fill out a missing-luggage report, you won't have to wrack your brain to remember exactly what they looked like. What's more, when your cases finally do show up, you'll be able to give the baggage-claim folks a positive I.D.

## ON THE DOUBLE

**I**f your luggage gets lost or delayed, you'll have two wardrobe choices: Live in your flying clothes for heaven knows how long, or fork out good money for new ones. When you're on the road with your spouse or a travelin' pal, you can both avoid that kind of hassle. How? Simple: Each of you should put one complete outfit in the other's suitcase. Even if one of your bags goes astray, it's not likely that both will.

## LOCK IT UP

**W**hen you buy a new suitcase, the first thing you should do is throw away the lock that came with it. (Those things are about as sturdy as the front door on a doll house.) Then go to your local hardware store and buy a tiny—but serious-strength—padlock. It'll cost just a couple of dollars, but it could save you hundreds if someone breaks into your hotel room and starts poking around. Of course, you'll have to remember to lock your case when you leave the room!

## DON'T PUT OUT THE WELCOME MAT

**E**ven if you've left your house in the hands of a trusted sitter, don't advertise your home address when you're on the road—it's like putting a "burglar-wanted" ad in the newspaper. Professional crooks pick up leads anyplace they can find them—including luggage tags that they or their roving accomplices "just happen" to see in airports, hotel lobbies, or anywhere else that travelers gather. So, outwit the sleazeballs: Instead of putting your home address on your luggage tags, use your business or destination address.

The same holds true for reading materials. How many of us throw a handful of magazines into our luggage to "catch up on" while on vacation? Well, that's fine, but before you start your trip, rip off the part of the magazine cover that contains your mailing label. That way, you can leave the magazine in your hotel room or out at the pool without a tell-tale address on it. It's just one more way to make your home safe while you're on the road.

# Beddin' Down for Less

**W**hile you could say that when you've seen one airplane seat, you've pretty much seen 'em all, that's sure not true of sleeping accommodations! When it comes to bunking down on the road, you've got more choices than you can shake a bedroll at. But whatever you prefer in the way of travelin' digs, there's no reason to shell out more bucks than you have to.

## Room at the Inn

When it comes to hotel rooms, there's a world of difference between the ones that rate a single star in the guidebooks and the ones that get four or five. Within rating categories, though, these bunkhouses have one thing in common with airplane seats: The rate for the very same room can bounce up and down like a 4-year-old on a bed. Here's how to catch those prices on the downward bounce.

## WONDERFUL WEEKENDS

**I**n a lot of cities, hotels make most of their bread and butter from business travelers who arrive on Monday morning and leave on Friday morning. So do big—and often fancy—motels that are near suburban campuses of major corporations. Rooms at these places usually carry hefty price tags from Monday through Thursday, but come Friday, it's a whole new ballgame. For a weekend stay, you can expect rates to drop by 35 percent or more. Often, the hotel will even throw in a whole slew of enticing extras, such as free breakfast, free cocktails, free admission to the health club, or discounts in its dining room, nearby restaurants, or even theaters and nightclubs. So what are you waiting for? Go live it up!

## GO FOR BROKE(R)

**J**ust like airlines with their seats, hotels often find themselves with more empty rooms than the corporate bean counters like. So what do they do? The same thing the airlines do, of course: They slash the prices and sell the rooms to consolidators, or brokers, who in turn sell them to you for as much as 50 percent off of the regular rate. Brokers focus mainly on major cities, though, so you're a lot more likely to find bargains in, say, Boston or San Francisco than in Laramie or Cedar Rapids. You'll find these low-price bed-finders in the Yellow Pages under "Travel Agencies and Bureaus."

## DOIN' THE WORK-WEEK RAG

**O**ut in the country, along any coast, and in any place that caters mainly to tourists, the hotel game is just the opposite of the city scene. There—in every accommodation price range—you'll generally get better rates during the week. And, when you're bedding down midweek in the off-season, you can expect some *real* deals!

### DON'T TOUCH THAT DIAL!

\* \* \* \* \*

The phone dial in your hotel room, that is. If you make only a local call or two, the extra fees can be high; for long-distance calls they'll really knock your socks off. Avoid the surcharges by arming yourself with a couple of prepaid phone cards. But take along your regular phone company calling card, too—that way, you'll have it to fall back on if (as sometimes happens) the prepaid cards don't work.

## MORE LAST-MINUTE MARVELS

**W**hen it gets right down to the wire, hotels often slash their prices big time, just to fill up those beds. If you can wait till the very last minute, you might get a rate that's better than a broker's price. Even if you're just around the corner from the hotel, though, don't simply stroll in and ask for a room; pick up a phone and call. Once they've got you in the door and standing at the check-in desk, your bargaining leverage will plummet.

# Broaden the Scope

When all I'm lookin' for is a place to lay my weary head after a long day on the road, any clean room with a comfortable bed and functional plumbing suits me just fine, and I have a hunch you feel the same. For a longer stay, though, it's nice to find a place with a little more character—and, of course, an attractive price tag.

## LET'S SWAP

**H**ere's one of the best travel deals I know of: house swapping. It's not really a new concept—for years, savvy penny-pinchers have been trading digs with each other. Usually, though, they had to make the arrangements themselves. Well, nowadays, there are registries that connect you with potential swappers all over the world. The details vary with the registry, but the basics couldn't be simpler: You pay a sign-up fee (usually minimal) and fill out an online form describing your home and your stomping ground, and listing the dates it'll be available. Then you peruse the listings to find a domicile that strikes your fancy. You can settle down in a beach house at Malibu, a condo in Manhattan, a thatched cottage in the Irish countryside—the world's your oyster! To explore the possibilities, crank up your favorite search engine and type in "house swapping" or "house exchanges."

## THE B WORDS

**I**t used to be that landing a room at a bed-and-breakfast establishment, a.k.a. a B & B, was a sure-fire moneysaver. Well, if you choose carefully— or get lucky—it still can be, but don't bet your bottom traveler's check on it. Overseas, B & Bs still tend to be better bargains than hotels. In the United States, though, a room at a clean, comfortable B & B will likely cost about what you'd pay at a decent motel (and these days, lots of motels even feed you in the morning). At some of the really highfalutin' B & Bs, you'll come close to droppin' more bucks than you'd spend on a stay at the Ritz!

## THE LAY OF THE LAND

**R**oom rates aside, there is one way that a good B & B can help you hang on to more of your travelin' dollars, and that's by sharing its local knowledge. The owner/operators of these places are right on the scene, and I've found that there's nothing they like better than pointing out all the fun—and often free—stuff there is to see and do in their neck of the woods. All you need to do is sit down with your hosts, and (as Grandma Putt used to say), chat 'em up. Tell 'em what your interests are, ask a few questions, and if it doesn't lead to adventures you'll be talking about for years to come, I'll eat my guidebook.

## HERE TODAY...

**A**nd maybe, gone tomorrow. There are exceptions, but B & Bs tend to have short life spans. (After all, they're usually one- or two-person operations, and entertaining the general public day after day can lead to burnout pretty quickly.) If you're headin' for the open road and plan to book your rooms as you go, take along a couple of the most up-to-date directories you can find. Your local bookstore should have plenty to choose from, but also check with state tourism offices for regional listings.

## PARK IT

**S**ome of the best lodging bargains I've found have been at State and National Parks and National Forests—and not just campgrounds

### A BREATH OF FRESH AIR!

\* \* \* \* \*

A cabin in the woods can be a great summer getaway—and a terrific bargain, to boot—but sometimes that rustic retreat comes equipped with a good old-fashioned two-holer where you might have hoped there would be indoor facilities. Well, here's a simple formula for reducing the, um, atmospheric aroma: Gather up some wood ashes from the campfire, and keep them in a bucket by the door, along with an old cup. Then, after each visit to the facility, sprinkle a cupful of ashes in the hole. It won't exactly have things smelling like a rose, but it *will* improve the air quality!

and bare-bones cabins, either. On public lands all over the country, you can find comfortable cottages, motels, and even fancy hotels and lodges. (Those can cost a pretty penny, but if you budget the rest of your trip carefully, you just might want to splurge.) For both plain and fancy places, you'll need to book far in advance, so don't dawdle. As soon as you know where you're headed, contact the state tourism office, the National Park Service, and the National Forest Service, and ask them to send you the rundown on lodgings.

# Goin' Places and Doin' Things

If you ask half a dozen people what makes a great vacation, chances are you'll get half a dozen answers. Well, folks, this isn't a travel guide—you'll find plenty of those at your local bookstore—so I'm not going to tell you where to go and what to do. Instead, I'll just pass on some tricks for saving greenbacks while you're goin' and doin'.

## It's a Wrap

There are more travel packages to more places—and in more price ranges—than you can shake a suitcase at. Are they bargains? Maybe yes, maybe no. To find the best prices on any kind of package, follow the same routine you would for landing deals on planes and hotels. For more kit-and-kaboodle travel information, read on.

# JUST SAY YES

To my way of thinking, there are times when a package tour makes great sense, even when you think you could shave a few bucks off the cost by going solo. I say sign up if:

☞ You want to trek to a part of the world that's a lot different from ours, and you don't know the lay of the land. For instance, if you've never been to Russia, you don't know a soul there, and you don't speak a word of the language, go with a group. You're likely to see a lot more than you would stumbling around on your own, and you'll probably save big bucks, besides. If the place catches your fancy, you can study up, make a few contacts, and go back on your own later.

☞ You find a tour that zeroes right in on a hobby or special interest—or that might launch you on a new one. Say you're a bird watcher (or think you might like to be), and you see a tour that's guided by an expert from the Audubon Society. Sure, you could probably explore the same places on your own for less cash, but you'd lose what amounts to an education-on-the-wing. (Sorry, I couldn't resist that cue!)

☞ The tour takes you to places you couldn't go to on your own at any price. For instance, outfits such as the National Trust for Historic Preservation run expert-guided tours that

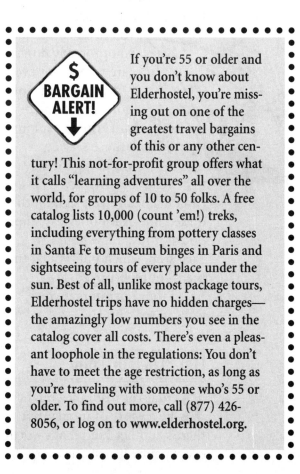

**BARGAIN ALERT!** If you're 55 or older and you don't know about Elderhostel, you're missing out on one of the greatest travel bargains of this or any other century! This not-for-profit group offers what it calls "learning adventures" all over the world, for groups of 10 to 50 folks. A free catalog lists 10,000 (count 'em!) treks, including everything from pottery classes in Santa Fe to museum binges in Paris and sightseeing tours of every place under the sun. Best of all, unlike most package tours, Elderhostel trips have no hidden charges—the amazingly low numbers you see in the catalog cover all costs. There's even a pleasant loophole in the regulations: You don't have to meet the age restriction, as long as you're traveling with someone who's 55 or older. To find out more, call (877) 426-8056, or log on to www.elderhostel.org.

include private homes and gardens where you couldn't even get in the door unescorted—or they take you behind the scenes at museums, theatres, and historical sites.

## DO THEY COVER THE WATERFRONT?

**S**ome folks go on cruises just because they love being out there on the deep blue sea. If you're one of them, you probably don't care where—or even if—the boat puts into shore. But if you're hankerin' to explore all those seaside towns along the way, read the itinerary very carefully before you sign on the dotted line. A lot of cruise ships dock for just a few hours at each stop, which puts you at the mercy of high-priced, fast-paced tour operators if you want to soak up any local color.

## FOR PEACE OF MIND

**R**ental-car insurance might be a waste of money, but there's another kind that's worth every penny it costs, at least to my way of thinking: traveler's insurance. If you have to cancel a package tour at the last minute, you stand a snowball's chance in you-know-where of getting a refund from the tour operator. For about 1 percent of the total package cost, though, you can buy a policy that will pay you back if your plans change due to circumstances beyond your control.

Before you sign on and write a check, though, make sure the policy covers you for *any* emergency. Some insurance companies pay off only for sudden medical problems. You want to make sure you're covered if, let's say, a crisis erupts at work, a big storm blows the roof off your house, or your daughter's baby arrives a month early and she needs your help.

# Road Trip

**For my money, there's no finer vacation than to get behind the wheel of a car and take off across the good old U.S.A. I do it every chance I get, and here are a few tricks I've learned for keepin' the costs under control. (That way, I can hit the road more often—for less dough!)**

## TAKE A BUDDY

**I**f you're not blessed (as I am) with a spouse who loves the open road, find a friend to go along with you. Besides sharing car expenses, you'll save big bucks on lodging. That's because, in most places, a single room costs almost as much as a double. So get the double and share the room. It'll translate into almost 50 percent savings for each of you!

## BE PICKY

**E**ven if your potential travelin' buddy is your best friend, take a short trial jaunt. You don't want to get a thousand miles from home and find out, for instance, that your pal wants to go out to dinner every night, and you'd rather eat sandwiches and play Scrabble in the room. You could wind up ruining a friendship as well as a vacation—and maybe even shelling out for a plane ticket home.

## CARRY THE CARD

**Y**our membership card, that is. Make that card*s*, plural. We all know that, just like the airlines, thousands of places (from famous theme parks to roadside souvenir shops) offer discounts for all kinds of affiliations. But you never know which one will land you the biggest bargain. It could be your AARP membership, it could be your veteran status, or it could be your union credentials. It could even be that a restaurant is giving away free lunches to folks who were born on a certain date, and it's *your* birthday. So cover your bases: Don't leave home without all the proof you've got.

## NO STRINGS ATTACHED

When you're on the road, keep an eye out for church suppers. You can get some great down-home cookin' for next to nothing. And you may even get to chew the fat with local folks who can clue you in on where to find the best bargains in town!

## GO BACK TO SCHOOL

**E**very time I get to a town that has a university in it, the first thing I do is head for the campus. I nearly always wind up hangin' around for a few days and having a great time for almost no money. Even in the summer, there's usually plenty going on that's open to the general public. Here are some of the free or almost-free treats I look for:

★ Museums, art galleries, and special exhibits

★ Concerts and recitals, either by student musicians or visiting performers

★ Seasonal festivals of all kinds

★ Historic buildings

★ Talks and lectures (often by famous visitors)

★ Botanical gardens

★ Student sports events

# Beyond Our Borders

**All of those road trip tips apply just as much to other countries as they do to ours, but here are some pointers that can save you a bundle when you're bound for foreign shores.**

## CHANGING CUSTOMS

**W**hen your trip is still in the planning stages, contact the U.S. Customs Service, and get the current lowdown on duty charges, as well as what you can and cannot bring back into the states. It changes occasionally, and not knowing this year's ropes can cost you big time. Look in the federal government pages of your phone directory, or log onto the Customs Service Web site at **www.customs.ustreas.gov/travel/travel.htm.**

**$ BARGAIN ALERT!**

If you find yourself near a culinary school or a university that has a food-service program, ask if there's a student-run restaurant. If the answer is yes, high-tail it over there. The budding chefs usually serve up first-class gourmet chow at coffee-shop prices.

# CLAIM YOUR REFUND

**M**any countries, including Canada, collect a hefty sales tax on goods and services. Usually, as a nonresident, you can apply for a refund after you return to the States. You must follow procedures exactly, though, and these change from time to time. Before you leave home, call the embassy or consulate of each country you plan to visit, and find out what the current policies are. Then make sure you follow them to the letter. Otherwise, your trip could cost a lot more than it needs to!

# DON'T BELIEVE EVERYTHING YOU READ

**H**ere's something the guidebook publishers don't tell you: Even in the most recent edition, the information is at least a year old. That's how long it takes for all that material to get collected, written up, verified, printed, and delivered to the bookstores. Of course, you can still count on a good travel guide for a lot of the basics. For instance, the address of Buckingham Palace or the height of the Eiffel Tower won't

change from one year to the next. Other things do change, though. For example, in the space of 12 months, hotel and restaurant ratings can plummet, their prices can soar, or they can even go out of business. An art festival that took place in June one year can switch to July the next. If you want to get the lowdown on what's happening *now*, read some newspapers and magazines from the place you'll be visiting. If you can't find what you want at your local library, try a large newsstand or a bookstore that caters to an international or expatriate crowd.

---

## PINCH PENNIES WITH PLASTIC

\* \* \* \* \*

We all know that carrying a credit card is safer than toting big amounts of cash. But on an international trip, there's another reason to say "Charge it!" every chance you get. Why? Because when you pay by credit card, or use your ATM card, you automatically get the official exchange rate of the day; when you pay by cash, you get whatever rate the establishment happens to be using—and it's often higher.

# Saving

# · PART II ·

# MONEY

# CHAPTER 7

# More Banquet for Your Buck

You wander into the kitchen for a midnight snack. You open the cabinet, reach through the jumble of jars, bottles, and boxes for the pretzels, and *bang!* Down comes an avalanche! *Crash! Splat!* There goes the salsa. You're still hungry—and there's a big mess to clean up. You've also got a floor covered with wasted food that you paid good money for—and all because your cupboard was about as well-organized as a 2-year-old's toy box.

In Chapter 1, I gave you the lowdown on savvy grocery shopping. Now I'm going to tell you how to stretch your food dollars even further. I'll show you how to turn your cupboards into neat storage spaces instead of disasters waiting to happen. I'll also give you tips for keeping food fresher, longer, and for making a little food go a long way. Plus, you'll find fabulous formulas for fending off bugs and other thugs—because you don't want to share your bounty with them!

# Sort It Out

Grandma Putt had a pantry that was lined with shelves from floor to ceiling. On one side she kept the fruits and vegetables she put by every fall, all sorted by type, and lined up in soldier-straight rows. On the other side were pots, pans, and dishes. Believe me, folks, when Grandma sent me to fetch, say, a jar of peaches or a mixing bowl, I didn't have to search high and low—I could lay my hands on it faster than you can say "suppertime." If your kitchen is only that well organized in your dreams, then read on.

## Clutter Busters

Nowadays, most folks don't have pantries. They have to make do with kitchen cupboards to corral their grub and gear—and you know how easy it is for clutter to build up behind closed doors! (As Grandma Putt would say, "Out of sight, out of mind.") Well, friends, here's how to stop clutter in its tracks.

## OUT OF THE CUPBOARD

Here's a dandy project for a rainy afternoon: Clean out your food cabinets. If you haven't looked at the back of those shelves since the last time you bought grape jelly in a Howdy Doody glass, you're probably thinking, "No way! There's no telling *what's* lurking in there!" Well relax, friends: It's probably not Godzilla. Just grit your teeth and grab some trash bags and boxes. Then open a door—any door—and start grabbing. As you pull out each item, assign it to one of the following categories:

☑ **Trash:** All bulging cans, any jar that's leaking or whose warning button on the lid has popped up, anything that's more than a few days past its printed sell-by date—and (of course) all those half-filled bags of limp snacks left over from last year's Super Bowl party.

✔ **Food bank:** Anything that's still good but you *know* you won't use—such as the canned crab meat that you've just learned you're allergic to or the bean soup that you've been meaning to eat for the past three months. (Be sure to get a receipt: Most likely your donation will be tax deductible.)

✔ **Use soon.** Food that you routinely use and that's still good, but that's gotten lost in the clutter.

✔ **Get creative—*now*:** Goodies that you bought on impulse, such as marinated artichoke hearts or pickled peppers, because you thought they'd be a great new taste treat. Well, they will be—*if* you eat them or work them into a recipe before they migrate to the "Trash" category. Otherwise, you'll just be throwing good money down the drain.

---

## EXPIRATION DATES: SCRIPTURE OR SUGGESTION?

\* \* \* \* \*

Typically, expiration dates on foods fall into two categories: "sell-by" dates and "freshness" dates. "Sell-by" dates, as the name implies, are deadlines for grocery stores. Foods cannot be sold past those dates. However, this is by no means a "use-by" date. Take milk, for example. If the date says, "Sell by August 3," you have a good week or so beyond that before it will actually be unsafe to drink. The "sell by" date is the last possible date a product may leave the store and still give consumers ample time to consume it.

The "freshness" date, on the other hand, is just that—a date provided by the manufacturer suggesting how long their product will be good to eat. It's a quality assurance date. Usually, a product will say something like "Best if used by August 3." Again, this is only a guide. If your bag of chips says "Best if used by," it doesn't mean that they're going to suddenly become inedible at midnight of that day. This, too, is just a guide, but it should be followed a bit more closely than the "sell-by" date.

For more information regarding freshness and food quality, see page 161.

## TO EACH ITS OWN

**W**e all know that food isn't the only clutter-causing culprit in the cupboards. It's no wonder that a jar of peanuts sits forgotten on a shelf for a year when it's surrounded by stacks of plates and towers of bowls that you only pull out once a year for Thanksgiving dinner! If you want to make *sure* that your food dollars don't go out with the trash, keep the gear and the edibles in separate places.

## ENOUGH IS ENOUGH!

**I**f the clutter in your kitchen is so out of hand that it's cutting into space you need for food, it's time to take action. How? It's simple. Start by memorizing my rule of thumb for conquering clutter: If you haven't used it in a year and it's not hanging on the wall, throw it out. Then follow these six simple steps to cleaning out clutter:

1. Rustle up some sturdy cardboard boxes. On the side of one of them, write "Up Front." Set this one aside for now. On another, write "Elsewhere." On a third, write "Goodwill/Garage Sale."

2. Take all of the nonedibles out of your cabinets and drawers. As you come across things you know you'll never use—three extra bottle openers, for instance, or a duplicate salad spinner—toss them into the "Goodwill/Garage Sale" box.

3. Everything that you do use, but not normally in the kitchen, goes into the "Elsewhere" box—for instance, your dog's Frisbee, small tools, or tins of shoe polish. Then take the box elsewhere. Pronto.

4. Fill the unlabeled boxes with all your kitchen gear, and keep them close at hand— say, on the shelves at the top of the cellar stairs. Then, as the need arises, grab a gadget. Making tacos? Pull out the old cheese grater. Toasting your team's victory? Go for the corkscrew. When you've finished using whatever

tool it was, put it back into the "Up Front" box. (**Hint:** You'll probably need several of these boxes!)

5. After a few weeks, examine the boxes. I'd bet my last pot holder that you've been pulling things from the "Up Front" boxes over and over again—and that there's a fair amount of stuff in the other cartons that you haven't even glanced at.

6. Organize the "Up Front" contents in whatever way works best in your kitchen, and get the other boxes out of the way for now—but not too far out of the way. As weeks or months go by, you'll no doubt be reaching for some of that gear. Whatever you do, don't toss out anything that's in those boxes until a full year has passed! Why not? Because (for instance) you don't want to give away your punch bowl in June, and then have to buy a new one in December for your New Year's Eve party!

## DOUBLE UP

✳   ✳   ✳   ✳   ✳

You can find a kitchen gadget for every purpose under the sun. If you're not careful, you can drop a whole lot of bucks outfittin' your kitchen with a lot of specialized gimcracks that you don't really need. Before you buy a new kitchen tool, check your inventory—chances are you have something that will do the job just fine. For instance:

◆ Any sharp knife will slice pizza as well as a fancy pizza cutter.

◆ A food processor does just about every chopping and grinding job there is, so if you have one, there's no need to splurge on one of those one-purpose gadgets like meat grinders and cheese shredders.

◆ A good old-fashioned potato peeler will pit cherries, hull strawberries, shave chocolate, and peel oranges and apples—so you can say "No thanks" to those pricey specialty gadgets!

◆ A colander sitting on top of a saucepan will get your broccoli and cauliflower just as tender-crisp as the most expensive veggie steamer.

# Ship Shape

If you've strolled through an upscale housewares shop lately—or even a discount store—you know that you could spend a fortune on gadgets to store your food in and corral your kitchen gear. But you don't have to. In this section, I'll clue you in on how to organize your bread and butter (and your bread and butter knives) without laying out a lot of cash.

## I SEE!

When it comes to storing dry goods, for my money, you can't beat big glass jars. Forget those labeled—and expensive—canisters that come in graduated sizes. (Whoever decided that you want to keep more flour than sugar on hand anyway?) My wife and I keep all of our flour, sugar, pasta, rice—and even tea bags, crackers, and dog biscuits—in clamp-top jars that we've picked up at garage sales for next to nothing. Thanks to the tight seals on the jars, the food inside stays fresh longer than it ever would in its original bags and boxes. Plus, we can see at a glance when we're running low on something—which means we always know which coupons to take along on our next trip to the supermarket.

## NO STRINGS ATTACHED

Restaurants and delicatessens buy pickles and other condiments in giant-size jars that make perfect, now-you-see-it storage containers for everything from corn flakes to jelly beans. The next time you're having lunch at your favorite deli, ask whether they have any empty jars to spare. I'll bet you bucks to bagels that they'll say, "Sure do! We were just about to toss half a dozen of 'em in the recycling bin, but now, they're all yours!"

## HANG IN THERE

Hanging pots and pans on the wall is a great way to free up cupboard space for food, but you can drop a *lot* of dough on a store-bought pot rack. So, do what I do: Make your own. Just buy some

¾-inch-diameter copper tubing, cut it to the size you need (or have the folks at the store do it), and fasten it to the wall with screw-in hooks. Then get some S-hooks that are big enough to go over the pipe and hold your pots. Presto! You're in business.

Stainless or galvanized steel will work just as well as copper tubing—it's all a matter of your taste and budget. Galvanized steel is the least expensive of the three (and you can spray-paint it any color you like); stainless is the highest-priced; copper's in the middle. Whichever you choose, just make sure you get it at a plumbing-supply shop— the stuff will cost at least three times as much at a hardware or home-improvement store.

## HANG IT ALL

**H**ow many times have you reached into a drawer for the tongs and pulled out a tangled mess of interlocked gadgets? Well, say goodbye to gadget gridlock: Hang all those oddly shaped tools on your homemade pot rack, alongside the pots and pans. I hang up cheese graters, measuring cups, potato mashers, and anything else that'll slide over an S-hook.

## GOING YOUR WAY

**B**efore you start reloading your clean, empty cupboards, take some time to plan the new arrangement.

---

**$ BARGAIN ALERT!**

Nobody likes to see a good restaurant go out of business—especially if it's been your favorite local hangout. There's a silver lining in that cloud, though: When a restaurant goes out of business, the owners usually sell the contents at rock-bottom prices. Sometimes, the owners handle the sale themselves; other times, an auction house does the job. Either way, you can pick up everything from tables to major appliances to great-looking glassware for pennies on the dollar—and it'll all be heavy-duty, commercial-grade gear that should last a lifetime. Watch your local newspaper for restaurant auctions and going-out-of-business sales.

Remember, though: There's no right or wrong way to organize a cupboard. All that matters is putting that food where you can put your hands on it quickly—before it turns into wasted cash. Here are three different systems that work for lots of folks I know:

1. **Categorically speaking.** For simplicity, you can't beat this old standby: Just arrange foods by category. For instance, group canned fruits and veggies on one shelf, canned fish and meats on another, and soups and stews on still another. Put all baking supplies together, all cereals in one place, and all snack treats together.

2. **We're all in this together.** If you like to put meals on the table *pronto*, this system is for you: Group together all the foods that you use to prepare a meal. For instance, keep the pasta with your favorite sauce makings, put the refried beans and salsa next to the taco shells, and gather all the broth and canned stew veggies into one big huddle.

3. **Alphabet soup.** If you like word games, you'll love this

---

## FANTASTIC FORMULA

### Cabinet Cleanser

Before you start reorganizing those cabinets and cupboards, you're gonna want to give them a good once-over with my celebrated cabinet cleanser. It's really simple.

> ½ cup of baking soda
> 1 gallon of hot water

Add the baking soda to the water and mix well. Then get yourself a sponge, and wipe away the built-up dirt and dust. You'll be amazed at all the filth your food has been living in!

---

scheme! You just organize your food alphabetically. Start with (let's say) apple sauce, then proceed through baked beans, cashews, dog biscuits—I think you get the picture.

# UP SHE GOES!

**R**egardless of what organizing system you use, if you have toddlin' tykes, cunning canines, or frisky felines around the house (or even if they're only frequent visitors), take my advice: Try a variation on the theme. Anything that you don't want little hands or paws dipping into or knocking over, put way up high, or even behind locked doors—because we all know that when the little rascals *really* want something, they'll use every trick in the book to get it!

## OVER THE RAINBOW

**F**rankly, I find this system a little kooky, but I know folks who swear by it—and it *is* simple, alright: You color-code your food. First, label each shelf with a color (or two, depending on how many shelves you've got). Then, arrange the cans, jars, and boxes accordingly. For example:

**Green shelf:** Pickles, relish, green beans, green chilis, peas, spinach, artichokes, asparagus, and green olives

**Yellow shelf:** Corn, yellow mustard, squash, pineapple, chicken broth, lemonade, and apple juice

**Red shelf:** Ketchup, salsa, spaghetti and pizza sauces, red beans, chili, strawberry jam, cherry and strawberry Jell-O, and canned tomatoes

**Orange shelf:** Carrots, yams, peaches, orange jam, orange-flavored drink mix, and Thousand Island salad dressing

**White shelf:** Pasta, popcorn, rice, sauerkraut, pears, white or light rye bread, saltine crackers, mayonnaise, canned tuna or chicken, and oatmeal

**Brown/black shelf:** Wheat, dark rye, or pumpernickel bread; barbecue, teriyaki, and soy sauce; dark mustard, nuts, canned sausages, cocoa, and black olives

---

### AND STAY OUT!

\* \* \* \* \*

You've spent good money on your chow, and a lot of time putting it in order. The *last* thing you need now is a parade of multi-legged munchers marching into the cupboards and helping themselves to your stash. So how do you keep the varmints out? Simple: Scatter some bay leaves across the shelves before you restock them. Wily weevils, beastly beetles, and other pesky pests will keep their distance.

# Stocking Up

Nobody—least of all a penny-pincher—likes to hear this, but it's true: Groceries start going downhill the minute they leave the processing plant. Although every product has a different life expectancy, if left uneaten long enough, everything from frozen meat to cans of soup will eventually have to go to your compost pile or (worse yet) the local landfill. Here's a rundown on how long you can safely store your favorite foods—and some storage tips to help you get the most banquet for your buck.

## Kitchen Keepers

I'd like to tell you that your food will last indefinitely if you follow my storage tips, but the truth is, sooner or later, you've got to toss out the stuff that didn't make it. But I *can* share my tips and tricks for getting the most life out of those hard-earned groceries. Read on!

## IF YOU CAN'T STAND THE HEAT...

You can get out of the kitchen, but you probably can't take your food with you. To keep it in good shape, try to keep the temperature in your food-storage area no higher than 72°F. On the other end of the heat scale, make sure the refrigerator temperature dips no lower than 32°F—except in the freezer, of course!

## IT'S ALL RELATIVE

Most dry foods keep best when the relative humidity is 15 percent or less, but unless you can look out your door and see a cactus or two, that level won't be easy to maintain. Keep the air as dry as you can, though. Running your air conditioner in the summer will help keep moisture at bay; so will stashing your dry goods in those glass jars we talked about a few pages back, or in plastic storage containers.

**Helpful hint:** To keep bread fresher, longer, tuck a stalk of celery into the bread bag to absorb moisture.

## LIGHTS OUT!

If you want to get your money's worth from all that healthy chow, keep it away from direct light. Both Ol' Sol's rays and artificial light can make the nutrients fade fast.

## ROUND AND ROUND

If you pay any attention to the "sell-by" dates in the grocery stores (and I sure hope you do!), you know that the folks who stock the shelves always tuck the new supplies at the back and slide the older ones up front. Well, you need to keep those cans and jars movin' at home, too! If you buy chicken soup, let's say, and you already have some in the cupboard, tuck the new cans behind the old ones. Otherwise, one of these days, you're just liable to dive into a bowl of chicken

soup that tastes like the tin can it came from, and trust me, friends—that chicken soup's not good for *anyone's* soul!

**NO STRINGS ATTACHED**

When it comes to handling, storing, and cooking food, some of the best advice I know of is absolutely free. What's more, it's just a simple phone call away, at your local Cooperative Extension Service. The office is staffed with professional home economists who can answer your questions and send you recipes and fact-filled pamphlets about everything from canning peaches to keeping food fresh on a camping trip. To find this gold mine of culinary lore, look in the county government section of your phone book, or call the home economics department at your local state university.

## READ THE NUMBERS

Most folks pay pretty close attention to the freshness dates that packagers put on perishable foods like milk, eggs, and lunch meats. It's easy to overlook those dates on less-fragile products, though. Keep these in mind when you're looking at packaged food:

1. When you pull something off the shelf, check for a date. Then abide by it. (Better safe than sorry!)

2. You can save big bucks by stocking up on your favorite foods when you see them on sale—but *only* if you know when to say when. Don't buy any more than you can consume before the expiration date rolls around. Otherwise, it's a good bet that you'll have spent far more than you saved!

## HOW LONG WILL IT LAST?

So, just how long can you count on your favorite grub staying fresh and tasty while it sits around unopened? Well, friends, it all depends. Here's a rundown of the life expectancies of some common, packaged edibles. (Bear in mind that these are approximate time frames. Also, the longevity of a particular food product can vary from one brand to another, so always check the date on the box, can, or jar before you chow down!)

| Good for up to 5 years | Good for up to 2 years | Good for 12 to 18 months | Good for 6 months or so | Eat within a month |
|---|---|---|---|---|
| Canned tuna | Canned beef, chicken, and ham | Baby food | Hot cereal | Bread |
| Canned chili | Canned fruits and vegetables | Barbecue sauce | Crackers | Ice cream |
| Refried beans | Canned soup | Cake mix | Dried herbs and spices | Potato chips |
| Tomato paste | Catsup | Canned and bottled juices | Flour | |
| | Chocolate syrup | Cooking oils | Mayonnaise | |
| | Mustard | Gelatin | Rice mixes | |
| | Pasta | Instant tea | | |
| | Pasta sauce | Jams and jellies | | |
| | Peanut butter | Oatmeal | | |
| | Peanuts | Quick-cook rice | | |
| | Popcorn | Salad dressing | | |
| | Powdered drinks | Salsa | | |
| | | Sugar | | |

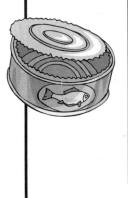

# Give 'Em Some TLC

Timing isn't everything, folks! No matter what the date on the package says or what the experts say about the storage life of fresh foods, you need to give each kind of food item the particular conditions it needs. Otherwise, it'll go downhill faster than you can say, "Where's the compost pile?" Read on for a roundup of tips that'll help you protect your edibles.

## FOREVER FRUIT

Well, maybe not forever, but for a little while, anyway! Here's how to give those fruits and berries the TLC they need to stay farm-fresh and flavorful.

| Fruit | Care |
|---|---|
| Apples | Store uncovered and unwashed in the refrigerator, away from onions and other odor-producing foods. Will stay fresh for up to 2 weeks. |
| Apricots | Keep uncovered at room temperature for up to 3 days, or refrigerate uncovered and unwashed for up to 1 week. |
| Blueberries | Spread in a single layer on a cookie tray, cover with paper towels, then cover with plastic wrap, and refrigerate. Will stay fresh for up to 5 days. |
| Cantaloupe | Store uncovered in the refrigerator before use. After cutting, store chunks in a plastic container or sealed plastic bag in the refrigerator. Will stay fresh for up to 5 days, whole or cut. |
| Cherries | Best if eaten upon purchase. Can store uncovered and unwashed in the refrigerator for up to 5 days. |
| Citrus fruits | Keep uncovered at room temperature for up to 3 days, or refrigerate uncovered for up to 2 weeks. |
| Peaches | Store uncovered and unwashed in the refrigerator. Will stay fresh for up to 1 week. |

## FOREVER FRUIT—*Continued*

| Fruit | Care |
|-------|------|
| Plums | Store uncovered and unwashed in the refrigerator. Very ripe plums will stay fresh for up to 1 week; less ripe will keep for up to 2 weeks. |
| Raspberries | Best if eaten upon purchase. Can store unwashed in the container they came in, covered with plastic wrap, in the refrigerator for up to 2 days. |
| Strawberries | Best if eaten upon purchase. Can store unwashed in the coolest part of the refrigerator for up to 3 days. |
| Watermelon | Store uncut at room temperature for up to 2 weeks. After cutting, store chunks in a sealed plastic bag in the refrigerator. Will stay fresh for up to 3 days. |

## ADD LIFE TO YOUR VEGGIES

When it comes to storage life, all veggies are not created equal. Some, such as carrots, have real staying power, while others—say, corn and peas—start losing flavor and nutrients the minute they're plucked from the plant. Here's a rundown of how to prolong the taste-filled lives of everybody's favorite veggies.

| Vegetable | Care |
|-----------|------|
| Broccoli | Store unwashed in a loose plastic bag in the refrigerator crisper. Will stay fresh for up to 5 days. Wash before cooking. |
| Cabbage | Store unwashed heads in a loose plastic bag in the refrigerator crisper. Will stay fresh for up to 2 weeks. Wash before cooking. |

*Continued on next page*

## ADD LIFE TO YOUR VEGGIES—*Continued*

| Vegetable | Care |
|---|---|
| Carrots | Wash well, place in a plastic bag, and refrigerate. Will stay fresh for up to 5 weeks. |
| Celery | Wrap tightly in aluminum foil and store in the refrigerator crisper. Will stay fresh for up to 1 month. Wash before eating. |
| Corn | Best if eaten upon purchase. Can store for a day or two in a sealed plastic bag in the refrigerator crisper. For longer storage, shuck corn, seal in a freezer bag, and store in the freezer for up to 1 month. |
| Iceburg lettuce | Wash thoroughly, drop into a pillowcase, and swing around outdoors to shake off the water. Store in a sealed plastic bag in the refrigerator crisper. Will stay fresh for up to 2 weeks. |
| Leaf lettuce | Wash and gently pat dry with paper towels. Store in a sealed plastic bag in the refrigerator crisper. Will stay fresh for up to 4 days. |
| Onions | Wrap individually in newspaper and store in a cool, dry, dark place for up to 1 month. Do not refrigerate. |
| Peas | Best if eaten upon purchase. Can store in a sealed plastic bag in the refrigerator crisper for up to 3 days. |
| Peppers | Store in the refrigerator crisper. Will stay fresh for up to 2 weeks. |
| Potatoes | Keep in a cool, dark place. Wash before cooking. |
| Squash | Store in a warm, dry place with good air circulation. (**Exception:** Acorn squash should be stored in a cool, moist environment.) Will stay fresh for up to 3 months. |
| Tomatoes | Keep at room temperature, away from direct sunlight. Will stay fresh for several days. Wash before serving. Refrigerate after cutting. |

# MEATY MATTERS

Most folks buy meat and poultry, and toss it into the freezer as soon as they get home. Well, that's not such a great idea. The package your meat comes in at the store isn't meant for long-term storage. So, if you're going to hold onto that steak or chicken breast for a while, here's the best way to do it.

| Meat | Care |
|------|------|
| Bacon | Once the package is opened, refrigerate remaining uncooked bacon in a zipper-lock plastic bag or tightly wrapped in plastic wrap for up to 1 week. |
| Beef steaks, cooked | Wrap tightly in aluminum foil and refrigerate for up to 1 week. |
| Beef steaks, uncooked | Refrigerate for up to 4 days or freeze for up to 12 months. Do not freeze in original packaging. Rewrap in heavy-duty freezer plastic wrap, heavy-duty aluminum foil, or freezer paper. Wrap tightly, then label with the date. |
| Chicken and turkey, cooked (whole or pieces) | Wrap tightly in aluminum foil and refrigerate for up to 1 week. |
| Chicken and turkey, uncooked (whole or pieces) | Refrigerate for up to 4 days or freeze for up to 12 months. Do not freeze in original packaging. Rewrap in heavy-duty freezer plastic wrap, heavy-duty aluminum foil, or freezer paper. Wrap tightly, then label with the date. |
| Hot dogs | Refrigerate in the original package for up to 1 week or freeze for up to 1 month. |
| Luncheon meats | Refrigerate in zipper-lock plastic bags or airtight plastic containers for up to 1 week. Do not freeze. |

## SOMETHING'S FISHY

O ur finny friends need a different set of storage rules than meat and poultry. Fish should be eaten ASAP, or it needs to be handled with TLC.

Refrigerate fish only if you are cooking it the same day you brought it home. Otherwise, wrap it tightly in heavy-duty freezer plastic wrap or freezer paper. It will keep well in the freezer for about three months.

## SHELL I TELL YOU?

S hellfish, such as clams, oysters, mussels, and scallops, can be refrigerated for one day before using. If you're going to store them in the freezer, do not cook them first, or they will be tough and chewy. Instead, simply wash them well in cold water to clean out the sand, then shell them. Save their liquid for packing. Pack the shellfish in airtight freezer containers and cover with liquid. If there isn't enough fish liquid, add cold water to cover. Leave about $\frac{1}{2}$ inch of headspace and seal the container tightly. They will keep in the freezer for up to four months.

## LET'S GO, SHRIMP

U ncooked shrimp should be refrigerated only if you are going to cook it the same day you brought it home. Otherwise, place them in a single layer on a cookie sheet, and put them in the freezer. When they are frozen hard, pack them in heavy-duty plastic freezer bags or in airtight freezer containers. They will keep for up to two months.

Cooked shrimp can be kept in the refrigerator, in tightly sealed zipper-lock plastic bags or plastic containers, for up to three days.

## PAPER, PLEASE

W hen it's mushroom-storin' time, say "no thanks" to plastic bags. The tasty fungi will stay fresh twice as long if you keep them in a paper bag in your refrigerator.

# FLOUR POWER

Flour will keep for about 15 months in an airtight container in a cool, dry place. If you want to hang onto the powdery stuff even longer, keep the container in the refrigerator. Just make sure you bring the flour back to room temperature before you use it in a recipe. (This storage routine works well for sugar and cornstarch, too.)

# MARSHMALLOW MAINTENANCE

Got some marshmallows left over after a family cookout? Instead of tossing them in the cupboard to get hard as rocks, freeze 'em.  Then, when barbecue time rolls around again, thaw 'em out— they'll taste as fresh as they did the day you bought 'em.

# THAT'S NUTS!

When it comes to snacks, there's nothin' I like better than nuts—cashews, almonds, walnuts, peanuts—

## BECOME AN EGGSPERT

\* \* \* \* \*

When you're keepin' a watchful eye on the old food budget, you can't find a better bargain than eggs. Cheap as they are, though, you still don't want to waste any—and you won't, if you keep these tips in mind.

- ✦ Ignore that special egg shelf in the fridge— your eggs will stay fresher, longer, if you keep them in their original carton.

- ✦ To find out whether an egg is still fresh, place it in a bowl of cold, salty water. If it sinks, start scrambling. If it rises to the surface, toss it out.

- ✦ To keep eggs from cracking as they boil, add a heaping teaspoon of salt to the water.

- ✦ If your eggs are a little past the expiration date, that doesn't mean you have to pitch 'em. Although I wouldn't recommend using them to make your famous Sunday-morning omelet, you can still boil them for use in salads or as deviled eggs for up to two weeks after their expiration date.

you name it. But these goodies don't come cheap, folks! That's why I keep my stash where they stay their freshest: in the freezer. About an hour before I want to serve them up to guests (or dip into them myself), I pull 'em out and let 'em thaw.

## SAY CHEESE!

**T**o keep your favorite hard cheese from going moldy before its time, wrap the block in a paper towel that's been dampened with vinegar. Then slide it into a zippered plastic bag, and put it in the fridge.

## HONEY DO

**I**t's important that you store Winnie-the-Pooh's favorite food in a dry place; otherwise, it tends to absorb moisture and granulate. If it does get dry and crumbly, though (and Winnie's on his way for tea), don't panic: Just sink the jar up to its neck in hot water. That honey'll be flowin' like liquid gold before you can ask, "Where's Piglet?"

### Save Me!

Unless you have a teenager in the house, I'll bet that you're tossing out tons of food that's still got a lot of life left in it. Here's how to get good mileage out of that grub—whether it's leftovers from last night's dinner or chow that's been sittin' on the cupboard shelf.

## NATURE'S CANDY

**R**aisins so hard you might as well be chewing on pebbles? Not a problem. Cover them with water, bring to a boil, and then remove the pan from the heat. Let stand for five minutes. Then drain off the water and gobble up those nice, soft raisins!

## FLORIDA SUNSHINE

**F**or my money, nothing beats freshly squeezed orange juice. But what do you do with all those rinds? Here's what:

☞ Shave off strips, and use them to garnish salads, or chicken or pork with orange sauce.

☞ Grate them, either by hand or in your food processor. Then freeze the gratings, and use them in muffins and quick breads.

☞ Dry the gratings on a screen, and add them to your favorite potpourri recipe.

☞ Put a big pot of water on the stove and get it boilin'. Then toss in your strips, along with a few cinnamon sticks and a handful of cloves—and stand by for the sweetest smell this side of heaven! (P.S. If you're lookin' to sell your house, pay special attention here, friends: Real estate surveys show that this and fresh-baked bread are the two aromas most likely to make potential buyers think, "Wow...this is the place!")

# TWICE OVER LIGHTLY

We all know that leftovers save you time and money—you reap the savings of buying in quantity, and you can eat a meal that's already been made. But there are some folks who think that leftovers are boring. Well, that doesn't have to be the case! Here are some of my favorite ways to enjoy my favorite foods—one more time:

**Wine.** Don't want that half-empty bottle languishing about for months? Don't pour it out; pour it into ice cube trays. Then use the cubes to perk up stews and casseroles.

**Meat.** Hot dogs, turkey, beef, chicken—you name it. Cut it into little pieces, stir in mayonnaise or salad dressing, salt and pepper to taste, and presto: instant sandwich makings!

**Stir-fry.** Toast a couple of bagels and spread with sweet and sour sauce, or sprinkle soy sauce on top. Add the leftover stir-fry, heat, and eat.

**Pork.** Freeze it, and when you have a few veggies to go with it, make eggrolls.

## GO APE OVER BANANAS!

\* \* \* \* \*

Bananas looking a little worse for wear? Well, count your lucky stars! You've got the makings for a delicious loaf of banana bread or yummy muffins! If your bananas are overly ripe when it's not convenient for you to make bread or muffins, that's okay, too. Just peel off the skins, and put the fruit into a plastic bag. Then tuck the bag into the freezer, and pull it out when you're ready to bake. As for those banana skins, they're the best friends your roses ever had! Bury 'em about 1 inch under the ground near each plant's main stem, then stand back and wait. The next time your roses bloom, expect them to be covered with flowers!

**Tortillas.** If they start to get a little crunchy on you, heat a little butter in a skillet, drop in the tortillas (one at a time) and warm 'em on both sides. They'll be good to go!

**French toast.** Freeze the slices separately in plastic zipper bags. When you're ready to eat, just pop 'em in the toaster.

**Fruit pie.** Apple, cherry, peach—I don't discriminate. Wrap it in foil and warm it in the oven at 350°F for 10 minutes. If you didn't know better, you'd swear it was freshly baked!

# DON'T GO YET!

Just because food starts headin' downhill doesn't mean you have to say goodbye just yet. There's good eatin' left in those vittles! Here's how to get the most out of the least:

★ Celery starting to wilt? Soak it in a bowl of ice water for 45 minutes.

★ Peppers about to go bad? Just seed, chop, and freeze them. The next time you

need chopped bell pepper, it'll be at your fingertips.

★ Too much milk on hand? Freeze it before it goes sour.

★ Stale bread? Toast it, tear the slices into cubes, and freeze 'em in a zipper-lock bag. Use 'em in stuffing, or crush 'em up for any recipe that calls for breadcrumbs. (This trick works with stale biscuits and bagels, too.)

★ Hard rolls too hard? To freshen 'em up, put them in a damp paper bag, and

## MELTING POT

* * * * *

There's nothing my wife and I like better than homemade vegetable soup, but chopping all the meat and veggies is mighty time-consuming. That's why we use this lazy-cook's version: We keep a big zippered bag in the freezer, and whenever we have any leftover cooked meat or vegetables, we toss 'em in the bag. When the bag's full, we empty it into a big pot of chicken broth and let 'er simmer. You can't find a simpler recipe than that!

heat them in the oven for 10 minutes at 350°F.

★ Soft crackers? Spread 'em on a baking sheet, heat them in a 300°F oven for five minutes, then cool completely. Bingo! Bring on the cheese!

# LET US GIVE THANKS

Here's my all-time favorite way to use those inevitable Thanksgiving leftovers: Grab a hunk of that turkey, a heaping spoonful of stuffing, and a little cranberry sauce, and put it all between two slices of bread. For my money, it almost beats the original feast!

# USE YOUR NOODLE

The next time you have leftover pasta, try something different: Put the cold noodles in a big bowl, and add your favorite diced raw veggies. (I like carrots, onions, broccoli, and peppers.) Toss it all with enough Italian dressing to coat, and let it sit for 20 minutes or so at room temperature, or for several hours in the fridge, until the flavors blend. Serve it up chilled or at room temperature. Now that's using your noodle!

# SUPER SIMPLE SPUDS

When I was a lad, I ate so many potatoes that Grandma Putt used to joke that if I didn't ease off, I'd turn *into* a tater. Well, I still gobble up those spuds like there's no tomorrow. Nowadays, though—much as I love 'em fresh from the oven—I enjoy getting creative with the leftovers even more. Here's a rundown of my favorite, um, artistic concepts:

**Mash it again, Jer.** Combine leftover mashed potatoes, chopped onion, and shredded cheese. Spoon the mixture into a baking dish, and bake until the top is golden brown. Yum!

**Soup's on!** Who doesn't love thick, creamy potato soup? Well, you can make it in a hurry with practically any kind of leftover spuds—mashed, baked, boiled, whatever. Just combine equal parts of potato, water, and milk or cream in a pot. Add your favorite herbs, and season to taste. (You can also jazz it up by adding cheese, bacon bits, or chopped onion, too.)

**Not just another pretty casserole.** Leftover mashed potatoes make a terrific topper on just about any casserole you care to name. Just spread a layer of taters on top, and bake until the surface begins to turn golden brown.

## FANTASTIC FORMULA

### Jerry's Potato Cakes

These take the cake, folks—especially if you've got plenty of leftover baked, roasted, or mashed potatoes on hand.

½ cup of flour

1 egg

2 teaspoons of baking powder

1½ cups of grated or mashed potatoes

Salt and pepper

Mix the flour, egg, and baking powder together. Stir in the potatoes, and season to taste. Drop dollops of the mixture onto a greased griddle or into an iron skillet, and cook them as you would pancakes. (This mixture works great for potato waffles, too.)

## IN A PICKLE

Once you've used up that jar of pickles, don't pitch the juice! That elixir can jazz up all sorts of edibles. Try a few of these tricks:

**Ham it up.** Pickle juice makes a great basting sauce for ham. Just stir cloves and mustard into the juice, and dribble it over the ham every 30 minutes until the meat's done.

**Hold the mayo.** Dress your macaroni salad with pickle juice and relish, instead of mayonnaise. You'll give that ol' pasta a zesty tang—with zero grams of fat!

**Zippy chip dip.** Combine pickle juice with cream cheese for a chip or veggie dip that'll make your guests sit up and say "Yum!"

**Eggzactly!** Make pickled eggs by adding hard-boiled eggs (still in their shells) to boiling pickle juice. Boil for about five minutes, then cool and serve.

**Calling all cukes.** Tired of potato salad? For your next

summer barbecue, try something different. Combine pickle juice, sour cream, and a pinch of sugar. Then pour it over paper-thin cucumber slices, and toss lightly.

## Accept Those Substitutes!

**It's as annoying as all get-out: You reach into the cupboard for something you're *sure* is there... and it's not. Well, don't hightail it to the supermarket, and don't get frazzled—get creative with some of these stunning stand-ins.**

### I CAN'T BELIEVE IT'S NOT BUTTER!

**W**hen I looked in the fridge and found an empty carton of butter, you'd better believe I was peeved. Then my

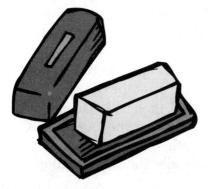

wife pointed out that I could use $7/8$ cup of solid shortening and $1/2$ teaspoon of salt as a substitute for 1 cup of butter. My world-famous cookies were just as delicious as ever!

### GREAT EGGSPECTATIONS

**W**ho says you can't bake a cake without eggs? If you're only one egg shy, just substitute 1 teaspoon of cornstarch. If you need two or more eggs, substitute 3 teaspoons of cooking oil for each egg that's missing in action.

### WE'RE ALL OUT OF HONEY, HONEY!

**S**o you forgot to put honey on the grocery list, and now you need it for a recipe? Not to worry: Just combine equal parts of sugar and water and you're good to go. Use exactly the same amount of this mixture as you would have used honey.

### HOW SWEET IT IS!

**E**very baker's been through this hassle: You've gathered all the ingredients for your favorite cake, and you discover that you're plum out of granulated sugar. So what do you do? Just go a shade darker. Brown sugar will work just fine. The finished product might have a slight molasses flavor, but so what? You might like it better than the original recipe!

## I'D RATHER BE IN PHILADELPHIA

Nothing goes better on a bagel than cream cheese. When you're fresh out, though, try this pinch hitter: Combine 1 cup of cottage cheese with ¼ cup of butter, and spread 'er on.

### FANTASTIC FORMULA

**Catch Up!**

I like catsup on just about everything. As fast as we can buy it, I can eat it, and that makes it hard to keep in stock. That's why I learned to make my own.

    1 cup of tomato sauce
    ¼ cup of brown sugar
    2 tablespoons of vinegar

Mix all of the ingredients together, then bring on the French fries!

## BREAKFAST OF CHAMPIONS

Making fried chicken and you're fresh out of bread crumbs? Grab a box of cereal. Crushed wheat, corn, or bran flakes will wake that chicken right up! Try 'em in stuffing or meatloaf, too.

## HALF A STRETCH

If you need a cup of whole milk, but there's only half a cup in the carton, don't fret! Just add ½ cup of water to the milk—in a recipe, you won't notice a difference.

## IT'S NOT PLAIN VANILLA

If you bake a lot, you know that a whole lot of great recipes call for vanilla extract. That's why it's so easy to run out. It's not the end of the world, though. In fact, it's not even the end of your cookies, muffins, or quick bread— just substitute a little ground cinnamon or nutmeg for each teaspoon of vanilla required, and you may invent a whole new taste sensation.

## NO SOURPUSSES HERE!

**M**akin' nachos and your sour cream's gone south of the border? Just mix 1 cup of plain yogurt with 3 tablespoons of melted butter. Then say "Olé!"

## PLAYING DRESS-UP

**I** don't know about you, but I can't eat a sandwich without some kind of spread. If you're out of mustard and mayo, try salad dressing. Ranch, Thousand Island, and blue cheese are terrific with any kind of meat. They even make a neat substitute for mayo in tuna salad.

## MAKE IT LAST

**E**veryone loves a meatloaf— the meal that just keeps on giving. Stretch a meatloaf out even longer by adding a little cooked rice to the mix. It should last you at least two meals, if not three.

### DO YOU OR DON'T YOU?

* * * * *

…Refrigerate your bread, that is. Here's the dilemma: Keeping that loaf in the fridge will keep mold at bay for up to two weeks, but the bread will start tasting stale after only a few days. At room temperature, mold starts forming in about a week—but the bread starts losing its freshness within about three days. The solution? If you're going to use it immediately, store it at room temperature for up to three days. If not, freeze it, instead of refrigerating it. Bread can remain in the freezer for up to a month. Then, simply thaw it, and it'll taste as good as the day it was bought. (By the way, folks, if you're used to using a bread box, the same rules apply as if you were keeping it, say, on top of your fridge. It's only good for three days, regardless of how expensive or high tech your box is.)

## MORE MEATLOAF

**T**o save time when making meatloaf, use spaghetti sauce instead of catsup.
Spaghetti sauce is filled to the rim with spices, so you don't have to take the time to add them to the mix.

## WHAT? NO CHOCOLATE?

It's hard to imagine a chocolate cake made without baking chocolate, but believe it or not, it can be done! Try this: For every square of unsweetened chocolate called for in the recipe, substitute 1 tablespoon of shortening plus 3 tablespoons of unsweetened cocoa. The result is heavenly!

# More Fantastic Formulas!

**We're winding down fast, folks, but never fear—here are a few more tips and tricks to help you get the most banquet for your buck.**

## SAVE THE SAUCE

I love alfredo sauce, but if you're not keeping an eye on it while it heats up, boy, can it

---

## HEALTHY SUBSTITUTES

Here are a few more substitutes for commonly used ingredients, but with a different slant—in addition to working in a pinch, these substitutes are actually *better for you than the food they're subbing for!*

| Instead of. . . | Try. . . |
| --- | --- |
| Butter | Olive oil (for savory dishes) or applesauce (for sweet dishes) |
| Cream cheese | Lowfat ricotta cheese |
| Sour cream | Plain yogurt |
| Heavy cream | Evaporated skim milk |
| 1 cup of whipped cream | 3 stiffly beaten egg whites |
| Nuts | Granola or rolled oats |
| Cottage cheese | Lowfat ricotta cheese |

ever curdle in a hurry! If your sauce heats up too fast, remove the pan from the heat immediately. Set the pan into a larger pan of cold water to stop the cooking, and stir vigorously until the sauce is smooth again.

# LEFTOVERS AND OVERS AND OVERS

**H**ere are a few more of my favorite uses for leftovers:

★ **Got oatmeal?** Save it, and add it to your meatloaf instead of using breadcrumbs. It's dee-licious!

★ **Got leftover ham?** Save it, and add it to an omelet the following morning.

★ **Got leftover chili?** Try warming it and using it as a topping for a baked potato.

It's like eating chili fries, only healthier!

★ **Got extra pie dough?** Simply roll it out, sprinkle with cinnamon and sugar, and bake it at 375°F until lightly browned. Yum!

| FANTASTIC FORMULA |
| --- |
| **Where's the Beef?** |
| It seems like we always end up with leftover roast, but my wife has the perfect solution. |
| Diced leftover roast beef |
| Diced onions |
| Chopped hardboiled egg |
| Mayonnaise to taste |
| Mix all of the ingredients together and *voilà!*, you've got yourself a heck of a sandwich filling. |

# CHAPTER 8

# Clothes Encounters of the Frugal Kind

Nowadays, it seems like clothing dollars go about as far as you can throw a feather. I don't know about you, but when I shell out $30 for a pair of jeans or a couple of hundred for a linen blazer, I expect those duds to last for years. But, what if you get a stubborn grass stain on those jeans the first time you wear them? Or, that blazer tumbles into a high-temperature wash load and shrinks a size or two?

In Chapter 2, I told you how to get great buys on all kinds of clothes. In this chapter, I'll tell you how to take care of them—thanks to Grandma Putt, who taught me that just a little commonsense TLC can make the difference between garments that barely survive their first wash and ones that you'll wear for years and years.

# The Best-Kept Closet

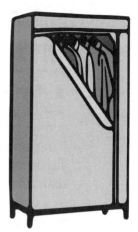

**M**aking clothes last starts with storing them smartly. We've all seen what a few hours in a suitcase can do to a carefully pressed dress or suit—but sometimes we mistakenly treat our clothes just as badly at home. Here's how to have your clothes in great shape when you need them—clean, fresh, pressed, and ready to wear.

## Welcoming Your New Clothes

**Take a few minutes to follow these steps *before* you put your new clothes in the closet, and I guarantee that when you're finally ready to wear 'em, they'll look as good as the day you bought 'em.**

### LABEL LINGO

**T**he sewn-in care label is Exhibit A when it comes to coddling your clothes. Read it well—and know that there's almost always a good reason why a manufacturer says "wash only in cold water" or "do not bleach." I keep clothes that need special care hung together at one end of the closet—especially those "dry-clean only"

jobs that require an outlay of cash every time I wear them.

By the way, unless a label is scratching the back of your neck and driving you nuts, don't remove it. You might be surprised at how quickly you forget the washing instructions—and you'd be surprised at how much harder it is to sell an unlabeled garment at a garage sale, too.

### PUT ON THE POLISH

**T**ake a minute to dab clear nail polish over the threads that hold the buttons on new shirts and jackets. The polish won't change the appearance of the buttons or thread, but it will protect the thread and help it hold up to much more wear and washing.

# HANG 'EM HIGH

**L**et's face facts: Clothes that you take off a hanger are almost always in better shape than those you pull out of a drawer. If you keep as much of your wardrobe as you can hanging in the closet, not only will those clothes look better on you, but they'll last longer because they'll be less wrinkled—which means you don't have to toil over them with a hot iron!

Now, not all clothes should be put on hangers in the same way. Here are a few rules for the most common articles of clothing that you'll hang:

**Cotton shirts.** Work shirts are the easiest—even wire hangers rarely do them any harm. Add a little starch when you iron them, and these will wait in the closet till you're good and ready to wear them. Dress shirts need a heavier hand with the starch to stay crisp and professional looking.

**Knit shirts.** I like to wear these because they're comfortable (and easy to clean after the occasional mishap in the garden), but I've discovered that they look 100 percent better if I hang them, folded, over the bottom of a plastic hanger, instead of hanging them on it by the shoulders. Knit shirts that are hung in the usual way often get puckers in the shoulders, and then require another round of washing to get out.

**Pants.** Years ago, I invested a few dollars in hangers designed for holding pants. They have clips on the bottom bar. Now I hang all my pants by the cuffs, and not only do they not have creases at the knees when I put them on, but the weight of the pants—when they're hung that way—helps keep wrinkles out of them indefinitely.

**Dresses.** Of course, I don't have any personal experience

## FANTASTIC FORMULA

### Color Keeper

Add ½ cup of white vinegar to the wash cycle the first time you launder new clothes. Not only will it help clean the manufacturer's chemicals out of the fabric, but the vinegar will also set the colors, so they'll last longer.

with dresses, but years ago, my wife let me in on this secret: Hang dresses—especially heavy ones—on two plastic hangers instead of one. The double hangers make a wide surface so the dress won't pucker in the shoulders or sleeves, and two hangers absorb the weight of the garment better than a single one does.

# Minding the Storage

**When you've stashed 'em the right way, clothes that you pull out of the attic or other storage area should look exactly as they did when they went in. When you don't store 'em properly, those duds may come out faded or full of insect holes, and that would be a waste of your hard-earned dollars—so store them right!**

**Whether you're retiring your summer clothes for a long winter's nap or safeguarding a precious heirloom for your kids or grandkids, follow these tips for safe storage.**

# RODS IN THE RAFTERS

**S**easons change, and so do clothing needs. That's why, twice a year, I haul my seasonal clothes out of the closet, and put them away in the attic until the temperature changes again. If you store your out-of-season clothes in the attic, too, here's a simple way to put them up with a minimum of hassle. Install a hanging rod in the attic—off the floor, away from the walls, and out of the way of your other storage. I put mine between rafters. Drape your hanging clothes with a sheet so they don't get dusty. Hanging your clothes keeps them free from wrinkles, so you won't spend the start of each season slaving over a hot iron!

# IN IT FOR THE LONG HAUL

**A**ttention pack rats! Can't bring yourself to put that old wardrobe out to pasture? Not a problem! Just follow these tips, and your old friends will be waiting for you, should you ever need them again.

☑ Always wash or dry-clean your clothing before putting it into storage. Just as you don't like going to bed dirty, neither do your clothes. (Any dry-cleaned clothes should be taken out of their plastic bags and aired out before storing, too.)

☑ Here are two words that should become part of your permanent vocabulary: acid free. Store clothing in a large, deep, acid-free box, and wrap them loosely in acid-free paper. Never use cardboard, because it promotes an acidic environment that breaks down clothing fibers over time.

☑ Make sure the clothes are wrinkle-free. Wrinkles in your clothes are just like the ones in your skin—they're deeper and harder to get rid of with age!

☑ Unless they're going to get rained on, avoid storing clothes in plastic bags. Plastic traps moisture, providing a cozy home for a variety of molds and mildew.

☑ For long-term storage, think horizontal, rather than vertical. Although vertical storage (hanging) reduces wrinkling, over time, it may result in stretched collars and misshapen shoulders.

## MOVE OVER, MOTHRA!

**M**oths are Enemy Number One to your clothes, and there's no place like storage for a full-fledged assault. To combat these critters (and keep your clothes from looking like oversize Swiss cheese), mothproof your clothes with a mixture of black pepper and rosemary. This mix works just like mothballs, but you don't have to worry about the health hazard or the unpleasant smell.

## KID-SIZE STORAGE SOLUTIONS

**I**f you've got little ones running around, you know that sometimes it's hard to find even a single clean outfit in the rubble of their dresser drawers. Here are a few simple ways to help kids keep their clothes available, clean, and in the right place. That way, your money won't be wasted on clothes that never get worn!

☞ **Label it.** Put labels on your children's dresser drawers, so they don't have to play eenie-meenie-miney-mo

**Pennypincher's Hall of Fame**

No doubt the best way to extend the life of children's clothes is to see that they get worn by more than one tyke. One famous American took that idea to extremes. John D. Rockefeller, the founder of Standard Oil and the richest man in the country in his day, insisted that his children wear hand-me-downs. In fact, his only son, the last of four surviving children, reportedly wore only his big sisters' outgrown clothes until he was 8 years old! When Rockefeller's kids got a little older and started pressing their old man for more expensive clothes and gadgets, the richest man in the United States—but still a practical guy after my own heart—is said to have chided them by saying, "Who do you think we are—Vanderbilts?" Now that's cheap!

when deciding how to put things away. For kids who aren't old enough to read, draw a picture (shirt, pants, and underwear are all easy to draw) to help them.

☞ **Color coordinate.** Families with more than one child can save time and money by buying all of each child's undergarments in their own color or pattern. For example, all pink underwear for one girl and all purple for another. As they come out of the wash, you can just toss them in the right piles without even looking at the tags. For clothes, try this: Assign each child a color, then use a permanent marker to make an X in their color on the tags of all their clothes. Not only will that make it easier for you to separate laundry, but it'll make it possible for kids to do that job, too.

☞ **Store by size.** Put outgrown children's clothing into storage in boxes sorted by size and gender. If you can quickly find all those size 4 boys' clothes when the next kid needs them, you'll save a fortune in new clothes.

# Laundry News You Can Use

We all know that even on the gentle cycle, washing and drying take their toll on clothes. In other words, getting the most wear and the least tear out of your garments boils down to keeping them clean without cleaning them to death. Here's what you need to know to keep your clothes in tip-top shape for years to come.

## Getting Ready

A little organization in the laundry room can go a long way toward reducing the time and energy you spend cleaning clothes. Plus, having the right stuff on hand to get the job done means that your clothes are getting the best possible care.

## PAINLESS SEPARATION

Doing laundry starts with deciding which clothes go in the washer together and which don't go in at all. Everyone knows how important it is to separate the light-colored clothes from the dark and bright ones—I think you only need to make one load of pink underwear in a lifetime to learn that lesson! But there are other items that don't mix well, either. Keeping them apart in the wash will help your clothes look better, longer—and that'll save you big bucks, too!

**Know the lint-makers and lint-takers.** Fabrics like terrycloth (towels), heavy jersey (sweatshirts), and chenille create tons of lint. Permanent press fabrics and corduroy pick it up. So, do yourself a favor, and wash "shedding" and "collecting" fabrics separately. Then you won't have to spend time delinting or rewashing, causing unnecessary wear and tear on your clothes.

**Defend the delicates.** Some clothes don't take the abuse of a wash and spin as well as others, and they're the reason for the delicate cycle. While your towels, jeans, and sheets may actually come out better after a rough ride through the normal wash cycle, bathing suits, sweaters, and hand-sewn clothes all need to be washed more gently. Wash delicate items on the gentlest cycle your machine has, and don't mix them with sturdier items, or the rough-and-ready materials will rub against the delicate ones, and damage them during the cycle.

**Segregate the soiled ones.** Some kinds of dirt—like the kinds that get caked on in the garden and the garage—deserve a wash cycle of their own. Washing machines do their best to get the grime from the clothes you give them, but the not-so-dirty stuff in your laundry basket will pick up that gardening grime and be ruined. I keep a special basket just inside the garage for my really dirty yard clothes, then I wash them separate from everything else.

# AN OUNCE OF PREVENTION

Now there are lots of special treatments for getting out hard-to-remove stains (and you'll find the best of them in this chapter), but the biggest mistake most of us make in getting out stains is just not giving them enough attention when we first make them.

We all get into things that are bad for our clothes—dirt, grass, food—they can't be avoided. Most of those stains are easily removed in the wash, though, *if*

Making your own laundry detergent is a piece of cake. Just mix equal parts of washing soda and borax (both can be found in the detergent aisle). Add ½ cup of this mixture to each load of laundry. Even though I use store-bought detergent for most loads, I do several loads of wash with this mixture at least once every month to get the detergent residue out of my clothes and give them longer life.

When it comes time for the rinse cycle, add ¼ cup of white vinegar to the load, and your clothes will come out just as soft as they do with a commercial fabric softener—and at a fraction of the price!

they are pretreated when they're new. To make sure clothing stains don't go untreated through your washer and dryer, try tying a stain-treatment stick to the lid of the dirty laundry basket. As you toss your clothes in, rub stains with the stick. The vast majority will come clean when you do the wash.

I'll tell you a little secret, though. I've found that stains rubbed with plain old soap come out clean just as often as the ones that got the stick treatment. Instead of using a stain stick, I just moisten a bar of Ivory soap, and dab stains on their way into the laundry basket. It costs just a few cents to treat months' worth of laundry, and the stains almost always come out.

## SOAP SMARTS

**Y**ou know, I'm a simple guy with no desire to spend 20 minutes in the detergent aisle at my discount store. (Of course, I'd never waste money buying marked-up detergent at the grocery store.) I want grab-and-go cleaning products, and I don't want to spend a fortune on them, either. Here's what I know that keeps it simple:

**Powder up.** Powdered detergents have two distinct advantages over liquids. Number one, consumer testing almost always shows they clean better. Number two, they cost less to use per load.

**Naming names.** You know that I usually buy generic products and have no complaints—but not when it comes to laundry detergent. Most store brands just don't clean clothes as well as the national brands do, and that means I end up cleaning things twice—or worse yet, making dust cloths out of clothes that have turned gray and dingy from bad detergent. So I always stock up on name-brand detergent when it's on sale and/or when I find coupons.

**Hand-some savings.** I make up some of the cost of brand-name detergents by not spending an extra dime on detergents for hand-washables. A squirt of clear dish soap (for the sink, not the dishwasher) is easy on delicate clothes and costs next to nothing for a sinkful of suds.

## ZIP IT

Close the zippers on clothes before you wash them and you'll keep them from snagging on (and damaging) other clothes. While you're at it, snap snaps, button buttons, and close Velcro closures for the same reason.

## SOCK IT TO ME

Do you have magic socks that seem to disappear whenever they go to the laundry? Me, too—when I was younger, I was hard-pressed to produce one complete pair! That's why I came up with a couple of ways to keep track of the little buggers:

★ Try washing socks with towels. Being cotton, towels don't have the same static problems as other fabrics. Plus, since towels are long and flat, it's hard for socks to find good hiding places!

★ Deposit dirty socks into a zippered pillowcase. When you're ready to wash, zip up the case and toss it into the washing machine. Do this faithfully, and I guarantee you'll have no more lonesome sock widows!

## CHECK THOSE POCKETS!

You can do more damage to your washing machine (not to mention the clothes in it) with the contents of one little kid's pockets than you will with 100 loads of laundry. (Think crayons, rocks, and little plastic, machine-jamming toys.) Heck, even a grown-up's undetected ballpoint pen can wreak havoc on a load of wash. So never put any article of clothing in the washing machine without making sure there's nothing going along for the ride. Teach your

### CLEAN CAPS

*  *  *  *  *

If you've ever faced the dilemma of whether to wear a dirty baseball cap or wash it and risk ruining its shape, here's the solution: Toss it in the dishwasher. Put your baseball caps on the top rack (the one designed for glasses) and run them through a normal cycle with just a smidgen of dishwasher detergent. The caps will come out perfectly clean—and they'll keep their shape, too!

spouse and kids to check their own pockets, but double-check them, too. As I always say, "If you want something done right, you have to do it yourself."

## Cleaning on the Cheap

**When it's time to turn on the washer, the money-saving measures end, right? Not a chance! Read on for ways to save on every load you put into the machine.**

## COOL IT

Washing clothes in cold water saves money two ways: First, on the bill that takes a beating for water heating, and second, in the longevity of your clothes. Whether you heat your water with gas or electricity, you'll save a bundle by switching to cold water for the wash and rinse cycles. Every now and again, I wash towels and whites in hot water to give them an extra-thorough cleaning, but for day-to-day laundry, I use cold water. It gets everything clean—and it doesn't fade colors or strain fabrics, either. Some

manufacturers estimate that clothes washed in cold water will last as much as twice as long as those washed in warm or hot. Now that's what I call great savings!

## LONGEVITY FOR JEANS

Want an easy way to add a year to the life of your jeans? Just turn 'em inside out every time they go in the wash. This quick turn will help keep the color where it belongs (in your pants) and reduce friction on the hard-worn parts of the fabric (think knees and seats), too.

## CUFF 'EM

Tighten stretched sweater cuffs by dipping them in hot water and drying them with a hair dryer. They'll be back in shape in no time!

## A PERFECT 10

If your washing machine has a timer, never set the wash cycle for more than 10 minutes. All the work of getting your clothes clean has been done at this point, and the clothes are simply agitating around and around for the remaining minutes.

# THE FINER THINGS

**S**ome clothing is just too delicate to toss in the machine unprotected. Here's how to keep your fine washables in shape:

☞ Use baby shampoo on your fine washables. Dilute a dime-size amount in a sinkful of water, and soak the garment. Drip dry or dry flat on a towel, depending upon the article and its instructions.

☞ Drop delicates in a pillowcase, knot it closed, and then wash on the gentle cycle. (This is safe for garments with beads or sequins.) Then hang them up to dry.

# LEATHER LORE

**O**ccasionally, I'll find cloth belts with leather ends. Now, I used to think that Cloth + Leather = Problem, but not since I found this solution: Wrap each leather end in plastic wrap, and hold it on with a rubber band. Then wash the belt

---

## FANTASTIC FORMULA

### Super Whitener

Here's a great recipe for keeping your white clothes, sheets, and towels bright white.

    4 aspirin tablets
    1 cup of hot water
    1 load of dirty laundry

Dissolve the aspirin in the hot water, then add the mixture to a warm-water load in the washing machine. For clothes that are already yellowed, let the load soak for 30 minutes before you put it through the wash cycle.

---

normally in cold water. The plastic will protect the leather while the cloth gets clean.

# FILL 'ER UP!

**N**othing saves more on laundry costs than matching the water level and cycle time to the load size. If your washing machine doesn't have variable water levels and cycle times, then always wash full loads. After all, every time the machine runs a full cycle, you pay the cost of the power for each and every minute— regardless of the amount of clothes that are in the machine.

## HARD-WATER WONDERS

* * * * *

Hard water does a number on your laundry, leaving it gray and worn out before its time. To find out if you've got hard water, fill a glass with tap water, add a pinch of detergent, and shake. If it makes lots of suds, your water's fine. If not—you guessed it.

So, how do you keep hard water from ruining your wash (without investing in a fancy, several-thousand-dollar water-softening system)? Just use half the recommended amount of laundry detergent for each load, and make up the difference with borax.

# Cutting Your Dryer Dollars

Ever wonder where all that lint in your dryer comes from? Well, it's generated when clothes are slammed together and rubbed against one another at high temperatures in the dryer. No wonder clothes don't hold up like they used to! The drying process is the number one reason that clothes fade and look worn as they get older. Here's how to use your dryer without letting it ruin your clothes.

## LOVE THAT LINE

Of course, the super-duper solar clothes dryer is my favorite—you know, the one strung across the backyard. Hanging your clothes on the line to dry doesn't cost a dime, and it makes clothes smell and feel cleaner than any fabric softener can.

If you like the dryer's softening effect on your clothes, try tumbling your clothes for just 10 minutes and then hanging them out to dry. Just those few minutes in the dryer will keep clothes from stiffening as they dry on the line.

## DRY MORE, SPIN LESS

**B**elieve it or not, hanging clothes out is actually easier if your garments don't go all the way through the last spin cycle in the wash. The longer clothes spin, the more wrinkles get set in. So, if you grab your clothes from the washer halfway into that last spin cycle, many will dry on the line looking like they've already been pressed.

## LOSE THE LINT

**E**mptying the lint trap after every load of laundry makes your dryer less of a fire hazard. It also saves you money on every single load. How? Well, the more lint the machine has collected in the lint trap, the more energy the dryer requires to get through a cycle. So keep it nice and clean!

## THROW IN THE TOWEL

**T**o speed up the drying process, run an extra spin cycle in your washing machine, and toss a dry, fluffy towel in the dryer along with your wet clothes, sheets, or towels. This can cut down on your drying time by 20 percent or more!

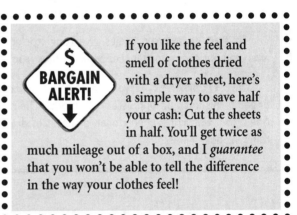

**$ BARGAIN ALERT!**

If you like the feel and smell of clothes dried with a dryer sheet, here's a simple way to save half your cash: Cut the sheets in half. You'll get twice as much mileage out of a box, and I *guarantee* that you won't be able to tell the difference in the way your clothes feel!

## OVERDONE CLOTHES

**W**e've all done it—walked away for just a few minutes, only to return an hour later to a dryer full of overdone, wrinkled clothes. Don't be tempted to toss them back in the washer—just toss a clean, damp towel in the dryer, and set it on warm. Your clothes will be back to normal in minutes.

## DOUBLE-DUTY DRYER SHEETS

\* \* \* \* \*

If you use commercial dryer sheets, think of them as just beginning their useful lives when they come out of the dryer. Here are a few more jobs you can give them before they retire:

**Dust cloth.** Dryer sheets don't just push dust around—they attract it. There's no better material for the job.

**Dish rag.** Sometimes, particularly stubborn pots and pans don't come clean after a good soak in soap and water. So, add a dryer sheet to the mix, and let it soak overnight in the sudsy water. In the morning, burned-on, stuck-on food will glide right off.

**Static remover.** Ladies, give your stockings a quick brush-over with a dryer sheet after you put them on. It'll keep your clothes from clinging to the nylon.

**Air freshener.** Dryer sheets can be used to freshen whole rooms (just put them under furnishings or upholstery cushions). Their specialty, though, is small spaces. Throw one into a wardrobe, linen closet, or chest of drawers to give a light, clean scent to everything inside.

# Ironing Dos and Don'ts

On a ranking of how I like my chores, ironing has a special place of honor—right at rock bottom. Could there be a more thankless job? Lucky for me, over the years, I've worked out a system to keep my hours chained to the ironing board to a minimum. Lucky for you, I'm happy to share it!

## WETTER'S BETTER

Okay, this is one tip you'll have to act on *before* you actually get to the ironing board. Remove clothes from the washing machine *before* the final spin cycle. Then hang them up to dry (if you don't have a place to hang clothes, try using your shower rod). Since they're wetter, they'll have fewer wrinkles and you can shape them better. If you do it well, you may not have to iron at all!

# KEEP IT CLEAN

There may be a worse feeling than the one that comes when you realize you've just ruined a good shirt with a dirty iron, but I can't think of one right now. Keep your iron clean by using a mixture of 2 tablespoons of salt and 2 tablespoons of vinegar to polish the plate. Once a year, rinse the water receptacle with vinegar, then flush it with water. This'll help prevent messy buildups.

# HEAT A SHEET

Put a sheet of aluminum foil, shiny side up, under your ironing board cover. It'll keep heat on the underside of your garments, and they'll press faster and more easily because of it.

# IRONING TLC

Some fabrics seem to hate to be ironed—but that doesn't mean they never need it! But, before you put iron to fabric,

give your garments some TLC. Iron silk, corduroy, and cashmere from the "wrong" side to avoid damaging them. For garments that are especially delicate, put a clean white T-shirt on top of them and iron through the shirt.

# SEAM SAVER

After you lower a hem, the holes from the first line of stitches can stand out like a sore thumb. To get them out, just

---

## FANTASTIC FORMULA

### Stir Up Starch

There are several ways to make your own laundry starch, but they all include the same secret ingredient: You've got to stir the bejeebers out of them to make sure they end up lump free. Here's my favorite formula:

1 tablespoon of cornstarch
½ cup of water

Mix the cornstarch and the water in a saucepan over medium heat (not boiling), until the mixture is smooth and transparent. Let it cool enough so you can safely pour it into a spray bottle, and you're ready to go.

moisten a clean white rag with a 50/50 mixture of water and distilled vinegar, set your fabric on top of the rag, and iron the stitching holes right out.

# Getting Stains Out

**My Grandma Putt used to say she never knew a stain she couldn't get out—just a few that wouldn't take a hint! For those, she'd bring out the big guns, trying each of the stain removers in her bag of tricks until she found the one that worked. Here are some of her favorites.**

## THE MAGIC POTION

If you've ever spent 5 or 6 bucks on a bottle of stain remover, you'll be glad to know that you can make your own for about 50 cents. Fill a clean spray bottle with two parts water and one part ammonia. Spray it on any stain (test for colorfastness first, please!), and most will wash right out.

## CREATE AN ESCAPE

Ever try to remove a stain and find you've just spread the darned thing around instead of getting it out? Try this: Set the garment, stain side down, on a clean white washcloth and treat it from the opposite side of the fabric. As the treatment goes through the material, it'll force the stain off the fabric and onto the washcloth. (Not bad for a formerly laundry-challenged guy, huh?)

## OUT, OUT, DARNED GRASS!

I've had a lot of practice getting out grass stains! Here are my four favorite methods:

1. **On jeans.** Make a paste of baking soda and water, rub it on the stain, then scrub with a toothbrush or hard plastic scrubbing brush. You could use toothpaste, instead, but baking soda works just as well and costs a lot less!

2. **On T-shirts.** Sponge the stain with rubbing alcohol, and let it dry. Then toss the shirt into the wash.

3. **On cotton dress slacks.** Apply shampoo or Murphy's

Oil Soap with a toothbrush. Then wash as usual. And by the way, just what were you thinking when you did yard work in your good clothes?

4. **All-over grass stains (like the kind you get when you're romping on the lawn with the grandkids).** Add ¼ cup of powdered dishwashing detergent to your regular laundry detergent, and wash the stained clothes in warm water.

# IN A LATHER OVER LEATHER

For heaven's sake, don't try to hand-wash leather in the sink! But don't fret—you *can* clean it at home. Rub a little Ivory soap on a clean, damp, white washcloth. Rub the leather coat, pants, handbag, or what-have-you only where it needs to be cleaned, then buff it dry with a piece of flannel or chamois.

## FIRE YOUR DRY-CLEANER!

\* \* \* \* \*

You know, the main reason I avoid dry-cleaning my clothes is because it's so expensive. Heck, you could pay for the same shirt two or three times over if you have to have it dry-cleaned at two or three bucks a pop every few weeks! But even if I were as rich as Midas, I'd still steer clear of dry-cleaning whenever I could. That's because the chemicals used in the process are toxic—some have even been linked to cancer. Now that's a risk I definitely don't want to have to pay for!

Of course, some clothes *do* have to be dry-cleaned—suits and sportcoats, for example, just won't survive any other kind of cleanup. But how do you know for sure what you can safely clean at home? Start by reading the label. If the label says, "Professionally Dry-Clean Only," there's no way around it, unless you're willing to risk ruining the clothes. If the label says, "Dry-Clean Only," though, there's hope. Here's how to approach those garments:

**Wash by hand.** Most of those "Dry-Clean Only" clothes can be washed by hand in cold water. Silks, cashmere, angora, chiffon, and even lace can all be hand-washed with care. Use a couple drops of clear dish soap, and gently work the suds through the garment. Don't tug or pull at the clothes.

**Roll 'em dry.** After hand-washing clothes, try this trick for getting excess water out: Lay the item flat on a clean white towel and roll it up. Press on the towel, then unroll it and let the garment dry flat.

## HOLD YOUR HORSES

**G**ot a stain that insists on sticking around? Don't give up if your first stain-fighting method doesn't work. And no matter what, don't throw that still-stained garment into the dryer! Once that stain's been in a hot dryer, it will be set and may never come out. Until you heat-set it, though, you can keep trying to get it out. Try repeating the stain-removal technique, or use one of my formulas in this chapter. There's a very good chance you'll hit upon a successful solution. And, if at first you don't succeed....

# Clothing Care

**N**ow, so far we've covered washing, drying, ironing, and stain removal. But wait, there's more! My Grandma Putt passed along so many neat tips and tricks for clothing care that I've just gotta share them with you. So read on for a little bit of this and a little bit of that—I *guarantee* you'll learn at least one new way to care for your clothes!

## Keeping Clothes Wearable

You already know that the way you clean and store clothing can add or subtract years from its life. But if you also know some of these simple clothing maintenance and repair tricks, you can be sure your wardrobe will be around a good long time.

## DON'T FORGET TO FLOSS

**I**f a button is already loose on a garment, or if you know the buttons are going to take a beating, consider sewing them on with dental floss. If the

## NO STRINGS ATTACHED

Dry cleaners have a bad rep, but did you know that some will actually replace buttons and zippers at no extra charge? That almost makes their prices seem reasonable, doesn't it?

original thread was white, the appearance won't be changed much. Floss is stronger than ordinary thread, and it'll hold up to wear and tear without giving an inch. (This works for buttons on pillows and cushions, too!)

## IT'S A SNAP

If the snaps on your clothing won't stay snapped, just set the snap on its edge on a hard surface, and tap the rounded part gently around the sides with a hammer. It'll be snug as a bug in a rug!

## THE MATCH GAME

Need a piece of cloth to repair a skirt or a pair of pants, but can't find an exact

match? Steal it from inside of the pocket or hem. You can replace the pilfered piece with practically anything, and no one will be the wiser.

## SEAL 'EM TIGHT

Keep clothing seams sealed—permanently—by putting a little Krazy Glue on the ends. This also works well with zippers: Just put a dab on the bottom of the zipper, where the zipper tape goes into the crotch of the pants.

## ZIP-A-DEE-DO-DA

It's hardly a wonderful day when your zipper gets stuck. No matter how much you pull and tug, it doesn't seem to do anything except get even more jammed. Try these tips, and soon you'll be singing "Zip-a-dee-yay!"

✦ If the zipper is caught up on some fabric, gently pull on the zipper tab with one hand, while you try to tug at the caught fabric with the other. Go slowly, or you could rip the fabric.

✦ If the zipper isn't stuck on fabric, try rubbing the teeth with a pencil; believe it or not, this actually helps it slide back and forth easier. Or, rub a bar of soap or a candle over the zipper teeth. Do this several times and things should get moving again.

---

## PANTYHOSE 9-1-1

\* \* \* \* \*

Not that I'd know personally, but I've heard that getting a run in her stockings can wreck a woman's day. Here are a few tips to prevent your pantyhose from running all over the place:

☑ **Freeze 'em.** Seriously—it'll make your pantyhose last and last. As soon as you buy a new pair of pantyhose, give them a rinse, wring them out, place them in a plastic bag, and toss 'em in the freezer. Once they're frozen, thaw, and hang them up to dry. Do this after each washing, too.

☑ **Block those toes.** If you've ever had your toes break through the end of sandal-foot hose, you'll appreciate this. Before you put on your pantyhose, use hairspray on the toes to keep those little piggies from breaking on through to the other side! Spray the heels, too, to prevent wear from shoes with heel straps.

☑ **Stop a run.** If you've already got a run, control it by using hairspray or clear nail polish. A little spray or dab at each end of the run should keep it in check.

---

## DON'T HEM AND HAW

In an emergency, you can "hem" pants using a roll of duct tape, but that's hardly a permanent solution. Instead, save time by using iron-on bonding net or hem tape. You simply apply the net or tape, roll the pant leg to the desired length, press with a hot iron, and *voilà*—instant hemming without the hawing! (The package comes with complete directions.)

## IF THE SHOE FITS...

Then keep on wearing it! Extend the life of your shoes by following these steps:

1. Always put shoe trees inside your shoes. If you don't have any shoe trees, don't worry; simply stuff your shoes with crumpled newspaper. The

idea here is to help your shoes retain their shape when they're not being worn.

2. When you put on your shoes, always use a shoe-horn. This helps prevent the smashed-down look that quickly develops when you repeatedly shove your foot in, instead of sliding your heel along the shoehorn.

3. Don't wear the same pair of shoes day after day. Have at least one other pair, if not two or three, to alternate with, so you can give your shoes a chance to air out and get back into shape between wearings.

# Recycling ABCs

**Now, I'm not talking about passing clothing down through the family tree, though you know that's a great moneysaving idea. What I'm getting at here is an answer to that nagging question, "What do you do with clothing that is really worse for wear?" It's too shabby to donate, but I can assure you that there's still some life left in those almost-rags. Read on.**

# IT'S IN THE JEANS

**I** know you hate to give up your favorite pair of jeans, but at some point, you've got to let them go. No, you don't have to throw them out; instead, consider one of these terrific new uses:

★ If your jeans are still in pretty good shape from the knees up, make cut-off shorts. Using pinking shears, cut off a couple of inches below the desired length, and roll 'em up. Now your favorite jeans will become your favorite shorts!

★ Use the legs of old jeans to make gift bags (perfect for golf clubs) or storage bags (perfect for a makeshift first-aid kit or to store jumper cables for your car). Just sew up one end, and either use pinking shears to give a decorative edge to the open end, or sew in a draw-string or ribbon so you can tie it closed.

★ Hit a home run with your kids by making a baseball base. Cut two equal squares from the legs of old jeans, and sew them together on three sides. Fill with sand, then sew up the fourth side. You can also cut smaller squares and make beanbags.

## GET SCRAPPY!

* * * * *

When you're done with a sewing project, don't throw out your old (or new) fabric scraps. Whether you want to spiff up an outfit, patch up an old quilt—or even make a new one—those chunks of cloth are worth their weight in gold. Try one of these on for size—and savings!

◆ Save scraps for making quilt patches or cushion covers.

◆ Cut up old T-shirts to make braided rugs.

◆ Use trimmings left over from shortening pants, skirts, or dresses to make great belts, scarves, headbands, or pocket squares that will match the original outfit perfectly!

◆ Cut up old, no-longer-wearable clothes to make all kinds of accessories like hats, handkerchiefs, ties, or hair bows.

## RIDE ON YOUR COATTAILS

You could always give an old coat to charity (and get that nifty tax write-off), but if you're thinking of tossing it out, don't! Instead, cut insoles for shoes out of it or make potholders. Or, if it's a down coat, use the stuffing to make throw pillows to dress up your sofa or bed.

## DON'T GET HOSED

Don't toss out those holey panty-hose. You'll be amazed at what they can help you do.

☑ Pantyhose are the perfect "brush" for suede clothing, because they attracts lint and other particles.

☑ Everyone hates to wash windows, but it's a lot easier if you put your soapy sponge inside a leg of an old pair of pantyhose. The rough texture of the nylon removes dirt effortlessly.

☑ Old pairs of pantyhose make great stuffing for pillows and stuffed animals—especially since they're washable!

# More Fantastic Formulas!

We're not through Grandma Putt's clothing-care and stain-fighting arsenal just yet! I've compiled a bunch of her favorite laundry formulas below. They've all worked well for me, so give 'em a try.

## VINEGAR TO THE RESCUE

**W**hiten whites and brighten brights by adding ½ cup of vinegar to the rinse cycle. And believe it or not, adding vinegar actually cuts down on the amount of time your clothes spend in the dryer. How's that for killing two birds with one stone?

## CLEAN AROUND THE COLLAR

**I** don't know what it is about that pesky ring around the collar, but it sure does show up a lot! Try one of these time-tested remedies:

✦ Rub a little shampoo into the collar stains, then throw the shirt in the washing machine. (Shampoos are made to dissolve body oils.)

## FANTASTIC FORMULA

### Mustard Blaster

I love a good hot dog, and as anyone can tell you, you can't eat a hot dog without a little mustard. If you're like me, it won't be long before you have a bright yellow stain on your shirt. Eliminate mustard stains by scrubbing them with a solution of two parts water and one part rubbing alcohol, then wash as usual.

✦ Mix equal amounts of liquid dish soap, ammonia, and water. This makes the perfect pretreatment spray, especially on shirt collars!

✦ Stir 2 tablespoons of baking soda and 2 tablespoons of vinegar together to make a thin paste. Rub the paste on the offending collar, wait half an hour, then wash as usual. I'd use this tip as a last resort (after all, rubbing in shampoo is both cheaper and easier), but it has never let me down.

## PAINT IT BLACK

**I**f your black clothes are starting to look a little on the brown side, try adding 2 tablespoons of coffee (ground coffee—not brewed) to the rinse cycle. You'll be back in the black in no time at all!

## MAKING UP IS HARD TO DO

To remove makeup stains, use hairspray. Just spray it on the stain, rub gently, and wipe with a damp cloth. Then wash as usual. To eliminate a light makeup smudge, take a slice of white bread, and wipe it across

## NO STRINGS ATTACHED

Here's a little secret no laundry product company would ever want you to know: Many, many stains come out quickly and easily when treated with nothing more than piping hot water. Yep, you read that right. Just good old, plain old $H_2O$. If you've got a stain on a durable fabric (cotton, denim, polyester/cotton blend, jersey, or the like), drape it over the sink or a bucket, then pour boiling water straight from a clean teapot through the fabric. The extreme heat of the water removes even some very stubborn stains from most materials.

the smudge. It'll be gone in a jiffy, and you won't have to throw the clothing in the wash.

## BRING IT TO A BOIL

Dirty white socks will come clean as a whistle if you soak them in a pot of boiling water with a slice of lemon. Let them boil for a couple of minutes, then wash as usual.

## TARRED AND FEATHERED

Here's one for all you roofers out there. Getting tar on your clothes is all in a day's work. But now you can get it out just as easily. Rub the tar stain with a little kerosene, and then wash as usual. Kerosene may remove the color from certain fabrics, so you should test this in an inconspicuous spot first. **Note:** Kerosene is flammable, so don't use it near any kind of open flame, and use kerosene only in a well-ventilated area.

## RUST IN PEACE

To get a rust stain out of colored clothes, apply a paste of salt and lemon juice, then put the clothes out to dry under the hot sun. To remove rust from white clothes, cover the stain with a paste of cream of tartar and water. Soak in hot water for 10 minutes, then wash as usual.

## GREASE IS THE WORD

**W**orking in the garage means dirty work, but somebody's got to do it. Try one of these grease-busters:

☞ Dab some dishwashing soap on the stain, rub with a damp sponge, and then soak for a good half-hour. Wash as usual.

☞ Put a little Goo Gone on the stain, and scrub. (Goo Gone is an all-purpose cleaner that you can find in the grocery store.) Wash as usual. This'll work even if you're treating a stain that has persisted after washing. You'll be as amazed as I was!

## FREEZE FRAME

**F**or those of us with small kids or grandkids, borax is our best friend—if we can get to the stain in time! Combat diaper and underwear stains by tossing the stained article into a

plastic bag and freezing it 'til you're good and ready to wash. Then rinse with cold water, pretreat with borax solution, and let it sit for 10 minutes or so. Wash normally.

### FANTASTIC FORMULA

**Sweaty Stain Solution**

Here's a laundry challenge that's been around as long as laundry itself: getting yellow perspiration stains out of shirt underarms. To treat white shirts, there's nothing better than this recipe.

$^1/_2$ cup of lemon juice, or 2 lemons

Hot water

1 additional lemon

Sunshine

**1.** Pour half a cup of lemon juice or squeeze two lemons into a half-full laundry tub of hot water. (If you're doing a full load, add twice as much lemon.)

**2.** Soak your clothes for an hour or overnight, then put them through the wash cycle.

**3.** Add the juice of one more lemon to the rinse cycle, then hang your clothes in the sun to dry. Lemon and sunshine combine to make nature's best bleach, and so far, nothing the detergent industry has come up with can top it!

## SALT SAVES COLORS

Clothes can start to lose their color after several washings. Rather than waste money on color-safe bleaches and brighteners, try adding a couple of pinches of table salt to your detergent. This'll help keep colors from fading away.

## DISAPPEARING INK

Ever have a pen burst in your pocket? Try one of these sure-fire remedies for removing ink stains:

★ Soak the ink stain in a dish of milk before washing, and it'll come right out.

★ Spray the stain with hairspray. It will dissolve away before your eyes. Then wash as usual.

★ Give the stain a rub with rubbing alcohol. Swab the stain gently, and it'll come right out.

## PUCKER UP!

Lipstick stains can be easily removed with—get this—petroleum jelly. Simply rub a small amount into the stain, and wash as usual.

## WAXING POETIC

What do you do if you get candle wax on your clothes? Scrape as much off as you possibly can with a knife. Then, put a white paper towel on top of and beneath the stain, and press with a warm iron. The excess residue should come right off.

## CHEW ON THIS

To remove stuck-on chewing gum from clothing, put the sticky garment in the freezer. After a couple of hours, you should be able to pull the hardened gum right off.

---

### FANTASTIC FORMULA

**Blood Buster**

If you can't get to a blood stain right away and it's had a chance to make itself at home, hydrogen peroxide may not do the trick (see "Insult to Injury" on page 205). Try this instead: Apply a paste of meat tenderizer and water to the stain, and scrub gently. The stain should begin to dissolve immediately.

## INSULT TO INJURY

The only thing worse than cutting your finger while you're fixing dinner is cutting your finger and getting blood on your shirt. If you get a bloodstain on your clothes, treat the injury and the stain at the same time. A little hydrogen peroxide will clean your wound *and* your shirt.

## CATCH UP!

Other than blood, no stain is more stubborn than catsup (or ketchup, as I like to spell it!). This requires immediate action. Rinse the stain with cold water, and let it sit for 30 minutes or so. Then rub in a bit of hydrogen peroxide, followed by another helping of cold water. Wash as usual.

## DON'T GET TAKEN TO THE CLEANERS

Here's something you may want to try when you have a stain on a dry-clean only garment. Gently scrub the stain with a baby wipe, then let the garment air dry. It works

### A LITTLE SOMETHING FROM THE GARAGE

\* \* \* \* \*

A wise old friend of mine recently suggested putting WD-40 on an oil stain I got on one of my "garage shirts." I thought he was nuts, but the stain came out! Simply spray oil stains with WD-40, rub it in, wait half an hour, then wash your clothes as usual. It works like a charm!

perfectly (and cuts down on your dry-cleaning bill).

## COFFEE TALK

I love the smell of coffee in the morning! I just don't like the stains it sometimes leaves on my shirts and pants. To get rid of coffee stains, soak the clothing in a sinkful of vinegar and water overnight. In the morning, while you're enjoying another cuppa' joe, lay the clothes out to dry in the sun.

# CHAPTER 9

# Long-Lived Appliances and Electronics

We of the D-I-Y (do-it-yourself) mentality think we can fix anything that goes wrong around the ol' homestead. Our confidence in our own abilities is *astounding!* And we certainly don't relish the idea of paying good money for something that we're sure we can take care of ourselves. But take it from me, my friends: When it comes to appliances and electronics, there are times when you need to call in the pros. Why? Because it seems like just about everything from toasters to radios runs on computer chips these days!

Now, not *every* little glitch needs expert repair, and that's what this chapter is all about. In Chapter 3, I told you how to get your appliances and electronics at low prices. Now, I'm going to tell you how to keep them running. And, while I won't be turning you into an electrician or master plumber, I *will* show you some simple maintenance techniques that will give you a leg up when it comes to keeping those appliances working better, longer, and for less money, too!

# Maintain and Prosper

An ounce of prevention is worth a pound of cure—everyone knows that. You brush your teeth so you don't get cavities. You change the oil in your car to keep it running well. But, do you clean your refrigerator's condenser coils once a year? Do you defragment (condense the files on) your computer on a regular basis? Do you clean the outdoor dryer vent twice a year?

If so, you get a gold star—maybe *you* should be writing this book! But if you're like most folks, you haven't given this kind of maintenance a second thought. Well, just as an apple a day can keep the doctor away, caring properly for your appliances and electronics can keep the repairman at bay and save you a bundle—so read on!

## Appliance Guidance

All appliances need a little fine-tuning every now and again—from your washer and dryer all the way down to your can opener. In this section, you'll find a load of maintenance tips to keep your appliances running like well-oiled machines. Remember: A little effort now will keep you from putting forth a lot more later on.

## HERE'S THE DISH

The dishwasher—the only sure-fire cure for dishpan hands! This dandy gadget sure has made a lot of lives easier, but it won't earn its keep unless you keep it in shape. Here are some quick and easy steps to help you keep yours running like a dream machine:

☑ If the water temperature isn't between 140° and 150°F, the soap won't dissolve; it'll just

build up until you've got a miniature mountain range of soap gunk—and dirty dishes, besides. To head off that unpleasantness, just run hot water in the kitchen sink for a minute or so *before* you turn on the dishwasher.

☑ If the tips of your dishwasher racks get rusty, just scrub off the rust with a steel wool soap pad. And to keep those racks spic and span, clean them once a month with a paste made of baking soda and water.

---

## FANTASTIC FORMULA

### Dishwasher Washer

A couple of times a year, stand 1 cup of vinegar in the upper rack and 1 cup of vinegar in the lower rack of your dishwasher, along with a full load of dishes. Run the dishwasher as usual. The vinegar will be dispersed throughout the machine, removing any mineral deposits or soap residue. Think of this as your 15,000-mile check up—it's just what your dishwasher needs to keep on truckin' for miles and miles.

☑ Every couple of months, lift out the strainer, put it into a sink full of hot, soapy water, and scrub it gently with a sponge.

☑ At least twice a year, clean the spray arm. Just pull it out of the machine and poke a strand of thin wire through each hole. When you're through, give the arm a gentle shake to make sure there's nothing else caught in there, and then scrub away the mineral deposits with a solution of vinegar and hot water.

## MINERALLY SPEAKING

Sometimes, the heating element in your dishwasher will become clogged with mineral deposits from all that water constantly running through it. Make a paste of vinegar and baking soda, and apply it generously to the area. Rinse with a little full-strength vinegar, and watch those deposits withdraw.

## IN HOT WATER

Yep, that's what you'll be in if you're using hot water when you run your garbage disposal. Why? Because instead of breaking up grease, hot water melts it, and eventually, all that melted grease hardens way down in the disposal's innards. That spells a big block-age—and a big plumbing bill. So always run cold water when you're grinding up your dinner remains, and keep that water running for at least 60 seconds after you flick off the switch.

# CUT THE CLOG

What if you've already run hot water down the dis-posal, and now all kinds of hardened who-knows-what is clogging it up? Fear not. Just mix up a concoction of equal parts vinegar, salt, and baking soda. Pour directly into the drain, and let the mixture sit for a good 10 minutes or so. Then rinse with 2 cups of boil-ing water. That should clear things up.

If that doesn't do the trick, try this: First, make sure the appliance is off. (You don't want to get a nasty surprise down there!) Then,

## JUST SAY YES—AND NO

\* \* \* \* \*

For as long as I can remember, people have been telling me *not* to put eggshells, potato peels, banana peels, and celery down the disposal. Well, they're half right. Whatever you do, folks, do *not* grind up banana peels or celery in your garbage disposal. Trust me on this—all those strings'll foul up the works big time! (You'll also be wasting some of the finest garden chow I can think of.) But don't be afraid to toss down those eggshells and 'tater skins. The warnings about them are just a bunch of old wives' tales. They won't harm your disposal. And coffee grounds actually help keep the blades sharp and the innards turning freely. So, by all means, give your disposal healthy helpings. (But save some for the compost pile!)

check to make sure the breaker switch didn't get tripped. If it's off, reset it. If not, you'll need to per-form a little minor surgery. Take the straight wrench that came with your dis-posal (it's usually hanging out underneath, waiting to be called to active duty), and manu-ally spin the motor. If that doesn't free it up, it's time to throw in your wrench and call a plumber.

## FANTASTIC FORMULA

### Odor-Be-Gone

Every once in a while, you may notice an unsavory odor creeping up from your garbage disposal and out the sink drain. Don't run for a room deodorizer. Instead, simply drop a few lemon or orange peels down the drain, and let the cold water run for a minute or two as you run the disposal. It'll be fresh again in no time.

## FREEZE, BABY, FREEZE!

Just like every other appliance, your garbage disposal runs its best (and most energy-miserly) when it's sparkling clean. To keep it ship-shape, drop in a tray's worth of ice cubes every week or so, and run cold water and the disposal for a minute or two. It works like a charm!

## RIDIN' THE RANGE

Your kitchen range is probably the hardest thing in the whole house—much less the kitchen—to keep clean. And the top can be a *real* dickens, with all those spills and splatters. But it's like mending a

fence out on the ranch: It's not half so hard if you keep on top of it. In this case, it just means that when a pot boils over, you need to hop to it with a moist sponge. For routine maintenance, wipe down the burners and range top once a day with a paste made of baking soda and water. If something really messy—like your world-famous marinara sauce—has spilled all over creation, you can clean the burners with steel wool pads. But keep them away from the range top itself, or it'll look like your cat used it as a scratching post!

## A PERFECT A-RANGE-MENT

Using your range properly can save you big bucks in energy costs. Here are a few tips to keep those bills in check:

☞ Match the size of the pan to the burner. A 6-inch pan on an 8-inch burner will waste more than 40 percent of the energy used.

☞ Don't open the oven door to preview the food. I know it's tempting, but each time you open the door, the oven temperature drops by 25°F. Keep your eye on the clock, instead.

☞ If you have a self-cleaning oven, try using the self-cleaning feature immediately after your food comes out of the oven. It won't take as much energy to reach the desired cleaning temperature.

☞ For electric stoves, try to use mostly flat-bottomed pans that make full contact with the burner. Rounded pans tend to waste most of the heat.

☞ Ovens are generally not efficient for cooking small- to medium-size meals. If a different cooking method can be used without sacrificing the flavor, then use your toaster oven or your microwave to cook smaller meals.

# EASY DOES IT

**W**ho needs those nasty— and expensive—oven cleaners? Instead, try my Grandma Putt's all-time favorite cleaner: baking soda paste. Simply add baking soda to a cup of hot water, and stir. When

the mixture reaches the consistency of toothpaste, it's ready to tackle those nasty oven stains— inside and out. It also does a great job of keeping the refrigerator, toaster, and any other appliance spic and span.

## HEAT 'N CLEAN

\* \* \* \* \*

When baking soda paste (see "Easy Does It," at left) won't do the trick, this routine will. First, set your oven on warm for about 20 minutes, then turn it off. Next, place a small pan of full-strength ammonia on the top shelf and a large pan of boiling water on the bottom shelf. Shut the door and let it all sit overnight. In the morning, open the oven, take out the pans, and let the oven air out. (It's a good idea to open the kitchen windows, too.) When all the fumes have flown, wash the inside surfaces with soap and water. Even the hard, baked-on grease will be gone before you can say, "Vamoose!"

## HOLD THAT HEAT!

If you're not careful, a lot of heat—and therefore, a lot of dollars—can fly right out through your oven door. Here are two ways to keep that energy where it belongs: in the oven, bakin' your food!

1. Never line the bottom of your oven with aluminum foil—it reduces airflow and can actually increase cooking time (and thus, the spending of energy dollars).

2. Once a year, check the oven gasket. If it's soft and malleable, you're in good shape. If it's brittle or tough, though, chances are that it's letting heat leak through the door. Most gaskets are attached with screws and clips. Just remove it, take it to the hardware store or appliance retailer, and buy a matching replacement. Install the new gasket, and you're good to go!

## IT'LL ALL COME OUT IN THE WASH

Your washing machine pretty much cleans itself on the inside, but that doesn't mean you're home free: Liquid fabric softeners, which are very waxy, can build up in the washer's innards and make a real mess. You can avoid the whole ball of wax in two ways: If your machine has a fabric-softener dispenser, pour in the recommended amount of softener and then add about $1/3$ cup of water. This will help the softener dissolve properly. For machines without dispensers, mix $2/3$ cup of softener with $1/3$ cup of water in a cup, and pour it into the washer tub.

## MORE IS BETTER

This advice might seem odd coming from an old tightwad like me, but trust me on this, folks: When you toss a load of clothes into the washing machine, always use more $H_2O$ than you think you need. If there's not enough water in the tub, the clothes can't circulate freely, and they'll get all wrapped around the agitator. That'll cause wear and tear on the agitator seal—not to mention the damage all that twisting and turning will do to your clothes. The extra pennies you might see on your water bill will be nothing compared to the cost of new clothes or a new washing machine!

## AND LESS IS MORE

**W**hen it comes to doin' laundry, lots of folks figure that the fuller they stuff the washing machine, the fewer loads they'll have to do. That's true, but so is this: The fuller you stuff a washer, the more washers you'll have to buy. *Never overload the machine!* Clothing should never come above the top of the agitator axle, and don't pack the clothes down to fit more in. Overloading your washer strains the motor and therefore, lowers your washer's life span.

### NO SMOKING!

\* \* \* \* \*

If your washing machine smells smoky (and you know nothing's burning), I'll bet my bottom soap flake that you've either put too many clothes or too little water in the tub. Stop the machine, make the appropriate adjustments to the water level or clothing amount, and then restart. And don't let that happen again!

## ON THE LEVEL

**M**ake sure that your washing machine stays on level footing. Otherwise, it may literally start to walk around the room with your clothes! That will not only ruin your floor, but can also wreak havoc on the inner workings of your washing machine.

Leveling the machine is easy—simply adjust the legs. To raise the legs of your washer, turn them clockwise. To lower them, turn them counterclockwise. It's that easy!

## WATCH THOSE HOSES!

**W**ashing machine hoses usually last 5 years or so, but they can go sooner—and a sudden rupture can mean expensive water damage to the old homestead. To be on the safe side, check your hoses once a month. If you see a small blister, it means trouble is headed your way. Hightail it to the hardware or plumbing-supply store, buy a new hose, and slip it on—*pronto!*

## THE CLOSED DOOR POLICY

A poorly sealed dryer door spells wasted heat. To make sure your seal is tight as a drum, hold a piece of tissue paper next to the door edge while the dryer is running. If it sucks the tissue in like a vacuum, you've got a problem. A quick trip to an appliance or hardware store will get you going again. (A new seal will probably run you around $15; just follow the instructions to install it, and you'll be all set.)

## LET GO, LINT!

Lint is a dryer's worst enemy, and it could be yours, too. Lint that builds up in the screens, filters, and dryer vents can do more than foul up the mechanism—it can cause a fire. To keep your dryer working— and a roof over your head— attend to these routine chores:

1. Clean out the lint screen after each load of laundry.

2. Every month or so, wash the lint screen in warm, soapy

---

**$ BARGAIN ALERT!**

You don't have to spend a lot of money to get the most out of your laundry appliances. Here are a few tips on energy efficiency that will make life a lot easier on your pocketbook:

★ **Position your washing machine close to the hot water tank.** This will reduce heat loss in long pipe runs.

★ **Keep your hot-water heater set at 120°F.** For every 10°F reduction in water temperature, you can reduce the cost of washing clothes by as much as 10 percent.

★ **Wash clothing in warm or cold water, and use hot only when absolutely necessary.** Using warm water rather than hot will reduce the load's energy use by half.

★ **Don't use a lot of detergent.** If your tub bubbleth over, it's just using that much more energy.

★ **Don't overwash clothes.** Delicates don't need to spend as much time in the washing machine as, say, those overalls you wore out in the garden last weekend.

water. Let it air-dry overnight, and come morning, it'll be ready for action.

3. Every four months or so, scrape built-up lint from the outdoor vent, using a stiff-bristled brush.

4. Twice a year, remove the exhaust duct from the dryer, and give it the once-over with a vacuum cleaner.

## IS YOUR REFRIGERATOR RUNNING?

**T**hen you'd better run and catch it! I'm sure you've heard that one before. But, have you heard the one about the leaky door gasket that cost the owner hundreds of dollars in energy bills *and* a new compressor? That joke's not quite so funny now, is it? Here's how to make sure the joke's not on you:

☞ As part of your routine kitchen cleaning, wipe down the door gasket with a mixture of 1 tablespoon of baking soda dissolved in 2 quarts of warm water. It'll remove dirt and odor, while keeping your gasket soft and flexible.

☞ Every 6 months or so, perform what I call the "George Washington Test." Just open the refrigerator door, and hold a dollar bill so that it reaches about halfway in at the top of the door. Close the door on the bill, and pull gently on the handle. If the bill slips down, you've got yourself a leaky gasket. Repeat the procedure all the way down the length of the door. If the gasket fails the GW Test at any spot, buy a new gasket at your local hardware store ASAP! At best, a loose gasket will waste energy and send your

---

### KNOCK ON WOOD

\* \* \* \* \*

Is your fridge sitting next to the stove or a wall oven? If so, you're probably paying too much in energy bills. Why? Because the heat from the range makes the refrigerator work overtime to keep your food cold. If you can't move the fridge to a new location, try this: Place a piece of plywood between the stove and the fridge to absorb the heat and keep your fridge running more efficiently.

electric bill soaring. At worst, it can shorten the life of your compressor—and that'll cost you *big* bucks!

## TILT!

**M**ake sure your fridge stays level or tilted slightly backward. It should never lean forward—the door could fail to shut completely, and that means higher electric bills.

## BE AN EFFICIENCY EXPERT

**A** full refrigerator is more efficient to run than an empty one, and in case of a power outage, fuller fridges stay

---

### NO STRINGS ATTACHED

If you're one of those folks who uses the top of the fridge as extra storage space, here's good news: You can cut your electric bill simply by taking that stuff off and stashing it someplace else. That excess weight makes your refrigerator burn more energy.

---

cooler longer. Most refrigerators will keep food sealed inside nice and cold for up to 48 hours, but full refrigerators will surpass even that. So don't be afraid to stock up! Just be sure to keep some space between items, so cool air can circulate under normal running conditions. Then the items will be nice and cold if and when the power does go out.

## COIL TOIL

**D**irty condenser coils make your refrigerator work harder—and use more energy in the process. So, at least once a year (twice a year if you have pets that shed), clean those coils! You can buy a special coil brush, but your vacuum cleaner will do the job just as well. Your refrigerator will run for shorter periods with clean coils, and that saves you money in efficiency. Oh—and while you're at it, get the dust on the wall behind the fridge, before it ends up on the coils.

## DON'T RUN ON EMPTY

**N**ever run the microwave without food inside it. I once came downstairs and caught my granddaughter practicing for a speech. Her timer of choice? The microwave—running on empty for a good 10 minutes! When there's nothing for the microwave to cook, the energy will feed back on itself, and that could eventually spell trouble for the microwave oven's working innards.

# CLEANLINESS IS NEXT TO SPEEDINESS

**A** microwave oven is a handy thing to have around the kitchen, but it's one of the most temperamental gadgets to come down the pike in a month of Sundays. If you don't keep the thing spotlessly clean, vapors from grease and spilled food can seep into the innards, causing rust and corrosion. Then, before you know it, your machine's gone belly up! To keep your microwave nukin' right along, make sure you put paper plates or paper towels over your food *and* under the dish before you press the Start button.

# OPEN SEZ ME!

**Y**our electric can opener might be the least pricey appliance in your kitchen, but

## FANTASTIC FORMULA

### Microwave Magic

Here's a super-simple formula for keeping your microwave spotless and smelling fresh: Just fill a bowl (microwave safe, of course) with water, and add a lemon wedge. Nuke the water for about 3 minutes, let it sit for another 5 minutes, then remove the bowl. Any dried-on particles on the oven walls will wipe away in a snap, and the interior will be odor free.

that's no reason to let it slowly drift off to the Big Garage Sale in the Sky. Just by wiping the blade with a damp sponge after every use, you can keep that little machine hummin' along for years.

# COFFEE ANYONE?

**I**'ve known folks who buy new coffee makers as often as I buy coffee filters—or at least it seems that way. They claim that after a while, the coffee starts tasting funny. Of course it does! But it wouldn't, if they cleaned the machine now and then. How often you need to do this depends on how hard your water is, but I guarantee it'll keep turnin' out cup after cup of great-tastin' brew if you use one of these simple methods:

◆ If you've got an aluminum percolator, add 2 table-spoons of cream of tartar to a full pot of water, and perk as usual.

◆ For electric-drip coffee makers, run a solution of half-water and half-vinegar through a brewing cycle. Then run a clean pot of water through before you make coffee again.

---

## LET OFF SOME STEAM!

\* \* \* \* \*

If your steam iron ain't steamin', chances are it's all clogged up with mineral deposits. To send 'em packing, fill the water reservoir with vinegar, and let it steam until it's empty. And from now on, use only distilled water in your iron. That way, you can kiss mineral buildup good-bye!

---

## AN IRON-CLAD PLAN

Steam irons might be small, but if you've glanced at their price tags lately, you know they're not cheap! One problem that sends plenty of irons to the gadget graveyard is melted polyester fabric that's stuck to the bottom heating plate. If that's what's mucking up your iron, don't give it its last rites just yet. Instead, turn it on low, and heat it until the material begins to melt. Then scrape off the gunk with a wooden spatula, a smooth scrap of wood, or half a wooden clothespin. That should clean it right up.

In the future, if you must iron polyester fabric, put an all-cotton cloth between it and the iron. After all, polyester is made from petroleum, and it is actually a kind of plastic—so, of course it'll melt under heat!

## Eternal Electronics

It seems that every time I call a store and ask about repairing some electronic gadget, I get the same answer: "Oh, we don't fix those anymore; just throw it out and buy a new one." Well, folks, if that idea doesn't ruffle your frugal feathers, I don't know what will! Here's a roundup of tips to help you hang onto those fancy chunks of machinery for as long as possible.

# AS EASY AS VCR!

**V**CRs are generally easy-going contraptions, but a defective tape can land your machine on its rear faster than you can say "I Love Lucy." If you want to keep playin' those reruns for years to come, keep these pointers in mind:

**Check 'em out.** Before you take any tape home from the video store, check it for obvious damage. If you hear bits of plastic banging around inside the tape case, or if the tape itself has obvious wrinkles, leave that tape right where it is.

**Speed it up.** Fast-forward any tape a little before you hit play. Most damage-causing culprits hang out at the very beginning, just due to general wear and tear on the tape. Often-times, when you first pop in a rental, the picture will be fuzzy or full of lines, regardless of the

Here's a case where a bargain ain't necessarily a bargain after all. I'm talking about generic (no-name) blank videotapes. They may have bargain-basement price tags, but trust me, friends, you'll get what you pay for if you buy them. Name-brand tapes have been manufactured to specific standards. Generic tapes have not, and they use poorer-quality tape, which can do permanent damage to your VCR. So, be willing to shell out a bit more money when it comes to buying blank videotapes, and you'll add life to your VCR.

tracking. But if you just fast-forward it a couple of minutes, the rest of the tape is usually as good as new.

# THRIFTY HEAD CLEANER

**D**o you regularly use a store-bought, VCR head cleaner? If so, you ought to have *your* head examined! Those pricey head cleaners can cost anywhere from $10 to $20, and for what? You can get the same results by simply putting a new, blank VHS tape into your machine and hitting fast forward for about 5 minutes. The tape picks up contaminants and cleans the heads. Don't rewind the tape, because rewinding will just reinsert any contaminants back into your machine. Next time you need to clean your heads (every three months or so, if you use your VCR regularly), reinsert the same tape, and repeat this process. Once the tape has progressed through its 90- or 120-minute running time, throw it away, and start with a fresh tape. (You can't rewind it and use it again, or else you'll release the contaminants back into the machine.)

---

## FIGHT THE URGE TO SURGE

\* \* \* \* \*

We all know that a power outage can spell disaster for any electronic device. The same is true even when lights blink on and off without actually going out. So it's important to protect your electronics by plugging them into surge protectors. Most surge protectors come in one long strip containing six outlets, and you probably don't need more than three surge protectors: one for your computer and all of its components (monitor, printer, scanner, etc.), one for your living room (to accommodate your TV, VCR, DVD player, stereo, etc.), and possibly one for your bedroom (again, for TVs, stereos, VCRs, etc.). You'll find surge protectors wherever electronics and appliances are sold.

---

# IT'S NOT ALL IN YOUR HEADS

If you've tried cleaning your VCR heads and you're still having problems, the machine might be dirty elsewhere. Here's how to clean up its act:

1. Unplug the unit, flip it over, and find the screws that hold the cover on (they'll be on the back or bottom of the machine).

2. Unscrew the screws, put them were you can find them, and gently pull off the VCR's cover.

3. Wipe the innards with a soft, dry cloth, or give it a once-over with your vacuum cleaner brush.

4. Screw the cover back into place, and you're good to go!

# TAPE TLC

To keep your videotapes runnin' their best, store them standing up on shelves, just as you do with books. For good measure, make sure that the spool holding the tape is at the bottom. Ideal tape-

## WATCH THE THERMOMETER

\* \* \* \* \*

When you go off on a winter vacation, it's only natural (and smart) to turn the house thermostat way down. After all, what do your TV and computer care if it's cold? Well, they don't care—up to a point. Electronic devices can handle cold or fluctuating temperatures just fine when they're not running. But before you turn them on again, bring the house back to normal room temperature. This is especially true for the TV—the picture tube must be at room temperature to perform effectively and ensure longevity.

storage temperature is around 70°F. If a tape has been out in the cold, let it warm up to room temperature before you play it.

## YOU OL' SOFTY!

**L**ooking for a miracle duster for your TV? Look in the laundry room! Your normal, run-of-the-mill fabric softener sheet works better than anything I've ever seen to get dust and dirt off both the TV screen and the cabinet.

## IT'S A WRAP

**I**f you've ever picked up the TV or other electronic remote control only to find sticky buttons, chances are that the remote was christened with someone's soda or other drink.

If your remote is still working after its bath, you're lucky. To avoid future disasters of the moist kind, wrap your remote controls in plastic wrap or put each one into a zipper-lock plastic bag to keep them protected. They'll send and receive signals right through the plastic, and they'll stay squeaky clean.

## MONITOR THE SITUATION

**I**f your computer monitor is flickerin' like an outdoor light show, chances are the culprit is just a poor connection. Take a gander at the back of your computer, and make sure that all the little pins and screws are in good and tight, and that

**ONLINE STEALS & DEALS**

**From the "I Love You" virus to the** "Jennifer" virus, they're out there, just waiting for an unsuspecting computer to prey upon. The bad news: Computer viruses can do anything from slowing your system down to a turtle's pace to wiping out your most important files. They're unrelenting in their destruction. The good news: You can protect your computer from viruses and not spend a dime. You can go online and download *free* virus detection software simply by visiting **www.thefreesite.com.** In addition to free virus software, this site also offers you access to free e-mail, all kinds of software, graphics, Web space—you name it, they've got it. So check it out.

nothing's bent. If the monitor is still blinking, it's time to call in a computer whiz to take a look.

## A CLEAN MOUSE IS A HAPPY MOUSE

When your computer mouse quits cold turkey—and you know the cord is plugged into the right hole on the back of the computer—chances are the tracking ball is dirty. What's that? Pick up your mouse and turn it over. See that little ball in there? That's the tracking ball.

Take it out of the mouse housing. (For some types, you'll need a tiny screwdriver; with others, you just twist off the cover with your fingers.) Then clean the mouse ball with a cotton swab dipped in a bit of warm water. Use your finger to move the rollers in the ball housing, then replace the mouse ball and secure the cover. Your mouse is now ready to roll!

## DVD—THE NEXT BIG THING

Does anyone out there remember Betamax? It was "the next big thing" back in the early '80s, and it became obsolete about as fast as the eight-track cassette did. Because of this, I'm always suspicious of new technological "breakthroughs," but it looks as though the DVD is here to stay, and those that own them swear by them. If you're new to DVDs, here are a few maintenance tips to get you up to speed:

★ Never move the player to a new location while it contains a disc. The disc could get cracked or broken. Believe you me, that's a sure-fire way to lose $20 (or more) in a hurry!

★ Don't put any cups containing liquid, candles, or metal objects on top of your DVD player—it's not a shelf.

★ When cleaning the DVD cabinet, make sure you disconnect the AC power cord. (Safety first!) Then wipe the player down with a soft cloth or a fabric softener sheet. Don't use any kind of liquid cleaner on or in your DVD. It could ruin the outside finish and short-circuit the player, if it gets inside.

★ Never place anything other than a disc in the disc tray.

★ Plug the unit into a surge protector. If you don't have one, make sure you unplug the DVD player during storms to prevent damage during a power outage.

★ Handle the discs carefully. Hold them by their edges, and don't place labels or adhesive tape on them.

# HOW DRY I AM

If you've ever put in a DVD (or CD, for that matter) and had the disc play for a bit and then stop abruptly, moisture may be the culprit. Start by cleaning the disk—just gently wipe it with a clean, dry cloth. If that doesn't do the trick, look inside the tray to see if there is any condensation. (The humidity level in your house can cause condensation in DVD and CD players.) If you see moisture, keep the tray open for at least an hour to let it dry out.

# Troubleshootin' Time

No matter how well you keep on top of routine maintenance, sooner or later, *something's* going to go wrong with an appliance or electronic gadget. Use the chart below to see at a glance whether you can fix the problem yourself, or whether you need to pull out your wallet, and call in a pro.

## APPLIANCES

| Appliance | Symptom | Try This |
|-----------|---------|----------|
| Dishwasher | It won't run. | Make sure the door is locked. |
| | | Make sure the timer and selector button are in the right positions. |
| | The dishes are still dirty. | Make sure the water is hot enough at the end of the cycle (between 140° and 150°F). |
| | | Make sure the dishes are stacked correctly and that all large clumps of food have been removed. |
| | The dishes aren't drying. | Check for mineral deposits on the heating element; wipe them away with vinegar. |
| | The dishwasher is noisy. | Check to see if the spray arm is hitting the dishes; if so, move them out of the way. |
| | | Check to see if there's enough water in the tub; stop using other faucets until the tub is full. |

| | APPLIANCES—*Continued* | |
|---|---|---|
| **Appliance** | **Symptom** | **Try This** |
| **Garbage Disposal** | It grinds things too slowly. | Run cold water for a minute or so while it's on and empty. |
| | It's noisy. | **Turn the power off,** then reach down and feel with your hand to determine if there's something trapped in there. |
| | You can't turn on the motor. | Check the fuse box or circuit breaker. |
| **Refrigerator** | It's stopped running, but the light is on. | Clean the condenser coils (see page 216). |
| | The refrigerator cycles on and off constantly. | Clean the condenser coils (see page 216). |
| | | Run the fridge on its own circuit to make sure it gets enough power. |
| | The refrigerator doesn't cool well. | Check the thermostat setting. |
| | | Clean the condenser coils (see page 216). |
| | | Check the gasket (see page 215). |
| | It smells moldy. | Clean the pan and disinfect it. |
| **Electric Range** | The oven lamp doesn't work. | Replace the bulb. |
| | The timer doesn't work. | Check the fuse. |
| | Condensation forms inside the oven. | Try preheating with the door slightly ajar, so that the moisture can escape. |
| | The self-cleaning cycle won't start. | Make sure the oven door is closed tightly and locked. |

*Continued on next page*

| APPLIANCES—*Continued* | | |
|---|---|---|
| **Appliance** | **Symptom** | **Try This** |
| **Gas Range** | A surface burner won't light. | Check to see if its pilot light is out; try relighting it. |
| | | If that doesn't work, call the gas company. |
| | The pilot flame won't stay lit. | Check for drafts. |
| | | Turn the gas off and use a small wire (like a coat hanger) to clean out the pilot port. |
| | You smell gas. | Open all windows and doors *pronto!* Then check the pilot light. If it's off, try relighting it. If it's on or it won't relight, send your kids and pets outside and call the gas company *NOW!* And do not turn on any electric switches. |
| | A burner is not working efficiently. | Clean the burner. |
| **Washing Machine** | It fills, runs, and then starts to fill again. | This is usually due to the location of the drain pipe. Make sure it's at least 35 inches off the ground. If it's not, adjust it upward. |
| | There is a squealing sound or a hot rubber odor. | Stop the washer and reduce the load. |
| | Water doesn't drain, or drains slowly. | Clean out and straighten the drain hose. |
| **Dryer** | It overheats or takes forever to dry clothes. | Clean the dryer vent (see page 215). |
| | Your clothes smell bad when you take them out. | Clean the lint tray (see page 214). |
| | Clothing is very wrinkled after the drying cycle. | Don't overload the dryer; remove items as soon as drying cycle ends. |

## ELECTRONICS

| Device | Symptom | Try This |
|--------|---------|----------|
| VCR | The tape won't record. | Check to see if the erase-prevention tab has been punched out. |
| | The timed recording isn't working. | Check to see if the VCR clock is set correctly. |
| | | Make sure the power is on. |
| | | Check that the timer is set to record correctly. |
| | The audio is working, but the picture is not. | Clean the heads with a blank videotape. |
| | The picture is snowy, or lines are flashing through it. | Adjust the tracking. |
| | Your recording is shaky and/or snowy. | Make sure the TV was set to the proper channel during recording. (For most VCRs, it should be Channel 3 or 4.) |
| | | Check the strength of the TV signal; adjust the antenna or check the cable connection. |
| | The remote control isn't working. | Check the batteries in the remote control. |
| | | Check the power cord on the VCR and the television. |
| | | Make sure you're close enough to the TV; generally, you need to be within 20 feet. |
| TV | There is no picture or sound. | See if the antenna or cable is disconnected. |
| | | Check every channel for a signal. |
| | The power turns off by itself. | Make sure the sleep timer hasn't been set. |

*Continued on next page*

| ELECTRONICS—*Continued* | | |
| --- | --- | --- |
| **Device** | **Symptom** | **Try This** |
| TV, *continued* | The remote control isn't working. | Move closer to the TV (see VCR entry, above). |
| | | Check the batteries in the remote. |
| | There are lines across the picture. | Move your VCR or DVD player farther away from the TV. (Other appliances or electronics could be interfering with it.) |
| | The picture is snowy. | Check the cable or antenna connection; make sure it's not disconnected or turned improperly. |
| | There's no sound. | Make sure the Mute button is off. |
| | | Check that any external speakers are connected correctly. |
| **Stereo** | Sound is coming from one direction more than another. | Adjust the Balance control. |
| | | Make sure any external speakers are connected correctly. |
| | You can't record from tape to tape. | Make sure the safety tabs have not been punctured. If they have, cover them with Scotch tape. |
| | The sound quality of all cassette tapes is poor. | Clean the heads of your tape deck with a cotton swab dipped in rubbing alcohol. |
| | The CD is skipping. | Clean the CD. |
| | | Wipe the CD tray with a soft cloth. |
| **Computer** | The PC won't turn on. | Make sure the power cord is securely plugged into the PC. |
| | | Make sure the power cord is plugged into a grounded, three-prong outlet; if it is, plug something else in to check for power. |

## ELECTRONICS—*Continued*

| Device | Symptom | Try This |
|---|---|---|
| **Computer,** *continued* | The monitor doesn't work. | Check the cable connection between the monitor and the computer. |
| | | Adjust the brightness and contrast controls. |
| | The keyboard doesn't work. | Make sure the keyboard is connected to the keyboard port, not the mouse port. |
| | The mouse doesn't work. | Make sure the mouse is connected to the mouse port, not the keyboard port. |
| | | Clean the mouse ball (see page 222). |
| | The printer won't print. | Check the cable connections. |
| | | Make sure it's not out of paper. |
| | | Make sure the ink cartridge isn't empty. |
| **DVD players** | Discs won't play. | Make sure the disc is positioned with the printed side up. |
| | | Check the type of disc. Some DVD players will not play audio discs. |
| | There is no picture. | Turn the TV to its Video Input channel. |
| | | Make sure all connections are secure. |
| | There is no sound, or sound is distorted. | Make sure all cables are inserted into the proper jacks. |
| | | Check the manual; it's normal for sound to be muted during still, frame advance, or slow-motion play. |

## FANTASTIC FORMULA

### Squeaky Clean Screens

Here's a great formula for keeping those TV and computer monitor screens squeaky clean:

$\frac{1}{4}$ cup of ammonia

2 quarts of warm water

Mix the ammonia and water, then apply sparingly with a soft cloth or sponge. All dirt and dust particles will be gone in a flash.

## FANTASTIC FORMULA

### Ultimate Range Cleaner

So, your spaghetti sauce splattered from here to Timbuktu, all over your burners and range. If the normal combo of baking soda and water doesn't work, try this:

3 tablespoons of baking soda

3 tablespoons of salt

A pinch of cream of tartar

Hydrogen peroxide

Combine the baking soda, salt, and cream of tartar in an old bowl. Add enough hydrogen peroxide to make a paste. Spread this concoction on the stains and let it set for a half-hour or so, then scrub with a sponge dipped in warm water.

# More Fantastic Formulas!

I know your head's probably spinning about now, but I've still got a few more tips and tricks up my sleeve that could prove quite useful in a pinch. Check them out.

## CHROME CLEAN-UP

Clean the chrome on your appliances by sprinkling a little white flour on a dry rag and polishing it off in a circular motion. The chrome shines up perfectly—and without any scratches!

## THAT'S ENTERTAINMENT!

If you've read through this chapter, you now know how to take care of the electronics *inside* the entertainment center, but what about the often overlooked cabinet itself? To spruce it up a bit, make a paste of baking soda and warm water, and apply with a soft cloth or sponge. Wipe dry with a clean rag. This is safe for virtually any finish.

## PHONE HOME

**H**ere's a quick way to disinfect your telephones. Combine equal parts vinegar and water, and dip a soft cloth into the liquid. Wring the cloth well, then rub over the handsets in a circular motion. Dry well with a clean cloth.

## SODA SOLUTION

**Y**ou can safely clean the exteriors of fax machines, printers, and computers with a paste of baking soda and water. First, be sure the computer is off before you start cleaning. And don't get any of the paste inside your computer, or it could wreak all kinds of havoc.

The safest way to clean a computer keyboard is to unplug it from your computer, turn it upside down, and gently shake it to get out any crumbs or loose dirt from between the keys. Then blow on the keys or use a commercial canned-air spray to clean them.

### FANTASTIC FORMULA

**Old-Time Oven Cleaner**

Do you have an oven that's not self-cleaning? Here's an old trick to get the grime off without a lot of scrubbing.

> ¼ cup of ammonia
>
> 2 cups of warm water
>
> Glass baking dish

Combine the ammonia and water in the baking dish. Put the dish in the oven, shut the door, and leave it overnight. In the morning, the grime will wipe away easily with a sponge—no elbow grease necessary!

# CHAPTER 10

# Furniture for All Time

I've got a couple of neighbors who buy new furniture more often than I buy new socks. Every time I see that big old delivery truck drive up and start unloading, I thank my lucky stars that Grandma Putt taught me the value of a dollar! She also taught me her golden rule for acquiring furniture—or anything else, for that matter—buy only what you really like and really need, buy the best quality that you can afford, and take care of it as though you expect it to last a lifetime. If you do, it will!

In Chapter 4, I told you all about how to get the best buys on furniture. Now I'm going to share with you all I know about taking care of those furniture pieces because, if you're anything like me, you don't want to be replacing them any time soon!

# Knock on Wood

We all know that well-made wood furniture can last a lifetime (or two!), but that doesn't mean you can neglect it. There's a lot more to caring for wood furniture than just spraying a little wood polish on the surface each week, and I'm here to tell you all about it. We'll start with a rundown on wood finishes ('cause you'll need to know exactly what you've got in order to clean it right), and then move on to some specific stain-removal techniques.

## From Start to Finish

There are six different types of wood finishes, and to keep your wood furniture looking its best, you need to give each one a slightly different kind of TLC. Now, wood finishes fall into two categories: soft (oiled) and hard (shellacked, varnished, lacquered, polyurethaned, or painted). Here's the lowdown.

## WOOD YOU KNOW?

Since the type of finish dictates how you care for the furniture, how do you tell what type of finish you've got? It's easy—just try one of these simple tests. (Make sure you test in an inconspicuous spot, such as a surface that's always against a wall, since two out of three of these tests may actually dissolve a bit of the finish.)

1. Drop a little boiled linseed oil onto the surface. If the oil soaks in, the wood has an oil finish. If it beads up, the wood has a hard finish.

2. Rub a little acetone onto the surface using a circular motion. If the finish begins to dissolve, it's lacquer. If it slides off like water, it's polyurethane. If it becomes sticky or gelatinous after a

minute or so, it's either varnish or shellac.

3. Drop a little denatured alcohol onto the surface. Shellac
will dissolve quickly, and
varnish more slowly.

# OIL'S WELL THAT STARTS WELL

**H**ere's the gold-
en rule for
furniture with oil fin-
ishes: *Never* treat them
with furniture polish or wax.
Instead, for regular cleaning,
just wipe away dust with a soft
cloth. Then, every few months,
give your oil-finished pieces a
dose of my Oiled Furniture
Formula (below left).

---

## FANTASTIC FORMULA

### Oiled Furniture Formula

16 ounces of gum turpentine
16 ounces of boiled linseed oil
6 ounces of white vinegar

Combine all the ingredients in a small bucket.
Then dip a sponge into the solution, and gently wipe the surface of the furniture. (Wear
gloves—this stuff is potent!) Let it stand for 5
minutes or so to loosen any tough dirt. Then
wipe away the excess with a soft cloth, and
buff to a shine. (Make sure you get all of the
formula off the wood, or you could wind up
with a gummy residue.) Wash out the sponge
and your gloves with hot, soapy water.

---

# A KNACK FOR SHELLAC

**Y**ou don't see shellac
finishes much on
newer furniture, but
it was hot stuff in
Grandma Putt's day.
If you've got some
vintage pieces in your house,
these pointers will help you
keep 'em shipshape:

☞ Moisture—even high
humidity—tends to make
shellac sticky. So never
clean shellacked pieces with
water, keep the air as dry as
you can, and make sure you
use coasters under those
iced tea glasses!

☞ For everyday cleaning, dust
shellacked furniture with a
dry cloth or the dusting
brush attachment of your
vacuum cleaner.

☞ To protect the finish, give
all your pieces a coat of my
Shellac Shape-Up formula
(at right), once a year or so.

# LACQUER LORE

Water + Lacquer = A sticky situation! So try to keep lacquered finishes away from humid areas, and steer clear of both water and oil for cleaning. Instead, use a soft, dry cloth. To maintain that perfect shine, rub a little liquid wax or polish onto the surface, using a gentle, circular motion. Then buff with a dry cloth. Repeat every six months or so.

For heavy cleaning, it's generally safe to use a solvent-based furniture cleaner or an oil soap. But always test in an inconspicuous spot before going hog wild—better safe than sorry!

# VARNISH VIGNETTE

When it comes to cleaning varnished furniture, everyday dusting can be done with a soft, dry cloth, but your duties don't stop there. Varnished finishes need big-time protection. Polish them regularly with furniture wax, and keep them away from liquids and foods. That means that if your varnished furniture gets a lot of use, you need to be sure to haul out the tablecloths, place mats, and coasters!

## FANTASTIC FORMULA

### Shellac Shape-Up

| 1 part boiled linseed oil |
| 1 part mineral spirits or paint thinner |

Mix the ingredients in a small bucket, then dip a sponge or soft cloth into the solution, and rub it evenly over the wood surface. (Make sure you wear gloves.) Wipe away the excess with a dry, soft cloth. If it's been more than a year since you've cleaned the furniture, you may need to repeat the process to remove all of the dirt. When you're through, wash your gloves and cleaning cloth in hot, soapy water.

When you wax varnished furniture, use a soft cloth and go slowly, one small area at a time. Excess wax is enemy Number 1 for varnish, so make sure you buff each area well with a dry cloth. To keep wax from building up, polish sparingly— once every couple of months at most. In between sessions, you can always re-buff the surface to keep that shine going.

## THE SAME OLD ROUTINE

If your furniture calls for polish, make sure you use the same kind of polish on the same piece of furniture every single time. Mixing and matching will leave your furniture hazy and streaked, and no matter how often you clean or dust it, it'll always look dirty.

## THERE'S ALWAYS ONE

Exception to the rule, that is! I started off this chapter giving you the dos and don'ts of caring for specific wood types. Well, here's one exception: If your varnished furniture is really dirty—we're talking dirtier than a gardener's clodhoppers—then some varnishes may be washed with mild dish soap and lukewarm water. But make sure you test the surface first in an inconspicuous spot. If you see anything out of the ordinary, such as streaking or discoloration, STOP! If everything looks okay, proceed cautiously, using a soft sponge or cloth, and dry the wood immediately with a clean, soft cloth.

## THOSE OLD SOFTIES!

When you reach for a soft cloth to clean your furniture, don't just dip into the rag bag and use whatever you grab first. What you want is a cloth that's 100 percent cotton with a soft, lofty texture. Old T-shirts work like a charm (just steer clear of any printed-on letters or decorations). Cloth diapers, flannel shirts or pajamas, and cotton socks'll do the trick, too. Whatever you do, avoid synthetic fabrics, especially nylon, rayon, and

### PROCEED WITH CAUTION!

\* \* \* \* \*

When you're working with mineral spirits (paint thinner), turpentine, boiled linseed oil, or any other strong or toxic substance, be sure to proceed with caution. Always wear gloves, and keep flammable substances away from heat and flames—and well beyond the reach of children and pets. And remember: Before you dispose of any oil- or spirit-soaked rags, spread them out in the sun to dry.

polyester. They don't absorb well, and some of them could even scratch your furniture.

## POLYURETHANE PROTECTION

**P**olyurethane finishes are a housekeeper's dream come true! They're tough, and they're not bothered one bit by heat or moisture. Unfortunately, they're not too easy to come by, because it takes a whale of a lot of work to apply them, plus they're slow as molasses to dry. But, if you're lucky enough to own furniture with this finish, enjoy. Aside from day-to-day dusting with a dry cloth, the only care polyurethane needs is a wipe with a damp cloth to remove fingerprints or water spots. And whatever you do, don't use wax on polyurethane; it can build up and cause you all kinds of headaches!

## DON'T LEAVE 'EM OUT IN THE COLD!

**C**old temperatures and damp air take their toll on wood furniture, warping the wood. When you're storing pieces that you don't use very often, such as

---

### BYE-BYE BUILDUP

\* \* \* \* \*

Here's good news: If you (or previous owners) have waxed your polyurethaned furniture and you're noticing a buildup, don't lose sleep over it. Mineral spirits will take that wax right off. Just put on your gloves, and go at the surface one small area at a time with mineral spirits and a cotton cloth. Just be sure to wipe each spot clean before moving on to the next one.

---

leaves for your dining room table, don't send them off to the basement or garage. Instead, stash them in the room they'll be used in—or as close to it as your closet space allows. That way, they'll experience the same temperatures and humidity levels as the rest of the table, and they'll fit right in when you need to use them.

## PAINT BY NUMBERS

**T**o keep painted furniture looking its spiffy best, just wipe it regularly with a soft, damp cloth. If the surface is especially dirty, use a solution of mild

dish soap and warm water. Clean slowly, one area at a time, and rinse and dry each area before you go on to the next.

Don't ever wax or polish painted furniture, and steer clear of oil, polish containing oil, and oil-treated cloths. If the paint chips here and there, sand the spots and retouch them with matching paint, or—if the result winds up looking patched—give the entire piece a fresh coat.

## DOS AND DON'TS

**H**ere's a roundup of rules for keeping all of your wood furniture looking its best:

- ✔ Keep wood furniture away from moisture, sunlight, and excessive heat or cold. All can damage the wood over time.

- ✔ Wipe up spills pronto; otherwise, you may find yourself with a sander in hand, wishing you'd been more of a Johnny-on-the-spot.

- ✔ When you're dusting, always pick up objects—never slide them across the surface.

- ✔ Open and close cabinet doors and drawers gently.

- ✔ Always lift furniture to move it—don't drag it.

- ✔ Never mix polishes, and don't polish any type of wood finish more than three or four times a year. If you do, you're practically begging for a sticky mess.

- ✔ Use pads, napkins, or coasters under glasses, vases, candles, and anything else that's wet or hot. Use felt under objects that could scratch the wood.

# Fighting Furniture Foes

**So now you know how to perform basic upkeep on your wood furniture, but what about those accidents that happen every now and then? Ink stains, nail polish stains, water rings, messes caused by milk, alcohol, or candle wax—you know, the usual suspects. Read on to find out how to fight these furniture foes.**

## THE DRINKS ARE ON US

**O**r, I should say, on the table! When you spill beer, white wine, or other alcoholic beverages on wooden furniture (and your shirt), you need to hop to it! Take a look at Chapter 8 to learn how to get the stains out of your clothes. To prevent stains on your wood furniture, wipe up the spill immediately, and rub the spot vigorously with the palm of your hand. Then, dip a soft cloth in a little furniture polish, rub the stain gently, and wipe with a dry cloth.

# RING AROUND THE TABLE

Water rings: The mere mention of the words makes me cringe. No matter how often I sing the praises of coasters or point out the benefits of putting a napkin down, those white circles always seem to spring up, as if by magic, whenever one of my grandkids has been around. Coincidence? I don't think so! Fortunately, I have a couple of sure-fire ways to get rid of rings.

☞ If the ring is fairly recent—within the past week or so—put a little mayonnaise, toothpaste, or salad oil on a soft cloth. Then rub your homemade weapon of choice over the ring, and wipe it dry with a clean, soft cloth.

☞ If the ring is large, cover it with a clean, thick blotter

## MOVIN' ON

\* \* \* \* \*

If you're like most people, you probably don't move your furniture around all that much. When you do, though, keep these tips in mind to avoid doing expensive-to-repair damage:

★ Before you move any piece of furniture, examine it for loose joints and then support any weak areas while you move it.

★ Move tables by their legs or the apron, not the top, because it could break off.

★ Lift chairs by their seats, not their arms or backs.

★ When moving furniture in a truck or van, always set it on its back or top, not the legs, and be sure to wrap it in moving blankets.

or a towel folded in half, and gently press down with a warm iron. Repeat until the ring has rung off.

☞ Try this stubborn-stain alternative: Dip a soft cloth into hot water, and add two or three drops of ammonia. Wring out the cloth well, and rub the ring lightly. It should disappear within a minute or so.

## WHAT'S MY LINE?

White lines or other white marks on furniture (other than water rings—see "Ring Around the Table" on page 239) are generally caused by one of three things: liquids containing alcohol (such as beverages and perfume), heat, or water. You should be able to get rid of them for good, but your method will vary depending upon the amount of damage done. Here are a few potential cures:

**Ashes to ashes.** Dip a soft, clean cloth in a mixture of cigarette or wood ashes (who knew smoking was actually *good* for something!) and lemon juice or salad oil. Wring the cloth out, and rub the white mark vigorously.

**Ammonia's the answer.** Alcohol spots often respond well to ammonia. Dip a soft, clean cloth into warm, sudsy water, and then add a few drops of ammonia. Wring out the cloth, and rub the white mark gently. Dry with a clean, soft cloth.

**Get serious.** If the methods above don't make the spots vamoose, call out the big guns. Moisten a soft cloth with lighter fluid, followed by a mixture of salad oil and rottenstone. Wring out the cloth, and rub the white mark gently. Then wipe it dry with a clean, soft cloth.

---

### ROTTEN WHAT?

\* \* \* \* \*

Throughout this chapter, I mention a substance called rottenstone. For those of you who aren't familiar with rottenstone, it is a silica-based limestone that's similar to pumice, but softer in texture. Rottenstone is generally used as an abrasive. It's not hazardous, but it's rough on the hands, so it's a good idea to use gloves when working with it. You'll find rottenstone in most hardware stores.

## THE WHOLE BALL OF WAX

**I** wouldn't call candle wax a stain exactly—but I'd sure call it a mess when it drips all over one of my favorite tables! The good news, though, is that wax is a snap to get off when you follow this simple routine: First, scrape off as much as possible with a plastic scraper or an old credit card. (This is a great use for those cards that keep showing up, uninvited, in the mail.) Then put a few ice cubes into a plastic bag, and hold it on the remaining wax. The stuff will crumble, and you can just wipe it away. Just make sure you wipe away any moisture that escapes from the ice bag, or soon you'll have *real* spots on your table!

Oh, and here's more good news: This trick works just as well with chewing gum as it does with wax.

## DON'T BURN, BABY!

**F** or my money, there are few sorrier sights than a cigarette burn on a great-looking wooden table. To get rid of the nasty thing, you have but two choices:

1. Rub the burn with a paste made of baking soda and boiled linseed oil, working with the grain until the spot disappears.

2. If that doesn't work, dip a cotton swab in paint thinner, dab the burn gently, and then scrape it away. Drip a couple of drops of clear nail polish into the dented area. Let it set for a few minutes, then continue to add nail polish until the burned area is level with the rest of the table.

## GREASE IS THE WORD

**G** etting rid of grease stains on wood furniture can be tricky, and the longer they set, the tougher it is. But I love a challenge, and my methods will arm you with the artillery you need to battle the greasy goo. Here's the plan of attack:

✦ If you're on the spot when grease and your furniture get together, grab some salt *pronto,* and pour it over the grease. Let it sit for a few minutes, to absorb the grease, then gently wipe it away with a soft cloth.

✦ For stains that attack behind your back, use the same blotter-and-iron tactic that works on water rings: Place a blotter (or folded towel) over the spot, and press with a warm iron until the spot disappears.

✦ If the heat technique above doesn't do the trick, turn to mineral spirits. Saturate the area with the spirits, and set an old cloth over it to soak up the grease. You may have to repeat this a couple of times, but I guarantee it'll send that grease packin' for good!

## NO STRINGS ATTACHED

There are a lot of terrific tips in this chapter, but if you've recently bought new furniture, don't overlook the great advice you got absolutely free from the furniture's manufacturer. As with most everything else you buy these days, furniture comes with a booklet containing all sorts of handy information to help you protect your investment. Keep those owner's manuals handy, so when cleaning time comes around—or a spill leaves your furniture with an unwelcome decoration—you'll know exactly what to do.

## HIT THE NAIL ON THE HEAD

So you've spilled a little nail polish. What's the best way to remove it? You'd think nail polish remover, but trust me folks, don't do it—it'll ruin your furniture's finish. Instead, blot the stain immediately. Then rub with extra-fine steel wool dipped in furniture wax, and wipe dry.

## INKY DINK

Ink can cause a lot of problems. It can explode in your shirt or pants pocket. It can seep onto your hands. And sometimes it can leak onto your wood table. When this happens, soak up the excess ink immediately. Then clean the surface with a damp cloth. Water-soluble ink should disappear. If the ink's not water-soluble, the stain will likely persist. Treat it with a mixture of rottenstone and vegetable oil. Rub the mixture into the ink stain, then dry with a clean, soft cloth.

## PAINT THE TOWN, NOT THE TABLE

**Y**ou may not cry over spilled milk, but spilled paint could be another story. If the paint's still wet, it's a snap to save the day: Just wipe away water-based paint with a damp cloth. For oil-based paints, use mineral spirits. If the paint has had time to dry, cover it with boiled linseed oil, and let it stand until the paint has softened. Then remove it with a cloth soaked in still more boiled linseed oil. Finally, scrape off any residue with a fingernail or a plastic knife. Whatever you do, don't use paint remover—it'll ruin your wood finish faster than you can say "Whoa, Nellie!"

# Upholstery Upkeep

**W**hile wood furniture can look good forever, its upholstered cousins can sure show a beating at a young age! But you don't have to resign yourself to replacing upholstered furniture every few years. Here's how to keep it clean and new-looking longer.

## Cushiony Clean

A friend of mine has found the end-all, be-all of easy—and cheap—upholstery care: She uses cotton slipcovers on all of her sofas, chairs, and ottomans. Then, when they're dirty, she just takes 'em off and tosses 'em into the washing machine. If you haven't taken that step yet, I highly recommend it. In the meantime, read on for other tips that'll keep your upholstered furniture looking great!

## MIND YOUR Ws, Ss, AND Xs

If you look closely, your upholstery is sending you a message that tells you how to care for it. All upholstered furniture comes with a tag containing a symbol: W, S, S-W, or X. These symbols are a code that the furniture industry came up with to tell folks the right way to clean each kind of fabric. Here's how to decode the code:

**W.** Spot-clean using only the foam of a water-based detergent or upholstery shampoo. Apply the foam with a soft brush or cloth, using a circular motion. Vacuum when dry.

**S.** Spot-clean using solvents only. Because solvents are toxic, never try this at home. Instead, fork over the bucks for a professional cleaning.

**S-W.** Spot-clean with a solvent or water-based detergent. (If you're doing this yourself, you'll want to use the detergent.)

**X.** Vacuum or dust with a soft brush only. No detergents, no solvents.

## FINISHING SCHOOL

When it comes to easy-care upholstery, the next best thing to slipcovers is one of the chemical finishes that fend off stains and dirt. They all perform basically the same work; the difference lies in when and how they're applied to the furniture. Here's a rundown on the three types:

**Zepel** is applied by the fabric manufacturer; you can't buy it and spray it on yourself.

**Teflon** is used by professional upholstery cleaners only.

**Scotchgard** is often applied by the manufacturer, but unlike Zepel and Teflon, you can also buy this stuff at your local hardware store. If you've just bought brand-new, untreated furniture, pick up a can or two of Scotchguard and spray it on ASAP—before anybody has a chance to spill a glass of wine or

drop a slice of pizza. If your furniture has been in residence for a while, you can still use the Scotchguard, but the upholstery must be spankin' clean. Otherwise, the Scotchgard will make any stains and surface dirt a permanent part of the picture.

# A CUSHY JOB

Sofa and chair cushions are dust magnets, and over time, dust takes a toll on fabric. That's why you need to go at them on a regular basis with your vacuum cleaner's brush attachment. Then, once a month or so, flip any detachable cushions so that they wear evenly on both sides. That way, they won't get that "sunken in" look. And while you're flipping, don't forget to vacuum underneath the cushions. Those little crevices are notorious for harboring all kinds of fugitives, and some of them—crumbs, for instance—are first-class lures for damage-causing insects.

# DOWN, BUT NOT OUT

Here's an exception to the vacuum routine I noted above: down pillows. Do *not* haul out the vacuum—dust down pillows or cushions with a soft brush; vacuuming can draw the down right out through the fabric, leaving you with a flat pillow and a clogged-up vacuum.

---

## FANTASTIC FORMULA

### Perfect Upholstery Shampoo

This simple formula will get your upholstered furniture clean quickly, gently, and for a fraction of the price you'd pay for store-bought upholstery shampoo.

> 1 cup of warm water
> ¼ cup of liquid dish soap

Combine the ingredients in a bowl. Then, using a wire whisk or a hand-held electric mixer, whip the solution until dry suds start to form. With a soft cloth or brush, slowly massage the dry suds into an inconspicuous spot on the upholstery, and let it dry. If you see no change in color or texture, keep cleaning. When you've finished the whole piece of furniture, let it dry, then wipe it with a soft cloth dipped in warm water and wrung dry. Make sure the fabric is completely dry before you let anyone take a seat—otherwise, it'll get dirty all over again! (To speed up the drying time, open some windows, or use a fan to "blow-dry" the fabric.)

## AT ARM'S LENGTH

So you know how to clean your upholstery, but what about those arm covers on your sofa and chairs? Simple: First, vacuum them while they're still on the furniture. Then take them outside and shake off any excess dust. If they're washable, pop them into the washing machine. (There should be a tag that tells you if they're machine-washable.) Wash in warm water with laundry detergent, but

wash only a few at a time, and use a lot of water. If the fabric is not washable, just clean the covers the same way you clean the rest of the furniture.

## THAT'S THE SPIRIT!

Spirits plural, I should say—mineral spirits, also known as paint thinner. This dandy (and cheap) stuff will get a variety of problem stains out of your upholstery, including:

★ Cosmetics (excluding lipstick and mascara)

★ Felt-tip markers

★ Grease

★ Oil

★ Shoe heel marks

---

### THE RESIDUALS

\* \* \* \* \*

When you use a water-based detergent to clean your upholstery, it's going to leave residue; that much is certain. What's not certain, however, is whether it'll leave the good (powder), the bad (oily), or the ugly (sticky). To determine what kind of residue your detergent of choice will leave, all you need is a glass pie dish and the detergent mixture. Place about ¼ inch of the detergent into the pan. Then place the dish in the sun. (If it's winter, you can use the oven—set it no higher than 150°F.) After all the liquid has evaporated, take a look at the residue. Is it powdery? Is it oily or sticky? If it's powdery, good for you—it'll vacuum up like crazy. But if it's oily or sticky, your upholstery will be stuck with it. I'd recommend you try a different detergent.

---

## TOUGH AS LEATHER

Leather may *look* tough, but actually, it's one big softy. In fact, it needs even more TLC than just about any fabric upholstery you can name. Here are a half-dozen things that can do big-time damage to leather if you're not careful:

## FABRIC FIRST-AID

What if you spill nail polish on your sofa, or a ballpoint pen explodes all over the armchair? Here's a handy-dandy chart to help you through a few of these trouble spots. A word of caution, though: Most of these will work only if you get the stain while it's fresh. Once it sets in, your best bet is to call in a professional furniture cleaner. (Before you use any of these solutions, test-clean an inconspicuous spot on the upholstery before you start in on the main stain. Otherwise, you could wind up with a worse-looking mess than you started with!)

| Your Problem | My Solution |
| --- | --- |
| Ink | Blot it up immediately. Then spray with hairspray and blot again. Repeat until the stain is gone. |
| Ice cream or milk | Scrub the area gently with a mixture of dish soap and warm water. Follow up with a solution of 2 tablespoons of ammonia to 4 cups of water (it'll be sudsy). Wash the area again with detergent and water. Finally, immerse a clean cloth in warm water, wring it out, and scrub gently. Let it dry thoroughly. |
| Gum | Toss a few ice cubes into a plastic bag, and rub it over the gum until it hardens. Then scrape off the stiff gum using a credit card or plastic scraper. |
| Soft drinks, tea, wine | First, use a little dish soap and warm water. Scrub gently with a soft cloth. Follow up with a little vinegar on a soft cloth. Finally, immerse a clean cloth in warm water, and wring it out. Scrub the area gently. Let it dry thoroughly. |

1. **Direct sunlight.** It'll fade leather over time, so pull those shades when Ol' Sol is shinin' through the windows!

2. **Smoke.** It, too, makes leather fade, so if you must smoke, don't do it near the furniture.

3. **Hot air.** Keep all leather pieces at least 2 feet away from radiators or other sources of heat.

4. **Sharp objects.** Pointy tools such as sewing needles, knives, and scissors can

make holes that you can't repair (at least not without noticeable scars). Don't use them when you're sitting on your leather furniture, and make darn sure you don't set them down on it!

5. **Dust buildup**. Keep it at bay by wiping your furniture once a week or so with a soft, dry cloth.

6. **Oils and all-purpose cleansers.** They can cause

major surface damage, so don't even think about using them.

So, how *do* you keep these prima donnas sleek and sassy? Simple: Get some leather cleaner (you'll find it at any place that sells leather goods), and follow the directions on the package. If you use your furniture regularly, it'll need cleaning about once a month. If you rarely use it, twice a year should do the trick.

• • • • • • • • • • • • • • • • • • • • • • • • • • • • • • • • • • • • • • •

# The Hard Stuff

**W**ell, friends, I've clued you in on how to make your wood and upholstered furniture last a lifetime (and then some). Chances are, though, that you've got at least a few pieces that don't fall into either of these catagories. Do you have a glass-topped table or two? What about metal or wicker furniture, or something with a marble surface? Read on for the dirty details.

## Keepin' It Clean

Glass, marble, metal, and wicker—these surfaces may be hard, but they still need regular care and cleaning to look their best. Here are my favorite easy-care tips.

## THROUGH THE LOOKING GLASS

**G**lass is pretty resilient, but it can scratch easily, so remember these three words: Lift, don't slide. Sliding objects (especially *glass* objects) across a glass surface is a sure-fire way to make your mark—permanently! Play it safe, and put felt under vases and other objects on your glass tabletops.

# DON'T LOSE YOUR MARBLE

For regular cleaning, wipe marble surfaces with a soft cloth dampened with lukewarm water. Then wipe dry with a clean, soft cloth. Every six months or so, go a step beyond and use a solution of liquid detergent and warm water, then rinse and wipe dry.

# A PROTECTIVE COAT...MAYBE

A light coat of wax will protect a marble surface, but don't try this trick with white marble—wax turns it yellow.

# WHOOPS!

Marble attracts spills like flowers attract bees. The sooner you spring into action with a damp cloth, the better chance you have for heading off permanent damage. For set-in stains, follow these guidelines:

**Tea, coffee, or soft drinks.** Make a 20 percent hydrogen peroxide/80 percent water solution, and apply with a soft cloth. Rinse with warm water, and dry immediately.

**Rust.** Use a commercial rust remover according to the package directions—but test in an inconspicuous area first.

**Butter, hand cream, or lotion.** Cover the stain with cornstarch, and let it stand for about 10 minutes. Brush it off, then add more. This time, leave it on for 24 hours, so the cornstarch can absorb the grease. Then brush the starch away, and clean the marble with soap and water, as described above.

## FANTASTIC FORMULA

### Glass Tabletop Cleaner

To keep your glass tabletops squeaky-clean, spray them with a solution of 2 tablespoons of ammonia mixed in 1 quart of water. Then dry them with a soft cloth. If the glass is surrounded by wood, spray the solution in the center of the glass and work slowly toward the sides—and be careful not to get any of the solution on the wood.

## HEAVY METAL

To keep wrought iron, chrome, or steel furniture looking nifty, dust it with a soft cloth dampened with warm water. When stronger measures are called for, use a solution of dish detergent and warm water, and apply it with a soft rag. Dry immediately to avoid water spots and (in the case of iron) rust.

---

### WONDERFUL WICKER

**\* \* \* \* \***

Rattan, reed, willow, and bamboo all sail under the name "wicker," and the care regime for all four types is the same:

☞ Dust regularly using a vacuum-cleaner attachment or a soft brush.

☞ Keep all wicker away from rain, drying drafts, and direct sunlight.

☞ If the air in your house is on the dry side, wipe your wicker pieces with a damp cloth now and then to stave off cracks and splits.

For more extensive cleaning, add mild detergent to 4 cups of warm water. Mix until the solution is frothy, and then apply the suds to the furniture, working slowly, one area at a time. Wipe away the suds with a clean, damp cloth. And don't sit on the furniture until it's good and dry!

---

## Quick Fixes

**Getting a scratch or a dent in your favorite chest or table might *seem* like the end of the world, but take it from me, folks: You can patch up most of those dings without batting an eye. Here are some of my favorite do-it-yourself remedies for doctoring wood furniture. Believe you me, they really work!**

## STARTING FROM SCRATCH

Probably no table in history has ever gone through life without a scratch or two. Sure as shootin', no table in *my* house ever has, and I'd bet my bottom dust cloth that you can say the same! The good news is that light scratches often vamoose if you rub them with a little paste wax. If that doesn't do the trick, turn to one of these stronger tactics:

☑ For light wood, use a natural shoe polish. Just push the polish directly into the scratch, and watch it vanish!

☑ For dark wood, reach for the nuts. Brazil nuts, pecans, and black walnuts are your best bets. Simply rub the nutmeat directly into the scratch, being careful to keep it away from the surrounding areas (so as not to darken them).

> ## DON'T TRY THIS AT HOME!
>
> \* \* \* \* \*
>
> When it comes to patchin' up marble, glass, or metal—or making major repairs to upholstered furniture—bite the bullet, and call in a pro. Unless you really know what you're doing, you'll probably wind up paying good money to have your misguided handiwork redone the *right* way after the fact.

## COLOR IT GONE

**W**hen it comes to camouflaging scratches, the handiest tool kit you can have is a big box of crayons—one with plenty of shades of brown. As a matter of fact, in a box of 64 crayons, you have the following shades to choose from: Brown, Mahogany, Burnt Sienna, Raw Sienna, Beaver, Chestnut, Sepia, Fuzzy Wuzzy Brown, Tumbleweed, Desert Sand, and Tan. And, if you want a big box of just the brown shades, minus the rest of the rainbow, head over to **www.crayola.com**, where you can *customize* your very own box! Then, the next time a table meets with an accident, haul out the crayons and match them to the color of the wood.

## DEPLORABLE DENTS

**I**t's your worst nightmare. Something (or someone) falls onto your beautiful wood table, and when you peel back the wreckage, there it is, plain as day—a dent the size of Wisconsin. At first glance, it doesn't seem like there's much you can do, but guess what, folks? In Jerry's world, there's *always* something you can do!

You've heard of steam opening the pores in your skin, right? Well, now it's going to open the pores in your wood. To remove a dent from your furniture, simply place several layers of damp cloth over the dent, and then press with a warm iron. The steam will open the wood's pores, causing the fibers of the wood to rise upward. Keep doing this until the dented area is level with the surface around it, and be prepared to repair the damage to your table's finish *after* you deal with the dent.

## FURNITURE FIRST AID

**W**hen your table winds up on the casualty list, reach for a bottle of good old iodine. New iodine will hide scratches in mahogany. For cherry-stained mahogany and cherry wood, use older iodine that's turned a dark brown. To mask scratches in maple, dilute brown iodine with a few drops of denatured alcohol. Just use a medicine dropper to drip the liquid directly into the scratch. It works like a charm!

## ALL OUT OF JOINT

**I**f you've ever tried to reglue a wood joint or refasten a piece of loose veneer, you know that the hardest part is getting rid of the old glue—after all, the directions on the glue bottle tell you everything else you need to know! Well, here's a trick I learned from a carpenter

**ONLINE**

**STEALS & DEALS**

**Extra, extra! Read all about it! The** folks at **www.furniturewizard.com** have built an informative site focused on helping you refinish your furniture. But that's not all. You name it, they've got it—home improvement tips, care and maintenance tips—they even recommend books and videos that'll help you with all of your furniture D-I-Y projects. And the best part? They sponsor an open discussion group where D-I-Yers from all over the world can ask questions and get answers to their toughest furniture how-to-fix-its. So check it out—you'll be glad you did!

neighbor of Grandma Putt's: If you're having trouble sanding off that ol' glue, rub a little vinegar on it. It'll soften up faster than you can say "marshmallow." Just make sure that both surfaces are completely dry before you start gluin'.

# More Fantastic Formulas!

**Well, folks, it's that time again—we're slowly winding down here, but I'm not going out without a fight. Below are still more of my fabulous furniture fixes, so don't put down the book just yet—I just may have saved the best for last!**

## FANTASTIC FORMULA

### Perfect Polish for Wood

Here's a great furniture polish recipe for all wood furniture:

$\frac{1}{2}$ cup of linseed oil

$\frac{1}{4}$ cup of malt vinegar

1 teaspoon of lemon or lavender oil (for scent)

A clean jar with a lid

Place the oil and vinegar in the jar, put on the lid, and shake vigorously. Add the lemon or lavender oil. In hot weather, you may want to reverse the proportions, so that you're combining $\frac{1}{2}$ cup of malt vinegar with $\frac{1}{4}$ cup of linseed oil, because the warm weather may make your furniture a little too, well, oily.

## GOT MILK?

**M**oo juice may do the body good, but it has the opposite effect on your wood furniture. If you spill a glass of milk, wipe it up immediately. However, if there is a lingering stain, put a few drops of ammonia on a dampened cloth, and rub gently. The milk should come right out. (You can also try baking soda mixed with a little mineral oil, if the ammonia doesn't work for you.)

## UP TO SCRATCH

**I**f you're fresh out of both shoe polish and crayons, here's yet another formula for removing scratches from wood fur-

## FANTASTIC FORMULA

### Surface Re-Sheener

Sometimes, in the process of removing a stain from wood furniture, you dull the sheen of the finish. When that happens, reach for this formula:

Pumice (available at hardware stores)
Boiled linseed oil

Make a paste from the pumice and oil. Then, using a soft cloth, rub the mixture over the entire surface, rubbing *with* the wood grain, not against it. Wipe away the residue with a clean cloth, and buff with a dry cloth. That finish'll be so shiny, you'll see your face in it!

niture: Mix equal parts of vegetable oil and lemon juice, and rub the mixture into the scratches, using a soft cloth. Repeat a couple of times; within minutes, the scratches should completely disappear.

## DUST IN THE WIND

The next time you go to pull out the furniture polish, try this all-natural alternative,

instead. Combine 2 tablespoons of lemon juice, 10 drops of lemon oil, and 4 drops of olive oil. Dip a soft cloth into the mixture, and apply it gently to your furniture with a circular motion.

## SHINE ON

When you want something to make dull metal furniture shine, try this formula. Combine $1\frac{1}{2}$ cups of vinegar with $1\frac{1}{2}$ cups of water in a spray bottle, and go to town. It'll shine up like a new diamond.

## HEAVY METAL

If you're looking for a metal polish, try this: Combine 1 tablespoon of flour, 1 tablespoon of salt, and 1 tablespoon of white vinegar into a thick paste. Apply with a damp sponge, and gently wipe the metal. Let the polish dry for about an hour. Rinse with warm water, and buff with a soft cloth.

# CHAPTER 11

# All Around the House

Like charity, thrift begins at home. But instead of depriving yourself of a tasty meal at your favorite restaurant or a night out on the town, see where you can cut back in other areas to free up funds for the things you like to do. One of the best—and easiest—ways to begin is to take a gander at all of that *stuff* you've got laying around the house!

The purpose of this chapter is twofold: First, I'll show you how to reuse and recycle products that would otherwise find their way to the garbage dump. (You won't believe the clever uses I've come up with for all that so-called trash!) Then, I'll tell you how to eliminate those expensive store-bought cleaners and disinfectants, while cleaning every room in your house for just pennies on the dollar. Best of all, you can find the materials you need for success under beds, in drawers, and inside cabinets—like I said before, all around your house!

# From Trash to Treasure

One man's trash may be another man's treasure, but I can find treasure in nearly *anyone's* garbage! Did you know that you can save money simply by knowing what *not* to toss out? Baby food jars, burned-out lightbulbs, paper bags, old pantyhose—these are just a few of the gems that all too often get kicked to the curb before their full potential can be realized. A lot of "garbage" can be reused and recycled in ways you've never even thought of. Some of it's clever, some of it's downright quirky, but all of it's practical and useful.

## New Life for Everyday Items

As you go around the house deciding what to keep and what checks out in a Hefty bag, don't be so quick to dispose of those household items that seem to have outlived their usefulness. You'll be surprised at what they can become in their next life!

## LET THERE BE LIGHT (BULBS)!

Eventually it happens—much like death and taxes, the day will surely come when your lightbulbs burn out. "So what?" you shrug. Toss 'em. Not much you can do with a burned-out lightbulb, right? Well, my friends, think again! Here are two super suggestions:

**Energy saver.** Reduce your electric bill by placing burned-out lightbulbs in every other socket of a multibulb light fixture. This saves money, and it's much safer than leaving the socket empty.

**Christmas ornaments.** If you're feeling creative, use burned-out bulbs to make Christmas ornaments. You can paint them, decorate them with ribbons, make faces, or whatever strikes your fancy. By the way, I recently saw some beautiful lightbulb ornaments in a very upscale home decor shop—so if you're really good at this, you could end up not only saving money, but making some moolah, too!

# SOCK IT TO ME!

**G**ot an old pair of socks lying around? You know the kind—worn heels, holes in the toes—most guys have at least one pair. (I know I do.) Well, here are a few alternatives to the trash can (and if you're not a fan of these ideas, remember—you can always make sock puppets!):

☞ Socks make great dusters. Just put a sock on your hand and you're a lean, mean, dustin' machine. Socks give you flexibility that dust rags just don't. Now you can get at all those hard-to-dust nooks and crannies. You can get behind the refrigerator, in and out of the details on your cabinets—you can even moisten the sock with water and clean the leaves of your cherished houseplants.

☞ Socks are wonderful storage containers. They work well for those fragile Christmas ornaments you have to pack and repack every year. Gently place an ornament inside, and then knot the top of the sock. (If you have really long socks, you may be able to fit two ornaments per sock, but don't cramp them—you don't want to squeeze them too tight and cause them to crack.)

☞ For those old socks that are still relatively intact (none that resemble Swiss cheese, please), you can make a savings bank for your kids. Simply dump their loose change inside and knot the top.

☞ Finally, if you're feeling crafty, you can make a dandy rag dispenser. (Again, no holey hosiery, please.) Just cut open the foot of the sock at the toe seam, and then sew around the top and bottom openings with elastic thread to create a tube with stretchy "mouths" at either end. Mount it someplace sensible, then cut your rags to about the size of a wash-cloth, so they fit inside. Drop 'em in the top and pull 'em out of the bottom, and you're good to go!

---

## PAPER OR PLASTIC?

* * * * *

**Use paper bags to:**

✦ pack your lunch (you can generally use the same paper bag for a good week or two to further economize)

✦ cover textbooks

✦ hold trash throughout the house or in your car

✦ wrap Christmas and birthday gifts (this works particularly well if you have to send a package through the mail)

✦ ripen fruit more quickly

**Use plastic bags to:**

✦ line trash cans

✦ dispose of used cat litter

✦ "waterproof" flashlights and radios on camping and boating trips (keep 'em under wraps, even while in use)

✦ take the place of those expensive flannel bags some folks buy to pack their shoes in when they travel

---

# CHECKS AND BALANCES

I don't know how it happens, but we always seem to end up with extra checkbook registers. For a while, I just scrapped them. Then one day, a lightbulb came on in my head. Now I use them for everything from making grocery lists, price books, and size charts (so I always know what to look for at thrift stores and yard sales), to making wish lists and to-do lists. Now I can't get enough of them—I even ask for extras when I go to the bank!

# FOILED AGAIN

Before you resort to buying expensive rust-removal products to clean up your car bumpers or wrought-iron outdoor furniture, give this old-fashioned technique a try: Grab a can of Coca-Cola and some aluminum foil. Crumple the foil into a ball, then pour the Coke over the rusty area. Scrub with the foil. It may take a bit of elbow grease, but folks have been shining metal this way for generations.

## SCRUB A DUB

**H**ere's another great use for aluminum foil. Take that piece of foil you heated the dinner rolls in and have it do double duty at the kitchen sink. A wad of foil makes the perfect scrubber for dirty pots and pans. Give it a try!

## CLOTHES ENCOUNTERS

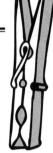

**P**eople don't use clothespins all that much anymore, yet they always seem to be lying around. Fortunately, clothespins have a number of practical uses. My personal favorite is the chip bag clip, but they also make great recipe and grocery list holders. Simply glue a magnet onto the back of the clothespin, and stick it on your fridge. This will allow you to consult recipes while you cook, or keep a running grocery list to ensure you don't forget anything at the store.

## A LIQUID ASSET

**L**iquid dish soap bottles are handy gadgets to keep around. Once the soap's gone, you can wash out the bottle and use it for everything from watering plants and dispensing cooking oil to squeezing out pancake batter in funky shapes. Plus, as my grandkids'll tell you, they make awesome squirt guns!

---

### THOSE YELLOW LEMON THINGIES

\* \* \* \* \*

I know—pretty scientific. But I don't know what else to call those little plastic lemons that typically hold lemon juice. I do know that they can double as soap dispensers, which is what my wife uses them for. I thought it was a little strange at first, but it works and she's happy, which, as you guys out there know, means that I'm happy, too!

---

## WHOA, BABY!

**P**eople use jars for everything under the sun, so why anyone would toss out baby food jars is beyond me. These small jars are perfect for holding a variety of things; in fact, if you do have an infant, consider yourself lucky—you'll have the opportunity to collect hundreds of these gems. They can be used to corral your workroom supplies. One jar can hold nails, another bolts, another screws, etc. Take it from me, they really help keep you organized.

What else can baby food jars hold?

How about votive candles? Or use them to store spices, homemade jellies and jams, or candy. Kids can decorate the jars with paint or glitter and use them to store hair clips, coins, or what-have-you. The options are endless!

## GIVE UNTO OTHERS

* * * * *

Still got stuff lying around? Don't toss it—if you really can't find a use for it, there's someone else out there who can. Here are a couple of ideas:

★ Return clothes hangers to stores or dry cleaners.

★ Donate old eyeglasses to churches or charity organizations.

★ Pass on old clothing to thrift stores, charities, or churches.

★ If you have excess yarn, cloth scraps, buttons, etc., check with your local schools and daycare centers. They're often on the lookout for these craft supplies. And check with your local craft store, too—some stores collect materials and turn them into quilts for the needy.

★ Books and magazines can be passed on to friends or donated to hospital or clinic waiting rooms.

In short, stick to my philosophy: When in doubt, don't throw it out! You can almost always find a home for your unwanted items.

# DON'T MESH AROUND

The next time you buy onions or fruit at the grocery store, don't be so quick to toss out the plastic mesh bag they came in—these bags can work wonders at the kitchen sink. Instead of spending money on those little plastic dish scrubbers, simply cut a recycled plastic mesh bag into halves or thirds—whatever's manageable for you—and *voilà!* Instant dish scrubbers. They work just as well and last just as long as the ones you buy at the store, but they cost nothing extra. Talk about the best of all worlds!

# IN A BINDER

When school gets out, don't toss out the supplies. Folders and binders can be reused year after year. And, if your kids are out of school altogether, you can use their old supplies to keep track of bank and credit card statements or your favorite recipes.

# BOTTLE BASICS

**N**othing makes my blood boil quite like seeing bottles in the trash. Those glass bottles are worth money—as much as 10 cents in some states, when recycled—and you wouldn't just toss a dime in the trash, would you? Didn't think so. So don't toss out your bottles, even if you can't collect a dime for them. Why? Because they have lots of practical uses.

For starters, you can turn them into vases, candleholders, or your own bottled water containers. For those of you with a creative flair, you can fill them with sand to make a doorstop. (A note to the artistic: This is especially nice if you use colored sand.)

And don't toss those plastic bottles, either. Cut the top off of a bottle, turn it upside down, and use it as a funnel. Or make an automatic watering system for garden plants by cutting the

## Pennypincher's Hall of Fame

I love to hear how different people reuse and recycle, so when Fatin Zayed of Chicago, Illinois, told me she had a collection of more than 300 baby wipe containers, I couldn't help but be impressed. What's more impressive, however, is why she has them. "With three kids, they build up pretty quickly. One day, you've got 10, and the next thing you know, the basement is flooded with them! I wasn't quite sure what I was going to do with them all, but when Amber asked for a set of Legos, it suddenly hit me," she says. "Why buy Legos or Lincoln Logs, when the baby wipe containers can double as the same thing? Except they're better, because the kids can actually play in, around, and under the structures they build. My kids love them, and having all these containers around saved me from spending an arm and a leg at the toy store! What could be better than that?" What indeed?

bottoms off of plastic bottles and turning the bottles upside down next to each plant. Push the neck of a bottle into the ground next to a plant, then fill the upside-down bottle with water. It will seep in as needed, and you won't have to be out there watering every day!

## BUCKLE UP

**I**f you have an old belt that's scratched up or torn, try using it to tie down young trees for support. Or cut it and fashion a dog collar for your best buddy. Just punch holes to fit, and your faithful canine is set to wear your hand-me-downs!

## BATTER UP

**M**aybe you're not playing baseball these days, but I'll bet you've got an old bat lying around somewhere. Don't toss it or sell it just yet. Baseball bats make very effective weapons against intruders. Lots of folks keep one under their bed for just such a reason. And, in a pinch, baseball bats make great supports for young plants and trees—until you can find something a little more permanent, such as a yardstick, baton, or broken broom handle. (Just make sure you insert your bat into the ground top down; otherwise your support will be top heavy and in need of its own support!)

## WAGON TRAIN

**A**h, the old red Radio Flyer wagons. I used to love them when I was a kid, and from the looks of it, they're still pretty popular today. But here's good news for you: Once your kids and grandkids outgrow the wagon, you'll be able to use it for all sorts of endeavors. Here are just a few examples:

☞ Let's start with my personal favorite—wagons are perfect for transporting gardening tools around your yard. You'll wonder how you ever lived without it!

☞ Use it to cart groceries from your car to your house. Just keep the wagon in your car's trunk, and pull it out when it's needed.

☞ Lug fireplace wood in from the great outdoors.

# HIT THE BOOKS

\* \* \* \* \*

It breaks my heart to see people toss out books and magazines—great literature is made to be enjoyed, not to clog up landfills. If you really don't want your old reading materials, at least donate them to a library, hospital, or school. Or head over to a half-price book-store and trade them for other books you haven't read. Here are a few other ideas for reusing the printed page:

☑ If you have textbooks, try selling them to other students.

☑ Use the pictures in magazines to make envelopes. Simply fold the page lengthwise in thirds, and then cut the top fold into a triangle. Place your letter inside, and seal all edges. (You'll need to attach your own address labels.)

☑ Keep magazines around, in case your kids or grandkids need to make a collage for school.

☑ Set up a book exchange at your office or church.

☑ Use magazine pages to make bath toys for your kids or grandkids. Simply cut the pictures out of magazines and seal them between two pieces of clear Contact paper. When they're wet, they'll stick to the bathtub tiles. Kids really get a kick out of this!

☞ Transport garbage and recycling from the house to the curb.

☞ Remove the wheels and handle, line it with a blanket, and use it as a bed for your dog or cat.

☞ Remove the wheels and use them as training wheels on a bike or replacement wheels on your lawnmower.

☞ Use it as a giant flowerpot that can be moved to new locations whenever you feel like a change of pace.

# SAVE THOSE HOSE!

Aside from causing millions of women discomfort on a daily basis, pantyhose actually have some unique—and very surprising—uses. How about using them to hang onions for storage? Simply drop an onion into the leg, tie a knot, drop another one in, and so on. You can also use them to remove nail polish. Just cut them into small, 1-inch rings, and use them in place of cotton or tissue with nail polish remover. My wife swears by them! Finally, use them as ties for staking small trees in your lawn and garden. They work like a charm.

# TEAR DOWN THE WALLS

If you're like me, you've got odds and ends of wallpaper sitting on a shelf somewhere. Wallpaper isn't cheap, and you just couldn't bear to throw it out, right? But what the heck can you do with the stuff? Try some of these suggestions:

✦ **Make place mats.** Just cut the wallpaper to the desired size, cover the front and back with clear Contact paper, and trim, leaving a 1/4-inch margin of Contact paper on all sides. This works great—

especially if the mats match the paper on your dining room walls!

✦ **Cover textbooks, scrapbooks, or boxes**. It's perfect for anything that could use a little sprucing up.

✦ **Make stationery.** Buy a pack of plain or lined writing paper, and cut the wallpaper to the size of the writing paper. Glue the paper to the wallpaper, write your letter, and then fold it in thirds, so the wallpaper is on the outside. Seal with tape or a sticker, use a white address label (so it's readable), add a stamp, and you're good to go.

✦ **Make decorator outlet covers.** Cut pieces of wallpaper small enough to cover outlet and light switch plates. If the paper is patterned, be sure to match up the pattern on the switch plate with the pattern on the wall.

# BEAN THERE, DONE THAT

Pinto beans. Probably not something you're typically figuring out new uses for, but (of course!) I've got a few. For example, if you ever play Bingo, the beans make wonderful markers. If you enjoy making crafts, you can dress up an inexpensive picture frame by hot-gluing pinto beans around the perimeter of the frame. And, if you like to fill your kitchen with decorative jars, just fill a baby food jar with pinto beans and place it on a shelf.

## TEA TIME

Got an old set of teacups lying around? Get them out of the cupboard and use them as candle holders—they make a nice decorative touch on windowsills.

## CREATE A CRAFT CLOSET

\* \* \* \* \*

Whenever my kids had a school project, we scrambled to find materials to make the Eiffel Tower or to build a medieval drawbridge. Let me tell you—I'm glad those days are over! Now, I watch in amazement as my grandkids drag their folks to the store to *buy* craft materials. Don't let this happen to you!

Make a craft closet or designate a craft shelf, or even just a craft storage box. Fill it with all those odds and ends you don't quite know what to do with, such as:

☑ pieces of foam packing material

☑ yarn, string, and ribbon

☑ old buttons and zippers

☑ beads from broken necklaces and bracelets

☑ old, nonworking watches (crack 'em open and use the innards)

☑ scraps of fabric and cloth

☑ pieces of cardboard, foil, and construction paper

I think you get the idea. Your kids (or grandkids) will be thrilled to have a treasure trove of materials on hand, and best of all, they're free!

# Use It Again and Again

As you find new uses for old stuff, I'm sure you'll keep turning up the same couple of items again and again—you know, like empty soda bottles, newspapers, jars, and so forth. It seems like everyone's house has a stash of this stuff, and it never gets used up. Well, I've got some super ideas for reusing these old standbys, so read on!

## MAGIC WITH MILK CARTONS

1. Use as seed starters.

2. Cut off the tops and bottoms, and press them into the soil around young plants to protect them from grubs and cutworms.

3. Cut off the front and the bottom, and use as a quickie dustpan.

4. Cut in half, and mix paint in the bottom half.

5. Cut in half, and place upside down on top of tent pegs when you go camping, so you don't bash your toes on them during the night.

6. Create a cheap air conditioner. Fill a carton with water, freeze it, and then place it in front of a fan to circulate cool air.

## FILM CANISTER FUN

If you have a camera that takes 35mm film, you know how those little plastic canisters start piling up. Here are some neat and novel uses:

**Traveling toothbrush container.** I know, it sounds a little weird, but trust me—it works. Just cut a small slit in the lid, so your toothbrush handle can fit through. Then open the container, put the head of your toothbrush into the bottom, and push the lid over the toothbrush handle until it meets the bottom. Press it closed, and your toothbrush is now protected from all things dirty and fuzzy!

**Lip gloss container.** Take that last little bit of lipstick you can never get to, combine it with a little

petroleum jelly, and then store your makeshift lip gloss in the film canister!

**Stamp dispenser.** Cut a small slit down the side of the base. Pop a stamp roll inside, and pull the end out through the slit. Put the lid on, and you're ready to stamp.

**Traveling condiment containers.** Store mayo, mustard, ketchup, etc., for picnics or for use in school or work lunches.

**All-around storage.** Store small office supplies (paper clips, thumbtacks, etc.) or loose buttons or beads; fill with quarters and keep in your purse or car for highway tolls and emergency phone calls.

# USE THOSE WIRE HANGERS!

Okay, now I *know* that every one of you out there has at least a dozen wire coat hangers hanging out in your closets. After all, it's common knowledge that if you put a coat hanger in a closet and shut the door, by morning, there'll be two more in there! Here's how to corral them into use:

1. Bend them into different shapes for Christmas,

---

## 6 EGG-STRA USES FOR EGG CARTONS

\* \* \* \* \*

1. Separate money at garage sales.

2. Store golf balls.

3. Store jewelry and other small items during travel.

4. Use as seed starters.

5. Use as a palette for watercolor paints.

6. Use as a desk organizer for paper clips, push pins, etc.

---

Halloween, and other holiday party decorations that can be hung on the walls or from light fixtures.

2. Unbend a few, and use them as hot dog or marshmallow sticks at a cookout.

3. Shape a hanger into a circle, and use as it as a wreath form. Attach greenery and other decorations.

# GREAT GARDEN HOSES

You know me—I wouldn't throw away a garden hose until I got every last bit of use out of it that I could think of! Here goes:

☞ Cut a short length of hose, and cut a slit down the side. Use it as a blade protector for knives and axes.

☞ Carry heavy buckets more easily. Just cut a length of hose to match the handle, cut a slit down the side, and cover the handle.

☞ Keep wire tree supports from rusting by covering them with lengths of hose.

☞ Use long lengths of old hose as driveway curbing. If you have a narrow driveway (or a new driver just getting behind the wheel), a hose "bumper" laid along the length of both sides of the driveway will alert the driver that they're at the edge, and it will protect your lawn from being run over.

# CRAFTY CDS

**I**'m talking about compact discs here, folks, not certificates of deposit! If you've got a few CDs lying

around that are too scratched to play, or you just don't like the music on them, don't toss them out. Believe it or not, I've found some handy uses for those unwanted CDs!

**Candle display.** Place the CD shiny side up, and put a votive candle in the middle. It makes a beautiful, reflective centerpiece.

**Driveway reflectors.** Fasten CDs, shiny side out, to wooden stakes, and use them as reflectors along your driveway.

**Template.** When you need to draw a perfect circle, but you can't find that compass, use a CD as a template.

**Coasters.** Glue felt to one side of the CD and use the other, uncovered side as a coaster.

**Bird deterrents.** Hang CDs from trees in your garden to scare birds away.

**Wall collage.** Glue several together and make a wall collage—perfect for a teenager's bedroom or a guest room.

And don't forget those plastic cases the CDs came in (officially known as "jewel cases"). Here's how to use them up:

**Dandy displays.** Use them to show off your butterfly, coin, or stamp collection.

**Picture frame.** Cut two photos to fit, and place them back to back in the case. Now you've got a double-sided picture frame, perfect for putting on a desk or table. Or insert just one photo and hang it on the wall.

**Desk calendar.** If you've got a calendar small enough to fit inside, great! If not, you can create one on your computer (or ask your grandkid to make one for you!). It makes a great stand-up desk calendar.

## A TISKET, A TASKET

* * * * *

Here's eight great uses for plastic berry baskets!

1. **Soap holder in the shower.** Just get two small suction cups on hooks, and hang the basket from them. Then you can keep anything within arm's reach—soaps, bath beads, your razor, and so on.

2. **Screwdriver or paintbrush organizer.** Just place the basket upside down on your tool bench, push the tool handles through the grid, and you're good to go.

3. **Easter basket.** Decorate with ribbons or other froufrou. Add a handle, if you'd like.

4. **Bulb protector.** Keep rodents away by planting bulbs inside mesh berry baskets that have been set into the ground.

5. **Seedling protector.** Place baskets upside down over new growth to ensure that no wascally wabbits dine out in your garden!

6. **Dishwasher basket.** Perfect for containing those little things that tend to slide around, such as small lids.

7. **Floppy disk holder.** A berry basket will hold plenty of 3½-inch disks.

8. **Bubble blower.** Kids love this. Mix up a large bucket of liquid dish soap and water, then dip the basket in. Wave it around in the air—it makes an amazing amount of bubbles!

# 8 GREAT WAYS TO USE IT AGAIN

* * * * *

## NEWSPAPERS

1. Line a bird cage.

2. Paper train a puppy.

3. Shred it and use as cat litter.

4. Ball it up and use in place of foam packing peanuts.

5. Roll into tight "logs" for the fireplace.

6. Lay down in the garden as mulch.

7. Shred and put it in your compost pile.

8. Use it as gift wrap (especially the comics section).

## PLASTIC 2-LITER BOTTLES

1. Make a flower vase.

2. Cut a slit near the top and use it as a coin bank.

3. Cut in half and use the bottom as a flowerpot.

4. Fill with water, freeze, and you'll always have a ready-made ice pack.

5. Cut the bottom off, turn upside down, and use it as a funnel. (This works great for oil changes!)

6. Use them as sandbag substitutes. If you ever use sandbags in the winter for additional weight in your car, you know how messy they can be when they break. Fill a few 2-liter bottles with sand instead.

7. Cut the top off and use as a salt scooper to de-ice sidewalks and driveways.

8. Use it to hold used cooking oil, bacon grease, etc., until it solidifies, then throw away the bottle.

## SHOEBOXES

1. Donate them to schools (so students can make shadowboxes).

2. Store pictures.

3. File old bills.

4. Store keepsakes, such as cards and letters.

5. File coupons.

6. Let children use them as building blocks (you may want to tape the lids down).

7. Remove the lid and let your cats play in it.

8. Cover with red and pink construction paper, doilies, etc., to make a Valentine's Day mailbox for school.

## CARDBOARD ROLLS

1. Make them into bird feeders. Hole-punch each end, and run two pieces of string through the holes. Dip each end in fat (you can ask for this at your grocery store meat counter), and then roll the fat-covered tubes in birdseed.

2. Roll up and store cross-stitch canvas inside.

3. Store pantyhose. (One pair per roll—this works especially well for travel because you don't have to worry about them getting snags.)

4. Make play binoculars—staple two toilet paper rolls together, and then punch holes in the top of each. Feed a piece of long string through the holes so kids can put them around their necks—they love it!

5. Store electrical/phone cords (one cord per roll—that way, they don't get all tangled).

6. Use them as makeshift megaphones for your kids (at your own risk, of course).

7. Store posters and important documents rolled up inside.

8. Stick them inside boots to help them hold their shape.

# Keep It Clean

I don't have to tell you that housecleaning is hard work. And it can be very expensive—there's a product out there for practically every surface in your house! Well, I'm here to tell you that you don't have to spend a penny on those "miracle" cleansers. Nearly everything you need to clean your home can be found in your own cupboards, cabinets, and pantry. If it can't, I guarantee that whatever you have to buy will be less expensive than any of those overpriced cleaning agents. So let's get scrubbing!

## In the Kitchen

Let's start with the kitchen. To me, the kitchen should be the cleanest room in the house. It should be a sterile environment—we're talking hospital clean here. If a cookie happens to slip out of your hand and fall onto your kitchen floor, there shouldn't be a question of whether to eat it or toss it out. You should have confidence that your floor, like every other surface in your kitchen, is—quite literally—clean enough to eat off. Here are some easy ways to get your kitchen spic and span, and keep it that way.

## BAKER'S TRIO

When it comes to cleaning your kitchen, nothing gets the job done quite like sodium bicarbonate. (For those of you, like me, who aren't exactly Bill Nye, the Science Guy, that's normal, run-of-the-mill baking soda.) Baking soda is a substance of powerful proportions—you can clean virtually any kitchen surface with it (including the kitchen sink). Here are three ideas:

1. The kitchen sink is, of course, the cornerstone of any kitchen. To clean the sink, simply sprinkle a little

baking soda followed by a bit of salt, like you would any other scouring agent. Scrub with a sponge, and rinse thoroughly.

2. The exteriors of all your appliances—refrigerator, oven, microwave, toaster, etc.—should be wiped down weekly with a paste of baking soda and water. Buff dry. You should be able to see your reflection when you're finished.

3. All countertops should be cleaned with a paste of baking soda and water. This will get out most stains, from coffee and tea to dried-on spaghetti sauce or chocolate. For heavy-duty stains, rub a drop of chlorine bleach into the stain until it disappears. Wash immediately with baking soda and water to prevent fading.

## SAFETY FIRST!

\* \* \* \* \*

If you know what you're doing, mixing chemicals is a cheap alternative to buying them at the grocery store. If you don't, it could mean trouble. Keep the following safety guidelines in mind whenever you're mixing up your concoctions:

◆ Never mix ammonia and bleach together. The combination is lethal.

◆ Keep all products away from curious little fingers. Even though these are homemade, that doesn't mean they're kid-safe. This goes especially for ammonia and alcohol.

◆ Before combining anything, always check the labels to make sure there are no explicit directions cautioning you about combining a certain product with another.

◆ Make sure that the area you are cleaning is well ventilated, and wear gloves to guard against skin irritation.

## IS IT FRESH?

**B**aking soda may be a modern miracle of a cleanser, but its powers are severely limited if it's not fresh. (The last thing you want to do is use the baking soda that's currently absorbing odors in your fridge to sanitize your kitchen… eewwwww!) So how do you tell if it's still fresh enough to use? Add 1 tablespoon of baking soda to ¼ cup of vinegar. If it fizzes, you're good to go. If it sits there like a bump on a log, then it's out with the old and in with the new!

# SOAK 'EM CLEAN

To clean really stubborn stains in pots and pans, and even on dishes, pour

## FANTASTIC FORMULA

### Wood Cabinet Polish

Cleaning your wooden kitchen cabinets is easy—just wipe them down with a paste made from a little water and baking soda, and call it an afternoon. But what about getting them to shine? Normally you'd reach for that can of Pledge, but now I'm going to make *you* a pledge: My special wood cabinet polish will make your cabinets shine so brightly that you're going to need to put on your sunglasses when you walk into the kitchen!

½ cup of malt vinegar

½ cup of linseed oil

1½ teaspoons of lemon juice

Combine the vinegar and linseed oil in a small jar or bowl. Add the lemon juice for scent. Apply the polish with a soft rag, adding a little elbow grease, and your cabinets will be the talk of the town (or at least the kitchen)!

1 tablespoon of dishwasher detergent (yes, the stuff you use in the dishwasher, not liquid dish soap) under warm running water until the sink is full. Then, place the offending cookware in  the sink so that it is totally submerged, and give it a good half-hour or so to soak. This should tackle any stain.

# COMPLETELY FLOORED

How you clean your kitchen floor depends on the kind of floor you have. You can't use the same agent on wood as you can on vinyl—that would be like using nail polish remover to brush your teeth! Here's the lowdown on how to get your kitchen floor looking its very best:

**Good, old-fashioned linoleum.** Combine a little liquid dish soap with a bucket of warm water, and use it to mop the floor. To protect the linoleum floor from those dreaded scuffs and scratches, you can also add a tablespoon of baby oil to the mop water.

**No-wax flooring.** Combine ½ cup of vinegar with a bucket of warm water, and use it to mop the floor.

**Wood flooring.** Mix a solution of equal parts vegetable oil and vinegar. Rub it into the wood well.

**Painted wood.** Mix 1 teaspoon of baking soda with 1 gallon of hot water, and use it to mop the floor.

**Brick or stone.** Add 1 cup of vinegar to a bucket of warm water, and use it to mop the floor. Rinse with clean water.

**Ceramic tile.** Mix ¼ cup of vinegar with a bucket of warm water, and use it to mop the floor.

**Rubber tiles.** Squirt a little liquid dish soap into a bucket of warm water, and use it to mop the floor.

# MORE FLOOR LORE

So now you know how to clean different types of floors, but what about those tough cleaning jobs? Try these:

★ To get rid of those black scuff marks from careless shoes, just rub them out with a rag or, if you're so inclined, even your sock. If they don't come out, try using a paste of baking soda and water.

★ To remove crayon marks, rub them with a damp cloth containing a bit of toothpaste.

★ To remove wax buildup, mix a 3:1 solution of water and rubbing alcohol. Scrub this in, and rinse thoroughly. (Make sure the area is well-ventilated before you begin.)

★ To remove tar, gently scrape up the excess with a dull knife, being careful not to scratch the floor. Then scrub any remaining mark with a paste of baking soda and water.

★ To remove grease stains from wood floors, immediately place an ice cube on the stain. The grease will harden, and then you can scrape it off with a dull knife.

# In the Bathroom

If there's one thing I can't stand, it's a dirty bathroom. Think about it—if the room that functions to promote good hygiene is dirtier than you are, then what's the point? Here's a host of home-made concoctions to help ensure your bathroom is as clean as mine. And believe me, that's no easy feat!

## THE TIDY BOWL

**A**h, the toilet. Everyone's favorite thing to clean—I know it's mine. (And if you believe that one, you really did just fall off the turnip truck yesterday!) But it has to be done. Here are a couple of great ways to make that porcelain shine up like a new dime:

✦ For a general cleaning, use baking soda and vinegar. Sprinkle a little baking soda into the bowl, and then douse with vinegar. Scrub with a toilet brush.

✦ For a stubborn toilet ring, try borax and lemon juice. Combine both ingredients

---

**$ BARGAIN ALERT!**

I'm sure that, just like me, you've often wondered if the cheaper, store-brand cleaning products do the same job as their more expensive, brand-name counterparts. Well, I'd have to say no. In my experience, using the cheaper generic brand of, say, dishwasher detergent—instead of a brand like Cascade—doesn't really save you money. Here's why: Take a box of Cascade that weighs in at 4.68 pounds and costs $3.89. Then take a no-name generic brand of dishwasher detergent, also weighing in at 4.68 pounds, but costing only $1.98. The cheaper brand's got to be the better buy, right? Wrong! It turns out that even though the no-name brand costs less, you end up having to use much more of the product to get the same cleaning results as the more expensive brand. The same holds true for liquid dish soaps.

On the other hand, there *are* bargains to be had in the cleaning department. Take bleach, for example. Bleach is bleach, so don't buy according to brand name—buy according to price. While you're at it, buy the cheapest brands of vinegar and baking soda, too.

into a paste and cover the ring. Let it sit for an hour, and scrub with a toilet brush. That ought to do the trick!

✦ For the base and back of the toilet, sprinkle a little cream of tartar on a damp cloth. It shines up porcelain perfectly!

# RUB-A-DUB-DUB

**H**ere's where you'll really appreciate my homemade concoctions. As you well know, there are few things worse than those fumes that come from those store-bought shower, tub, and tile cleaners. I used to have to take breaks from cleaning the bathroom just to breathe in a little fresh air, but no more. Here's everything you need to tend to your tub and tiles:

☞ Before tackling the bathroom, run a little hot water from the shower head into your tub or shower stall. Leave it on for five minutes or so. This will loosen up the dirt and make cleaning much easier. (It's like a shower for your shower!)

☞ To clean the tub, sprinkle a little baking soda like you would any typical scouring powder. Scrub with a sponge or brush, and rinse thoroughly.

☞ To remove mineral deposits from faucets, simply soak a few paper towels in full-strength vinegar, and lay the wet towels over the deposits. For showerheads, remove the head, and completely submerge it in vinegar. Let it sit for about an hour.

☞ For rings around the bathtub, clean it with vinegar first. Then follow with a little baking soda. Scrub, and rinse thoroughly.

☞ To clean ceramic tile, combine 1/4 cup of vinegar with 1 gallon of water. Mix together, and sponge the solution onto the tile. Scrub, then rinse thoroughly.

☞ To clean grout, make a paste of 3 tablespoons of baking soda and 1 cup of warm water. Scrub the paste into the grout with an old toothbrush. Rinse thoroughly.

☞ To clean shower doors, simply wipe them down with a

little vinegar. They'll shine like the morning sun.

☞ To remove mildew, dilute ½ cup of chlorine bleach in 1 gallon of water. Sponge the mixture onto the tile and grout, then scrub. Rinse thoroughly.

---

### DID YOU KNOW?

**\* \* \* \* \***

The average American home contains anywhere from 3 to 10 gallons of hazardous products, and store-bought cleaning agents can be serious offenders. My homemade concoctions are not only cheaper, but they're also safer for you and your family. That's something you can take to the bank!

---

## SPIT AND POLISH

When it comes to cleaning the bathroom sink, you'll most likely find little dried toothpaste deposits—they're a dime a dozen at my house! How strange, then, that the best way to clean your sink is…with toothpaste! I'm completely serious. Just dab some on, and then brush it onto the surface with an old toothbrush. Rinse thoroughly—you won't believe the shine!

## DOWN THE DRAIN

When you're constantly fishing clumps of long hair out of your bathroom drains, you learn a thing or two really fast. Here are two ways to help you keep your drains free and clear from any obstacles (and that goes for kitchen drains, too):

**Prevention is key**. In bathrooms, use a drain strainer to trap that long hair, so you don't find yourself digging it out months from now (this isn't very much fun!) In the kitchen, pour a kettle of boiling water down the drain once every few weeks to melt any fat deposits that may be accumulating. A little baking soda or vinegar down the drain does the trick, as well.

**Break out the plunger.** It's not just for toilets anymore! A plunger will generally break up any drain clog and allow it to float away.

## MIRROR, MIRROR, ON THE WALL

It's tough enough to keep mirrors clean, but when you

throw hairspray into the mix, it's darn near impossible. To get rid of that built-up hairspray haze that tends to attach itself to bathroom mirrors, just dab on a little rubbing alcohol, then wipe with a soft cloth. Now you're looking *really* good!

## MIXTURE FOR FIXTURES

**S**o you know how to clean the sink, tub, and toilet, but what about the water faucets, soap dishes, and toilet handle? To clean stainless steel, ceramic, enamel, chrome, or porcelain fixtures, the answer's the same: Simply dissolve 2 tablespoons of baking soda in 1 quart of water. A little dab'll do ya, and they'll shine right up.

## IT'S CURTAINS!

**S**hower curtains can be washed in the laundry and tumbled dry. You probably knew that, right? But did you know that those vinyl curtain liners can be tossed in the wash,

---

## LET'S CLEAR THE AIR

✳ ✳ ✳ ✳ ✳

Store-bought air fresheners are costly and unnecessary. You can do much better by making your own at home. Here's how:

✦ To eliminate strong cooking odors, place a few saucers filled with vinegar around the room. It negates any odor.

✦ Soak a cotton ball in pure vanilla extract, and place it on a small saucer.

✦ Simmer a mixture of cinnamon sticks and cloves in a pot of water on the stove. Your home will smell heavenly!

✦ To guard against garbage odor, sprinkle a little borax in the bottom of your garbage can. You'll be glad you did.

✦ To guard against fridge odors, just place an open box of baking soda on one of the shelves. It absorbs all odors.

---

too? This is great news, because nothing gets grimier than that curtain liner—heck, even I'm tempted to toss it out half of the time. But after a quick cycle through the laundry, it's good as new. Just make sure you hang it to dry—it'll melt in the dryer!

# The Rest of the Rooms

**Now that you're an expert when it comes to cleaning your kitchen and bathroom—and saving money in the process—what money-saving secrets do I have to share for the rest of the house? Read on, my friends!**

## RUG RESCUE

**G**eneral carpet care falls under Common Sense 101—if you know how to use a vacuum, that's half the battle. If you spill something, wipe it up immediately. But there's a bit more you should know in order to keep your carpets and rugs looking their best.

**General spills.** If something spills, blot it up immediately. Soak up the excess stain, and then add a little vinegar. Scrub the area gently. If you want, you can also sprinkle a little baking soda over the carpet, then vacuum to eliminate lingering odors.

**Blood stains.** Blot up immediately and follow with cold water or club soda. Repeat as often as necessary, until the stain's gone for good.

**Ink stains.** (For light-colored carpets only.) Sprinkle a little cream of tartar on the stain and follow with a few drops of lemon juice. Rub into the stain, and brush away the powder. Wash immediately with warm water. Repeat as necessary.

**Ground-in dirt.** Just add salt. Allow it to sit 20 minutes or so, and then vacuum.

**Urine stains.** Blot up excess urine. Add a little liquid dish soap, and scrub into the stain. Follow with 1/4 cup of vinegar diluted in 1 quart of warm water. Let it stand an hour or so. Blot up again with paper towels, and allow to dry completely.

## HARDWOOD WOES

**I** love hardwood floors. They're beyond beautiful. But for all their beauty, they can be a real pain to care for. Earlier in this chapter, I told you how to keep wood floors clean and shiny. But how do you get rid of stains? Here are a few pointers:

**Water stains.** Dry immediately. If a spot remains, lightly sand with fine sandpaper and then refinish.

**Cigarette burns.** Try a little steel wool moistened with soap and water. If the burn is serious, you may need to seek the advice of a professional.

**Heel marks.** Use a little steel wool followed by soap and water. Wipe it dry with a clean, soft cloth.

**Chewing gum.** Rub ice over the gum until it hardens. It should come right off.

**Ink.** Treat just like a water stain. Sand with fine sandpaper, then refinish.

## THE ITSY-BITSY SPIDER

**C**obwebs—they're the most dreaded sight in my house. It's no secret that spiders and I have never been on good terms, so you'd best believe I get rid of them as soon as I see that first string dangle down from the ceiling. To get cobwebs in those hard-to-reach places, simply put an old sock on the end of a yardstick, and sweep it around the ceiling. *Voila!*

## BLIND AS A BAT

**C**leaning my horizontal and vertical blinds is right up there with cleaning the toilet: Not exactly my idea of a fun way to spend an afternoon. To clean your blinds, just use a soft cloth moistened with a little water. Start at the top, and then work your way down toward the bottom. Don't forget to do both sides. **Hint:** An old, clean sock works well for this. Just wear it like a mitt and you can grab onto the blinds and clean both sides at the same time.

---

### WINDOW WASHING 101

* * * * *

Here's how to keep your windows squeaky clean, easy as 1-2-3!

**1.** Never wash windows while the sun is shining directly on them. It will cause the solution to dry too quickly and leave streaks.

**2.** Use newspaper if you don't have any soft cleaning cloths. I've found that it works just as well, if not better.

**3.** Use up-and-down strokes on one side of the window and side-to-side strokes on the other; that way, you can tell which side needs further attention.

## WALL OF FAME

**Y**ou clean your windows. You vacuum your carpet. And you dust every piece of furniture. But how often do you wash down your walls? If you're anything like me, not often. But you should do it occasionally, just to remove any handprints or dirt that's accumulated. Dissolve 2 ounces of borax with 1 teaspoon of ammonia in a bucket of water. Scrub from the top down. Dry immediately.

A word of warning, though—if you live in a recently built home that was painted by the builder, chances are that the paint was sprayed on. This means there's only a very thin coat of paint on the wall and, if you wash the wall, you'll likely end up looking at bare drywall patches!

## PAMPERED PAPER

**S**o it's easy to wash painted walls, but what about wallpapered walls? Well, wallpaper accumulates dirt and dust just like anything else. Some wallpaper can't be washed at all—only dusted with a soft, dry rag. To determine if yours is safe to clean, select an inconspicuous area to test. Wash the spot with

**Here's a Web site after my own heart—www. pioneerliving.com.** As the name suggests, it hearkens back to a time when life was simple, when vinegar and baking soda were held in high regard and no one would think of shelling out hard-earned cash for cleaning products! Actually, the fact that this site exists on the Web is nearly an oxymoron! Here you'll find all kinds of natural remedies to clean just about everything in your home. In addition, the site also offers tips on beauty, health care, cooking, crafts, and ways to take care of your home and family. It's truly a site pioneers would be proud of!

a little baking soda and water. If it's safe, proceed from the top down, just as you would with painted walls. If the paper starts to discolor, abandon the wet wash and simply dust occasionally with a soft, dry cloth.

# EASEL DOES IT

**I**f you have kids or grandkids, it'll probably happen: They'll grow tired of the coloring books you've given them and turn to the hundreds of feet of vacant space before them— your walls! Here are some ideas to get rid of pen, pencil, and crayon stains from your walls and washable wallpaper. (If your wallpaper isn't washable, you'll need to call in an expert.)

**Pen and pencil marks.** Wipe with a damp sponge and a little dish detergent. Pencil marks should come off easily. Pens may take a bit longer to completely disappear. You can also try lightly scrubbing with a paste of baking soda and water, then rinsing.

**Crayon marks.** Scrape off what you can with a dull knife, being careful not to scratch the wall. Then take several paper towels, place them over the crayon stain, and run a warm iron over them. The towels will absorb the crayon.

# MORE FUN WITH CRAYONS...

**H**ere's another way to get crayon marks off your walls. Use a dryer sheet. Just run the sheet over crayon-marked walls, and they'll come clean in a hurry!

# HANDS ACROSS YOUR LIVING ROOM

**H**andprints on the walls. I don't know how it happens. Maybe they missed the light switch. Maybe they just weren't paying attention. But sooner or later, you're bound to find yourself faced with the task of cleaning greasy paw prints off of your walls. How do you do it? The same way you get rid of crayon marks. Cover the grease with several paper towels, and run a warm iron over the stain. The paper towels will absorb the grease.

# More Fantastic Formulas!

**This is my favorite part—even more terrific tips, tricks, and tonics to help you clean all around your house!**

## ALL-PURPOSE DISINFECTANT

**H**ere's a multipurpose disinfectant recipe that you can use on everything from cutting boards and kitchen counters to toilets and baby bottoms! Just combine the following ingredients in a spray bottle, and let loose:

---

### FANTASTIC FORMULA

**One-Shot Cleaner**

Here's a great recipe for a multipurpose cleaner:

2 quarts of water

2 cups of rubbing alcohol

1 tablespoon of ammonia

1 tablespoon of dishwashing liquid

Combine all ingredients in a spray bottle, then go to town. (Incidentally, this super-duper concoction will beat commercial, streakless glass-cleaning products hands down!)

---

2 cups of water, 2 tablespoons of liquid dish soap, and 30 drops of tea tree oil (available at most health food stores).

## A SILVER LINING

**T**o clean your cherished silver, you don't have to buy some expensive cleaner at the store. Simply put a layer of aluminum foil over a very clean kitchen sink, and sprinkle 2 tablespoons of salt on the foil. Place your silverware on top of the salt and pour 6 cups of very hot water over it. Like magic, the tarnish will disappear from your silver and reappear on the aluminum foil—it's truly amazing!

## DUST IN THE WIND

**L**ooking for a top-notch furniture polish you can use to dust wood furniture? Just combine 1 cup of vegetable oil with $1/2$ cup of lemon juice. Rub it into your furniture with a soft cloth, and buff to a shine.

## ANIMAL, VEGETABLE, OR MINERAL?

**I**n the case of your toilet, definitely mineral—deposits, that is. To get rid of them, just drop a couple of denture-cleaning tablets into the bowl, and let them do the dirty work for you. Once they've stopped fizzing, simply flush.

## STRONG ENOUGH FOR A MAN...

**B**ut made for your carpet. Well, not really, but it *is* true that shaving cream can be a wonderful stain remover, especially for fresh food stains. Just cover the stain with shaving cream, let it dissolve into the stain, and then wipe away. (You may have to repeat more than once.)

## LIQUID PLUMBER

**G**ot a clog that a plunger just won't budge? Try my patented (well, not really, but it works) clog-buster formula: Dump about ½ cup of baking soda

### FANTASTIC FORMULA

**Play Misty for Me**

You've seen the ads: "Just spray a little on your shower walls, and you'll never have to scrub again." That's a pretty lofty claim, and I've yet to find a product that lives up to it. I do have a concoction that comes close, though. Try this recipe:

> 3 cups of water
> 1 tablespoon of liquid laundry detergent
> ½ cup of rubbing alcohol

Combine the ingredients into a spray bottle and—here's the key, folks—spray your shower down with the concoction on a daily basis. And just for the record, you will have to scrub again—you just won't have to do it as often, and you won't have to worry about mold and mildew.

down the drain, and follow with ½ cup of vinegar. Allow it to sit. While you're waiting, boil a large pot of water. After 10 minutes or so, dump the boiling water down the drain. Flush thoroughly with cool water.

## FANTASTIC FORMULA

### Plumb Fed Up

So your clog is *really* stubborn—we're talking the granddaddy of all clogs—enormous, tough, and a pain in the you-know-what. It's time to bring out the big guns. Try this:

> ½ cup of salt
>
> ½ cup of baking soda
>
> 1 pot of boiling water

Pour the salt down the drain, followed by the baking soda. Then pour in the boiling water. The salt serves as an additional abrasive to help dissolve the clog.

# HOME IS WHERE THE HEARTH IS

If you're lucky enough to have a fireplace, then you ought to know how to clean it! For brick fireplaces, combine 1 ounce of liquid dish soap and 1 ounce of salt with a little water. The mixture should be fairly thick. With a soft sponge, apply the mixture to the brick. Let it stand for 30 minutes, then remove with a sponge soaked in warm water.

If you have a stone fireplace, add 2 tablespoons of liquid dish soap to a bucket of water. Sponge the mixture onto the fireplace, working from the top down. Dry with a soft cloth.

# KISS MY GLASS

A lot of folks say, "I don't do windows" because it's so frustrating to get out there and wash and rub, only to see a ton of streaks when the sun shines in. Well, my solution to the streak problem is simple—vinegar! It's great for cleaning glass. Just combine equal parts vinegar and water, and apply to windows with a soft cloth. Dry with a second soft cloth. This will leave your windows sparkly and virtually streak-free.

# UNSCENTED SHINE

If you don't particularly like the idea of using pungent vinegar to clean your windows, try using borax, instead. Just combine 1 tablespoon of borax with 2 cups of water. Apply to the surface with a soft cloth and dry with a second soft cloth.

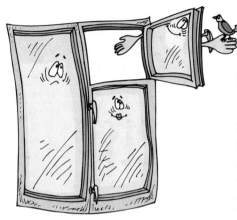

soft cloth and dry with a second soft cloth. Your windows will sparkle, and nothing beats that fresh lemon scent.

**Go clubbing.** If you're not fond of scented windows, clean them with a little club soda on a soft cloth. Dry immediately with a second soft cloth for a perfect view.

## MORE WINDOW WONDERS

There are all sorts of schools of thought on window and glass cleaners. As mentioned earlier, there's vinegar and borax. But here are some other potions that'll work wonders for your windows:

**Lemon up.** Combine 1 tablespoon of lemon juice with 3 cups of water. Apply with a

## SCRATCH THE SCRATCH

Now this one's going to surprise you. How can you get small scratches out of glass without some serious polishing? Simple—you scratch it back! Rub a little toothpaste (the white kind, not gel) into the scratch with a toothpick. Then polish with a soft cloth. Another neat trick: Use 0000 steel wool to gently rub out the scratches.

# CHAPTER 12

# Personal Care and Grooming Secrets

All across this great land of ours, health and beauty stores are making a mint. And I just don't get it. Now, something like a hardware store, I can see. After all, unless you're McGuyver, you're hardly going to make your own circular saw from a coffee can and a pencil. But you *can* make your own shampoo, conditioner, toothpaste, and other beauty products for pennies on the dollar.

In this chapter, you'll find a whole host of homemade beauty products. These formulas are easy to make, and you don't have to spend a lot of moolah to make them. And whenever a recipe calls for soap, olive oil, or another household product, use the least expensive brand you can find, and your beauty products will still turn out just fine!

One word of caution: Before using any product on your skin, test it on a small area of your face or inner arm, wait 24 hours, and check for signs of irritation. If there are any, don't use another drop!

# The One-Stop Beauty Shop

All you have to do is turn on the TV or flip through a magazine to see ad after ad for beauty products that seem to be targeted expressly at you. And they all promise instant results! Whether it's dry hair, oily hair, no hair, gray hair, dandruff, oily skin, dry skin, skin without its proper pH, wrinkles, bad breath, off-white smiles, circles under eyes, puffy eyes—you get the picture. No matter what you've got, there's a boatload of products out there for darn near anything you can think of—for a price. But don't waste your hard-earned cash—it's fast, fun, and easy to make your own shampoos, conditioners, hair sprays, skin creams, and other beauty products at a fraction of the cost—and from ingredients you've already got lying around the house.

## Hair Care for Less

A quick look at the hair care section of your local grocery, drug, or discount store will have your hair standing on end! There are so many choices, and they all sound good, so how do you know which one is right for you? While all of those products probably do what they say they do (for the most part, anyway), the truth of the matter is that you don't need any of them. I'll show you how to clean and pamper your hair with your very own homemade products that are cheap and easy to make. Read on!

## SHAMPOO YOU

Unless you're made of money, you're better off making your own shampoo. Sure, salon shampoos work great, but they're also unbelievably expensive. And your run-of-the-mill, store-bought shampoos? The sad truth of it, folks, is that most aren't even good for your hair! Here are a few alternatives:

**Egg on your hair!**
Separate 1 large egg. In a mixing bowl, use an electric mixer to beat the egg white until foamy. Then add 2 tablespoons of castile soap and the egg yolk. Blend on low. Rub half the mixture into your hair. Let it stand for one minute.

Rinse thoroughly, and repeat the process with the second half. (You'll find castile soap in health and beauty stores.)

**Oil's well that ends well.** Here's a sure-fire recipe for success: Combine 1 egg, 1 teaspoon of lemon juice, 1 teaspoon of olive oil, $\frac{1}{2}$ cup of water, and 2 tablespoons of castile soap in a blender. Whip until creamy. Shampoo using warm water. You can store the unused portion in the refrigerator and use it the next day.

**An herbal essence.** Brew a pot of your favorite herbal tea, and combine $\frac{1}{4}$ cup of it in a small saucepot with 1 cup of castile soap. Stir over low heat until blended. Store any unused shampoo in a capped bottle.

# JUST ADD WATER

It's true that you can make store-bought shampoo last twice as long by pouring half of the contents into a separate bottle and adding an equal amount of water. But is it as effective? Certainly. In fact, it's actually better for your hair that way. Oftentimes, the animal fat and other ingredients in over-the-

---

## FANTASTIC FORMULA

### All the Tea in China

Here's a great shampoo that you can bottle and store for up to two weeks:

2 cups of boiling water

4 chamomile tea bags

4 tablespoons of pure soap flakes

$1\frac{1}{2}$ tablespoons of glycerin

Pour the boiling water into a bowl. Add the tea bags and allow them to steep for 5 to 10 minutes. Remove the tea bags, and add the soap flakes to the remaining liquid. Let stand until the soap becomes soft. Add the glycerin, and mix until well-blended. Pour into a bottle, and store in a cool, dark place.

counter shampoos are detrimental to your hair, weighing it down with all kinds of chemicals. Diluting store-bought shampoo with water will benefit your hair and your pocketbook, although the best way to go is to save even more money and make your own shampoo.

## ENOUGH WITH THE DANDRUFF!

**N**o matter how subtle you try to be, we can all see you brushing those little white flakes off your shoulders. Over-the-counter shampoos may help, but those flakes are resilient little buggers. Here are two all-natural remedies to help you stop looking over your shoulder—literally.

☞ Boil 1 cup of apple cider vinegar, 1 of cup water, and ¼ cup of fresh mint leaves. Strain and pour into an airtight container. Let it cool, then gently massage the solution into your scalp, and allow it to dry. Do not shampoo or rinse for at least 12 hours.

☞ Boil 4 tablespoons of thyme in 1½ cups of water for five minutes. Cool and strain into an airtight container, and store in a cool, dry place. (It'll keep for up to one week.) To use, shampoo your hair normally and towel dry. Pour half the thyme mixture over towel-dried hair. Massage into your scalp thoroughly; do not rinse.

## TAKE A BREAK

**H**ere's something to try in your fight against dandruff—take a break from shampoo. Replace any shampoo you've been using with baking soda for a 30-day period. Just wet your hair, massage a few handfuls of baking soda through your scalp, and rinse. The baking soda will absorb all of the oil from your scalp and loosen the dead skin. It will initially make your hair very dry, but after the 30 days are up, the dandruff will be gone and your hair will be silky and shiny.

## TRY AN OLD STANDBY

**V**inegar—it's good for everything else, so it shouldn't be a surprise that it's also a cure for dandruff. Simply pour 1 cup onto your hair, let it sit for 30 minutes, and then shampoo normally. Repeat this process daily until the dandruff disappears (usually within a few weeks).

# UNDER ONE CONDITION...

Conditioner. Personally, I've never used it. (Just look at me—why would I need conditioner?) But my wife insists on

| FANTASTIC FORMULA |
| --- |
| **Burning the Midnight Oil** |
| Here's a substitute for those hot oil treatments you're always seeing advertised on TV. |
| ½ cup of olive oil<br>½ cup of boiling water |
| Combine the olive oil and boiling water in a bottle with a lid. Wrap a towel around the bottle (to avoid burning yourself), and shake it thoroughly. Let it cool for a few minutes. Then massage the mixture into your hair, being careful not to burn your scalp. Cover your hair with a shower cap or plastic bag, and cover that with a hot towel (preferably just out of the dryer). Leave the mixture on for 30 minutes. Then shampoo as usual. |

it; otherwise, her hair looks like "a wasp's nest." (Those are her words, folks—not mine. I want to live to see my next book!) But you don't need to use store-bought conditioners—a lot of them are animal fat-based and only make your hair oily and greasy, adding deposits that the shampoo is supposed to be taking away. Try this instead:

Beat 1 egg yolk until it thickens. Slowly add ½ teaspoon of olive oil, then ¾ cup of warm water, continuing to beat the mixture well. Store in an airtight container. When you're ready to use it, shampoo your hair normally, then follow with this conditioner. Leave the conditioner on for a few minutes before rinsing thoroughly.

# BOILED IN OIL

Here's another hot oil substitute. Combine 2 tablespoons of olive oil and 2 tablespoons of honey in a small, heat-proof bottle. Then place the bottle inside a cup of hot water to warm it. Apply the warmed oil-and-honey mix to your hair,

**$ BARGAIN ALERT!**

I'll keep on saying it, folks: You don't have to spend a lot of money to keep your hair looking good. Here are a few more moneysaving ideas for terrific tresses:

✦ Don't wash your hair every day. Every two days is more than sufficient and, if you can stand it, twice a week is optimal. Not only is this best for your hair, but it really saves you money on the cost of hair products. (And it makes your homemade ones last longer—not to mention all that hot water you won't be paying for!) Which brings us to…

✦ Don't use hot water to wash and rinse your hair. The cooler, the better—hot water can damage and dry out your hair.

✦ Always use natural-bristle brushes to reduce the static in your hair. Nylon brushes create static, giving you that much-feared "Bride of Frankenstein" look. (Okay, you may not see right away how this one will save you money, 'cause natural-bristle brushes do cost more than plastic ones. But natural bristles will make your hair more manageable, which will save you money on those fancy de-frizzing products you see in the stores.)

✦ Clean your brushes and combs regularly. What good is it to have clean hair, when your accessories are filthy? Just soak them in a little baking soda mixed with warm water once a week or so. Your brushes and combs will be sparkling clean, and you won't be tempted to toss them out and buy new ones.

and massage the concoction into your scalp. Wrap your head in a shower cap, cover it with a warm towel, and wait 30 minutes for the oil to work its magic. Then wash your hair as usual.

## THE POWER OF PROTEIN

**H**ere's a deep conditioning treatment you *can* beat! Beat 1 egg white until foamy, and then add 4 tablespoons of

plain yogurt. Divide your hair into equal sections, and apply the mixture one section at a time. Leave in for 15 minutes, then rinse thoroughly.

## ADD MAYO, HOLD THE MUSTARD

**I**'d always heard that mayonnaise makes a good hair conditioner. Turns out, those old wives' tales are true. Simply shampoo your hair normally, towel dry, and massage regular mayonnaise (not the miracle salad dressing stuff) into your hair. Let it sit for 15 minutes or so, shampoo again, and rinse thoroughly.

## SPLITTING HAIRS

If I've heard it once, I've heard it a million times: "I'm just going to get all the split ends cut off." Now that doesn't sound like a big deal, but in the worst case, you could be talking about chopping off as much as 6 inches of hair! Before you let your mane get that out of control, try one of these recipes to tame split ends:

**Sweet and spicy.** Wash hair normally and towel dry. Combine 1 teaspoon of honey with 2 tablespoons of garlic oil. Then beat in 1 egg yolk. Rub the mixture into your hair a small section at a time. Then cover your hair with a shower cap (or a plastic bag) for 30 minutes. Rinse thoroughly, then shampoo as usual.

**Overnight oil.** Massage your hair with 1 cup of warm olive oil. Cover your hair with a shower cap or plastic bag, and then cover with a towel. Secure the towel well, and leave it on overnight. In the morning, shampoo your hair normally, and rinse with a 50/50 mix of white vinegar and water.

## SPRAY FOR STRAYS

Some people prefer to let their hair blow where it may. But for those of you looking for something to keep those stray hairs from wandering, check out this citrus hair spray concoction:

Finely chop one peeled orange. Add it to 2 cups of boiling water. Boil until about half of the original amount of liquid remains. Cool, strain out the oranges, and store the remaining liquid in a spray bottle. If it becomes too sticky, you can add a little more water. If you plan to keep it around a while, add 1 ounce of rubbing alcohol, and store the spray in the refrigerator. It'll keep for 2 to 3 weeks.

## LET'S GEL

For a great hair gel, simply mix unflavored gelatin with half as much water as the instructions specify. It'll allow you to sculpt your hair into nearly any style.

# THAT'LL BE THE DAY... THAT I DYE

**W**hen my wife first started coloring her hair, she went to a salon. "After all," she rationalized, "anything worth doing is worth doing right." But is it really worth doing at 50 bucks a pop? (And that was a bargain, folks—a lot of salons in town charged $60 for coloring.)

That led me to do a little research and, sure enough, I've come up with homemade coloring alternatives that cost next to nothing, yet work as effectively as anything you'll find in a salon. Whether you believe blondes have more fun, or are just looking to cover up the gray, I've got a little something for everyone!

## Blonde Highlights

★ Combine 1 cup of lemon juice with 3 cups of brewed (and cooled) chamomile tea. Pour over damp hair, and then head outdoors. Sit in the sun for an hour or so, and then rinse thoroughly.

---

## FANTASTIC FORMULA

### Lemon-Fresh Hair Spray

2 cups of water

2 lemons

1 tablespoon of vodka

Boil the water in a saucepot. While the water is boiling, peel and finely chop the lemons. Add the lemons to the boiling water, and simmer over low heat until the lemons are soft. Cool, strain, and pour into a spray bottle. Add the vodka, and shake well. If the hair spray is too sticky, dilute it with a little water.

---

Follow up with a good conditioner. Repeat until you reach the desired shade.

★ Combine 3 tablespoons of chopped rhubarb with 3 cups of hot water. Simmer for 10 minutes, strain, cool, and then use as a rinse after each shampoo.

## Red Highlights

★ After shampooing, rinse with strong black coffee (cooled) or strong rosehip tea (also cooled). Leave the tea on your hair for 15 minutes, and then rinse thoroughly with cool water.

### Brunette Highlights

★ Cook an unpeeled potato in boiling water. Cool it in the pot until the water is tepid.

---

## OTHER HAIR-BRAINED SCHEMES

\* \* \* \* \*

You didn't think I was through with my hair-coloring ideas, did you? Take a gander at this list of tasty hair solutions:

✦ Have teenagers that are dyeing for a new color? Don't let them waste their money (or yours!) at expensive salons. Powdered drink mixes (Kool-Aid, Tang, etc.) and food coloring provide safe, natural, and—most importantly—*temporary* solutions! Mix with about half as much water as recommended to make a drink (or dilute food coloring until you like the color), then apply to hair. Leave on until it's reached the desired color intensity, then rinse with cool water.

✦ Are you facing a recession—of hair, that is? Simmer ½ cup of dried catnip in 2 cups of water for about 20 minutes, then steep for several hours. Strain, then use the catnip water as a rinse after each shampoo to promote hair growth and shine.

✦ Want to help make thinning hair fuller? Boil 1 tablespoon of dried rosemary in water, and let it steep for three hours. Strain, cool, then use as a rinse after shampooing. It won't work miracles, but it will do the trick over time.

---

Dip a pastry brush into the water, and use it to saturate your hair (being careful not to get any in your eyes or on your skin). Leave the potato water on your hair for 30 minutes; then rinse thoroughly with cool water.

### To Cover Gray

★ Combine 1 tablespoon of apple cider vinegar with 1 gallon of warm water, and use as a final rinse after each shampoo.

★ Simmer ½ cup of dried sage in 2 cups of water for 20 minutes; remove from the stove, and steep for several hours. Strain, then apply the sage water to damp hair. Let your hair dry completely, then rinse thoroughly. Repeat weekly until you reach the desired hue, and then repeat monthly to maintain the color.

# Affordable Skin Care

**What's the largest organ in the human body? Most people think it's the large intestine, which, uncoiled, runs several feet long. But that's wrong!**

It's your skin, which is a living, breathing organ that needs all kinds of maintenance to work right. And the good news is, it doesn't have to be expensive maintenance! From cosmetics to cleansers, I've got the scoop on affordable skin care. Read on.

## STRETCH YOUR COSMETICS

**M**ake those expensive store-bought cosmetics last as long as possible by following these simple suggestions:

☞ Put your eyeliner and lip pencils in the freezer for 20 minutes before sharpening them. They won't break as easily.

☞ Mix a small amount of water with your foundation before applying; it'll help the supply last longer, and it'll go on your skin more smoothly.

☞ Use a lipstick brush to get at that hard-to-reach residue at the bottom of a tube. This can extend the life of your lipstick by up to 50 percent!

## HOMEMADE BEAUTY

**D**on't spend big bucks on beauty products you can make at home. Here are three easy-as-pie substitutes:

☑ Instead of buying colored lip gloss, just apply a thin layer of petroleum jelly over your lipstick. It works just as well, plus it prevents chapping

**ONLINE STEALS & DEALS**

**Ladies, you're gonna love this! Next time you're** near a computer, log on to **www.free-makeup-samples.com.** As the name implies, you can request free—that's right, free—samples from nationally known cosmetic companies. And, as if that weren't enough, you can also register for free beauty catalogs and peruse the site's natural beauty tips. So check it out—you'll be glad you did, and your husband will be even gladder!

and cold sores! Use it alone for that natural look.

✔ Out of face powder? Use cornstarch, instead. (But be careful—if you use too much, you'll look like you stepped out of 1776!)

✔ Keep stray eyebrows going in the right direction by applying a little petroleum jelly or hair gel—they work just as well as those high-priced, eyebrow-taming gels.

## THIS ONE'S REALLY CORNY

This works well to clean oily skin: Pour a little liquid castile soap into the palm of

### FANTASTIC FORMULA

**Milky Way Skin Cleanser**

Here's a cleanser that's great for oily skin.

½ cup of buttermilk

2 tablespoons of crushed fennel seeds

Combine the milk and fennel seeds, and heat in the top portion of a double boiler for 30 minutes. Turn off the heat, and let the mixture steep for three hours. Strain, cool, and pour into a bottle. Keep refrigerated.

your hand, and add about 1 teaspoon of cornmeal. Massage it into your face until it lathers, being careful to avoid your eyes. Rinse with warm water, and pat dry.

If you've got dry skin, substitute 1 teaspoon of honey for the cornmeal.

## FACE THE FACTS

When washing your face, don't overscrub! Overscrubbing can irritate your skin and cause it to break out. Instead, wash gently with a circular motion—you may not even want to use a washcloth. Your fingertips work just as well, and there's less chance of irritation.

## DRINK UP!

This is a skin-care must: Drink lots of water. You can put all kinds of products on your skin to keep it healthy, but it's what's inside that counts. Besides, water is the cheapest beauty trick there is!

# A WRINKLE IN TIME

**M**ost people don't find crow's feet or laugh lines (or any facial lines, for that matter) anything to laugh about. Here are a few tips to help eliminate those seemingly inevitable wrinkles and lines:

★ Apply egg whites to the lines under your eyes and around your mouth. It temporarily tightens up the skin as it dries, decreasing the appearance of fine lines.

★ Here's another one for those wrinkles around the eyes: Dab a little castor oil in the creases. This will also work on folds around the throat.

★ For overall skin rejuvenation, prick 3 to 5 vitamin E capsules, and drain the contents into a small bowl. Add 2 teaspoons of plain yogurt, $\frac{1}{2}$ teaspoon of honey, and $\frac{1}{2}$ teaspoon of lemon juice. Apply to your face with a cotton ball or tissue. Leave on your skin for about 10 minutes, and then rinse thoroughly with warm water.

---

## FANTASTIC FORMULA

### Almond Joy Cleanser

Give dry skin a moisturizing drink with this cleanser.

2 tablespoons of almonds
2 tablespoons of milk
$\frac{1}{2}$ teaspoon of flour
$\frac{1}{2}$ teaspoon of honey

Chop the almonds in a blender, slowly adding the milk, flour, and honey. Blend until a thick paste forms. Massage the concoction into your skin, and rinse with warm water.

---

# MARVELOUS MOISTURIZERS

**M**oisturizers are supposed to be the key to supple, young-looking skin. Here are a few alternatives to those expensive, store-bought concoctions:

**Peaches and cream.** Peel a large, ripe peach. Mash it through a sieve to get as much juice as possible. Then mix the peach juice with an equal amount of fresh cream. Massage a small amount into your skin. Refrigerate any unused portion, and use within a week.

**Eggcelente.** Combine 1 egg yolk with $\frac{3}{4}$ cup of milk. Apply

# FAVORITE FACIALS

**\* \* \* \* \***

Most women swear by facials. Some do it to look younger, while others just like the way their skin feels when they're done. There are all kinds of natural formulas for facials out there, and my wife has tried just about all of them. Here are some of her favorites:

## Go Bananas

1 banana
1 avocado

Using a blender, make a puree of the banana and avocado. Apply the mixture to your skin, and leave it on for at least 20 minutes. Rinse with warm water, and pat dry. If you have dry skin, follow with a moisturizer.

## Fruit Loops

6 strawberries
1/2 pear
1/2 apple
1 ounce of orange juice
Honey

Puree the fruits with the orange juice in a blender. Apply a thin layer of honey to your face, then apply the fruit mixture. Leave it on your skin for at least 30 minutes, then rinse with warm water, and pat dry.

## Sweet Avocado

2 tablespoons of mashed avocado
2 tablespoons of honey
1 egg yolk

Mix all the ingredients together thoroughly, and apply to your face. Leave it on your skin for 30 minutes, rinse with warm water, and pat dry.

## Sweet Avocado: Take 2

2 tablespoons of mashed avocado
1 tablespoon of crushed almonds
1/2 teaspoon of honey

Combine all the ingredients until creamy. Apply to your skin, and leave on for 30 minutes or so. Rinse with warm water, then pat dry.

to your face with your finger-tips, using a circular motion. Leave it on for about five minutes. Store any unused portion in the refrigerator, and use within a week.

**Oil of olive.** Rub olive oil (or peanut, sesame, or avocado oil) on your face for a natural moisturizer. Leave it on for about 10 minutes, then rinse with warm water, and pat dry.

# BYE-BYE TO BOTHERSOME BLEMISHES

**P**imples and blackheads aren't just problems for teens. Here's how to conceal and eliminate bothersome blemishes.

**Part with Pimples**

★ Peel and mash six cloves of garlic. Apply to the affected areas (avoiding the eyes). Leave on for about 10 minutes. Rinse with warm water, and pat dry.

★ Apply a little wine with a cotton ball to the affected areas (white for a fair complexion, red for a darker complexion). Then toast to your clearer skin.

---

**FANTASTIC FORMULA**

**Ahhh Aftershave**

All right guys—this one's for you. Here's an easy recipe for aftershave that will make the women in your life go "Ahhh."

2 cups of rubbing alcohol

1 tablespoon of glycerin

1 tablespoon of dried lavender

1 teaspoon of dried rosemary

1 teaspoon of ground cloves

Mix all the ingredients well, pour into a bottle with a tight-fitting cap, and refrigerate. Shake well before using, and strain as you use it. This aftershave will keep, refrigerated, for up to two months.

---

★ Make a paste of equal parts baking soda and wheat germ, plus a little water. Rub onto the affected areas, and leave on for about 10 minutes. Rinse with warm water, and pat dry.

★ Squeeze the juice from a lemon, and dilute it with a little water. Dab it on the affected areas with a cotton ball or tissue. Don't rinse; just pat dry.

### Banish Blackheads

★ Make a paste of oatmeal and water. Apply directly to the affected areas. Leave on for about 10 minutes, rinse with warm water, and pat dry.

★ Rub affected areas with a slice or two of tomato.

★ Make a paste of oatmeal, honey, and egg white. Apply to your skin, and let it sit for 10 minutes or so. Rinse with warm water, and pat dry.

★ Heat a little honey and apply it directly to the affected areas. Let it sit for a minute or two, then wash it off with warm water and rinse with cool water. Pat dry.

### GOT FRECKLES?

* * * * *

Why is it that people who don't have freckles think they're so darn adorable, but people who do have them wish they didn't? If you're flocked with freckles that haven't faded with age, try this favorite remedy. Dissolve a little sugar in 2 tablespoons of lemon juice. Apply the mixture to each freckle with a cotton ball or tissue. Repeat this process once every couple of days, and the freckles should fade—fast!

## BROWN SPOTS BE GONE!

Nothing can turn back the hands of time, but you can diminish the appearance of brown spots on your hands and face. Try this regimen: Apply vitamin E to the spots daily. At night, apply castor oil. The spots will begin to fade after a few weeks.

## Savings to Smile About

I'm sure you've heard that baking soda makes a great toothpaste, and it does— but it's even more effective when combined with other common household products. Here's more great ideas on alternatives to store-bought toothpastes and mouthwashes.

## THE POWER OF $H_2O$

It's important to brush your teeth, and it's a good idea to floss and use mouthwash. But did you know that the best way to guard against cavities and tooth decay is to drink lots of water? Why? Because, unlike when I was growing up, the public drinking water in most communities today contains fluoride. Many of the bottled waters available in stores also contain fluoride. And fluoride is the most powerful weapon against tooth-decay out there. So drink up!

# WHITER WHITES

**T**his concoction might seem a bit gritty, but it's great for whitening your teeth. Just combine 1 tablespoon of honey with 1 tablespoon of ground charcoal. Your smile will be sweeter and your teeth will be whiter in no time at all.

# STRAWBERRY FIELDS FOREVER

**O**kay, I admit that this "toothpaste" description had me scratching my head, but don't knock it 'til you try it! Simply mash three large strawberries, and then use as you would any other toothpaste. Rinse well to get out any little seed parts. It'll leave your teeth feeling fresh and clean. Try it—I'm not kidding!

## TOTALLY TOOTHPASTE

\* \* \* \* \*

In a pinch, baking soda will clean your teeth effectively. But clean teeth are only half of the equation—you also want fresh breath. Here are a few of my favorite homemade toothpaste recipes that'll have your breath kissin' sweet. As with any toothpaste, be careful not to ingest the ingredients.

### Hydromatic!

1 teaspoon of baking soda
$1/4$ teaspoon of hydrogen peroxide

Combine the ingredients into a paste, and brush your teeth. Your mouth will feel squeaky clean.

### Perfect Peppermint

$1\frac{1}{2}$ teaspoons of baking soda
1 teaspoon of glycerin
4 drops of peppermint oil
Dash of salt

Combine the ingredients until you achieve a toothpaste consistency. This one's my all-time favorite—you'll love how fresh your mouth feels!

# BASIC BREATH FRESHENERS

**I**f you're one of those folks who plunks down a dollar a week on those little tins of breath mints, keep George Washington in your pocket with these substitutes:

☞ Chew fresh parsley after a meal. It contains an antiseptic that kills tooth-decay causing bacteria.

☞ Chew fennel seeds or anise seeds—both are instant breath fresheners.

☞ Drink a nice hot cup of peppermint tea.

☞ Dip a toothpick in peppermint oil, and chew on that for a while. (This is perfect for after meals.)

## FANTASTIC FORMULA

### Magnificent Mouthwash

Mouthwash is one of the most unnecessary purchases you can make, because it's just so darned easy to make your own. Here's one of my favorite recipes:

$^3/_4$ cup of vodka
20 drops of lemon juice
Distilled water

Combine the vodka and lemon juice in a bottle with a tight cap, shake well, and allow it to sit for one week at room temperature. When you're ready to use it, dilute with 2 parts distilled water to 1 part mixture. Gargle with this, and you'll have fresh breath like never before. (For a nonalcoholic mouthwash, see page 312.)

# The Best of the Rest

**So far we've covered your hair, skin, and teeth, but how about those eyes? Those feet? Those fingernails? In this section, I'll share my homegrown hints on everything from how to shrink swollen, puffy eyes to recipes for hand cream and fingernail treatments.**

# GREAT EYE-DEAS

**T**hey say the eyes are the windows to your soul. And maybe they are, but who can tell through those dark circles and all that puffiness? If you've got dark circles or puffy eyes, here's how to make those peepers look like a million bucks—on the cheap, of course!

## Dark Circles

★ Cut a fresh fig in half. Then lie down in a comfortable place, and put one fig half over each eye for about 10 minutes.

★ Wrap a grated, raw potato in cheesecloth, and apply to your eyelids for 20 minutes. Then rinse with warm water.

★ Cut two cucumber slices, lie down in a comfortable place, and put one cucumber over each eye for about 10 minutes.

## Puffy, Swollen Eyes

★ Soak two herbal tea bags in cool water, lie down in a comfortable place, and put a tea bag over each eye for about 15 minutes.

★ Put 4 tablespoons of grated raw potato in a wet cloth. Lie down in a comfortable place,

**FANTASTIC FORMULA**

**Terrific Tootsie Treat**

Pamper your toes with this soothing potion.

> 1 ripe banana
>
> 2 tablespoons of honey
>
> 2 tablespoons of margarine
>
> 1 tablespoon of lemon juice

Smash the banana. Then add the rest of the ingredients, and mix until creamy. Massage onto clean, dry feet, paying particular attention to any cracked, flaky areas. Pull on a pair of cotton socks, and wear overnight. (This works for dry hands, too.)

and put the cloth over your eyes for about 15 minutes. Rinse with cold water.

★ Take two metal spoons, and run them under cold water. Place the bowl of one spoon over each eye for about 60 seconds.

★ Apply hemorrhoid cream to the puffy areas. (Don't laugh—it works on those other puffy areas….)

## Tired, Irritated Eyes

★ Soak two cotton balls or a soft cloth in cold skim milk,

lie down in a comfortable place, and put one cotton ball over each eye for 10 minutes. Rinse with warm, then cool, water.

★ Soak two cotton balls in ice water, lie down in a comfortable place, and put one cotton ball over each eye for about five minutes.

# HAND IT OVER

As you well know, working in the yard and garden can make your hands really rough. But the cost of those store-bought, super-duper hand lotions can put your budget in bad shape! Here's a make-it-yourself concoction that'll leave your hands soft and smooth, while leaving money in your wallet. Combine 1 tablespoon of dried rosemary, 2 tablespoons of dried chamomile flowers, and 4 cups of water. Boil in a small, uncovered pan over medium heat for about 10 minutes. Cool to room temperature, and then strain. Store in a bottle and refrigerate. Apply with a cotton ball (or, if you have a spray bottle, you can spray it on instead), and let your hands air dry.

# TOUGH AS NAILS

When you're pampering your hands, don't overlook your nails. They need some special attention to look their best. Here's how:

☞ Combine 2 teaspoons of castor oil, 2 teaspoons of salt, and 1 teaspoon of wheat germ. Mix well, and pour into a bottle. Shake well before using. Apply to nails with a cotton ball to strengthen them and give them shine.

☞ Beat 1 egg yolk in a small bowl; soak your fingernails for about five minutes, then rinse and buff dry.

☞ Mix 1 tablespoon of castile soap and 1 cup of water in a small bowl. Soak hands and nails for about 10 minutes, then rinse and dry.

☞ To quickly dry fingernail polish, dip your painted nails in ice water several times. The polish will harden much faster than by air drying.

# More Fantastic Formulas!

Once again, we're coming to the end of the road, but you know me—I always believe in a strong finish! Try these tips and tonics on for size.

## A BALANCING ACT

**P**eople often use the term "pH balanced" when they talk about skin care, but what does it really mean? The term refers to skin that is perfectly balanced—no dry areas, no oily areas, and nothing shiny or flaky. But most of us have combination skin, and a simple cleanser can help restore a sense of balance to your face. Here's the recipe for the best balancer I've ever found. (My wife swears by it.)

Combine 3 cups of distilled water with ½ cup of apple cider vinegar. Apply evenly to your face with a cotton ball, avoiding the eye area. (It won't do any permanent eye damage, but it'll burn like the dickens!)

## ASTRINGENTS AND TIGHTENERS AND TONERS, OH MY!

**I**'m always amazed at what people think they need to buy to take care of their skin. Astringents? Toners? What are these things? From what I can tell, astringents, tighteners, and toners all pretty much function the same way—they remove dirt and other particles from skin and they close up pores. If you think you need this for your skin, don't waste your

---

### ☕ FANTASTIC FORMULA

**All Eyes on You**

Here's a great formula for a gentle and soothing eye-makeup remover:

1 tablespoon of olive oil
1 tablespoon of castor oil
2 teaspoons of canola oil

Mix all of the ingredients together. Apply with a tissue or cotton ball to remove eye shadow, eyeliner, or mascara safely and without irritation.

money on the store-bought versions. Try these instead:

**Go suck on a lemon!**
Combine ½ cup of lemon juice, 1 cup of distilled water, and ⅓ cup of witch hazel. Pour into a clean bottle, and shake well. Apply with a cotton ball or tissue. (Shake well before each application.)

**Sage advice.** Steep 4 teaspoons of dried sage in 4 teaspoons of vodka for 2 weeks. Strain. Dissolve ¼ teaspoon of

borax in 3 teaspoons of witch hazel, then stir in the vodka/sage liquid and 3 to 4 teaspoons of honey. Pour into a clean bottle, and shake well. Apply with a cotton ball or tissue. (Shake well before each application.)

# IT'S MILLER TIME

**M**ake hair more manageable and add shine to spiritless hair by combining 1 cup of warm water with 3 cups of beer. Use as a final rinse. Blot gently with a towel. (And don't worry—you won't smell like a brewery. The beer smell will disappear as your hair dries.)

# YOU OLD SALT

**H**ere's a quick and easy formula for basic bath salts. Mix together 1 cup each of table salt, Epsom salts, and baking soda. Store in an airtight container at room temperature. To use, add about 2 tablespoons to your bath water. If you'd like, you can add a few drops of your favorite essential oil as the tub fills.

---

## FANTASTIC FORMULA

### Face the World

Here's a great face cleanser that works well for oily skin *and* won't break the bank.

2 cups of rolled oats

1 cup of almonds

2 teaspoons of dried peppermint

2 teaspoons of dried lavender

Combine the ingredients in a blender or food processor and chop until they form a fine powder. Mix a heaping teaspoon of the mixture with just enough water to make a paste, and then massage gently into your skin, avoiding your eyes. Rinse with warm water, and pat dry. Store in a covered container.

# RUB-A-DUB-DUB

\* \* \* \* \*

Bubble baths. Milk baths. Bath oils. All are music to a woman's ears. Well, now you don't have to wait for Calgon to take you away; you can do it yourself using products you'll find throughout your house. Here are a few simple recipes:

## Luxurious Bath Oil

> 2 cups of milk
> 1 cup of honey
> 1 cup of salt
> ¼ cup of baking soda
> ½ cup of baby oil

Combine the milk, honey, salt, and baking soda in a large bowl. Fill your bathtub with water, and pour in the mixture, then add the baby oil (and, if you'd like, a few drops of your favorite fragrance for scent).

## Soothing Bath Oil

> 1 egg
> ¼ cup of milk
> ½ cup of baby oil
> ¼ cup of vodka
> 2 tablespoons of honey

Mix the ingredients in a blender for 45 seconds. Fill your bathtub with water and pour in the mixture. Store leftovers in an airtight container in the refrigerator.

## Bring on the Bubbles!

> 1 gallon of water
> 2 cups of soap flakes
> ½ cup of glycerin
> 2 cups of shampoo
> Scented oil of your choice
> (optional)

Mix the water, soap, and 2 tablespoons of the glycerin in a pot over low heat, stirring until the soap flakes have dissolved. In a large bowl, add this mixture to the rest of the glycerin, the shampoo and, if you'd like, scented oil. Store in quart containers at room temperature. To use, add about 1 cup to your bathwater as the tub is filling.

## The Milky Way

> 2 cups of dry milk powder
> 1 cup of cornstarch
> Scented oil of your choice
> (optional)

Mix all of the ingredients in a blender. Store in an airtight container at room temperature. To use, add ½ cup to hot bath water, and enjoy.

# SESAME SCRUB

This facial scrub for dry skin is simple. Just apply a little sesame oil to your face and neck. Scrub gently with a warm, damp wash cloth. Rinse with warm water, and pat dry.

# EGGSTRAORDINARY

If you're battling oily skin, here's a mix that can't be beat! Mix 1 beaten egg white

---

**FANTASTIC FORMULA**

### Creamy Chamomile Cleanser

Here's a gentle cleanser that works well for dry and sensitive skin.

⅓ cup of heavy cream

⅓ cup of milk

2 tablespoons of dried chamomile
    flowers

Simmer the ingredients in the top portion of a double boiler for 30 minutes. Turn off the heat, and let steep for three hours. Strain out the flowers, let the remaining liquid cool, and then refrigerate in a bottle with a tight cap. To use, apply evenly to your face using a circular motion, rinse with warm water, and pat dry.

---

with the juice from half a lemon. Apply gently to your face, avoiding your eyes. Leave it on for about 15 minutes, rinse with warm water, and pat dry.

# WHITE, WHEAT, OR RYE?

I don't know how you take your sandwiches, but when it comes to taking care of your face, trust me—it's wheat you want! Add 1 teaspoon of wheat germ to a palm full of honey. Mix between your hands, and apply gently to your face. Leave it on about five minutes, rinse with warm water, and pat dry. This formula works well for oily or blemished skin.

# OATMEAL—NOT JUST FOR BREAKFAST ANYMORE!

Who says oatmeal's only for eating? Not me! It also makes a great facial cleanser for oily skin. Give this a try: Combine enough water to ½ cup of uncooked oatmeal to make a creamy paste. Apply to your face using a circular motion. Leave it on for 20 minutes or so, rinse with warm water, and pat dry.

## PORE SHRINKER

**H**ere's a simple mix that will tighten up enlarged pores. Mix a little buttermilk and table salt into a paste. Apply to your face, and massage well. Leave it on for about five minutes, rinse with warm water, and pat dry.

## Y NOT YOGURT?

**T**his one's an easy answer for oily skin. Get yourself a small container of plain yogurt and rub a few tablespoons of it directly onto your face. Let it sit for 10 minutes or so, rinse with warm water, and pat dry. If you wish, you can add a little oatmeal to make it a scrub.

## COOL AS A CUCUMBER

**H**ere's a soothing facial for all skin types. Puree half of a cucumber in a blender. Mix in 1 tablespoon of plain yogurt,

---

### FANTASTIC FORMULA

#### Oranges and Oats

Here's a face-wash recipe that's perfect for all skin types, and you can put it together in a flash.

1 cup of uncooked oatmeal
1 cup of almonds
1 cup of dried orange peel

Place the ingredients in a blender or food processor and chop until they form a fine powder. Place some in the palm of your hand, and add a few drops of water to moisten. Rub gently onto your face, being careful not to get any in your eyes. Rinse with warm water, and pat dry. Store in an airtight container at room temperature.

---

apply to your face, and leave on for about 30 minutes. Rinse with warm water, and pat dry.

## PERFECT PAPAYA

**I**f you've got dry, flaky skin, don't despair. This concoction will give your skin the moisture it needs at a fraction of the cost of those store-bought moisturizers. Simply puree one papaya using a blender or food processor.

## FANTASTIC FORMULA

### Alcohol-Free Mouthwash

Here's a mouthwash recipe that doesn't contain any alcohol, but I guarantee that it'll make your mouth wake up and take notice!

2 cups of distilled water
1 teaspoon of dried rosemary leaves
1 teaspoon of fresh mint leaves
1 teaspoon of dried anise seeds

Boil the water, add the herbs and seeds, and steep for 15 minutes. Cool, strain, and bottle. Store in the refrigerator between uses. (You can double or triple the recipe to suit your needs.)

## FANTASTIC FORMULA

### Foot Soother and Smoother

Say good-bye to rough, cracked skin on your feet with this soothing solution.

1 tablespoon of almond oil
1 tablespoon of olive oil
1 teaspoon of wheat germ

Combine the ingredients and store in a bottle with a tight cap. Shake well before using. Rub generously into feet and heels, especially the dry parts. Your tootsies will love you for it!

Then gently rub the smashed papaya onto your face, being careful not to get any in your eyes. Rinse with warm water, and pat dry. Refrigerate any unused papaya in a sealed container for up to three days.

# CARROT FACIAL

This incredible, edible formula makes a great facial for oily skin—just be sure to try it on an inconspicuous spot, first, to be sure it won't cause your skin to turn slightly (and temporarily!) orange.

Boil 3 large carrots until they're soft. Mash them, and add 5 tablespoons of honey. Massage gently onto your face, using a circular motion, and leave on for 20 minutes or so. Rinse with warm water, and pat dry. Discard any of the remaining carrot mash.

# CHAPTER 13

# The Great Outdoors

Back when I finally said good-bye to apartment living and bought my first little house, Grandma Putt sent me a card congratulating me on this major rite of passage. She signed it with one of her classic reminders (only semi-tongue-in-cheek). It said, "Renters work from sun to sun, but a homeowner's work is never done." Well, folks, over the years, I've learned how true that old saying is! But I've also learned how to keep that never-ending maintenance from taking such a big chunk out of the old bank account.

In Chapter 5, I told you how to stake your claim on your own piece of the great outdoors without spending a fortune. Now, I'm going to let you in on some of my frugal secrets for keeping your home's exterior in tip-top shape. So, let's get to it!

# Outdoor Housekeeping

As I've said many times, Grandma Putt was a real stickler for keeping the house neat and tidy—and take it from me, friends: Her good housekeeping didn't stop at the front door (or the back door, for that matter). She made sure that the outside of our house stayed as spic-and-span as the inside. In this section, I'm going to pass along some of Grandma Putt's old-fangled methods for outdoor housekeeping, along with a scrub bucket full of tips and tricks that I've picked up myself over the years.

## Siding Secrets

No matter what it's made of, the face your house presents to the world needs attention now and then if it's going to look its best and do its job of keeping Mother Nature's elements at bay. Here are some of my favorite methods for keeping exterior siding in tip-top shape.

## CLEAN UP ITS ACT

If your aluminum or vinyl siding is in good shape, all it needs is an annual cleaning.

Start by giving it a good, strong spray from a garden hose. Then, go at any spots with a scrub brush and a solution of ¼ cup of laundry detergent and 2 gallons of water.

Whatever you do, though, don't use abrasive cleansers on aluminum siding—they could easily damage the finish. They're fine on vinyl siding, though, because the color isn't just surface-deep, as it is with aluminum—it actually permeates the vinyl.

# POWER UP

If your siding has gotten *really* dirty, or if you're prepping it for painting, rent some power-washing gear, and let 'er rip. Try to schedule your cleanup for a weekday—you're likely to get a better deal on the price. If the minimum rental period is a full day and it won't take you that long to finish your house, see if you can find a neighbor who'd like to go halfsies on the time—and the cost.

# BLAST!

Be careful when you're wielding your power-washing wand on aluminum siding. Too much water pressure can make the surface coating buckle and peel. If you do get a tad carried away, though, don't despair—you can patch up bald spots in no time. Here's what you'll need:

✔ 600-grit sandpaper (from the bodywork section of an auto-parts store)

✔ Exterior spray paint that's the same color as your siding

✔ A transparent sealer such as Plasti Dip Spray-On (available at hardware stores)

## FANTASTIC FORMULA

### Super Siding Solution

For really stubborn spots, use this super-simple recipe.

3 quarts of water

1 quart of household bleach

⅔ cup of TSP (trisodium phosphate, found in paint and hardware stores)

⅓ cup of laundry detergent

Mix the ingredients together in a bucket. Use to wash the siding, then immediately rinse it down with a hose.

Sand the damaged area so that it blends smoothly with the surrounding siding. Then spray on the paint. When it's dry, apply the Plasti Dip according to the instructions on the can, and *presto*, your siding's as good as new!

# DENT REPAIR

If you wind up with a dent in your aluminum siding, you can patch it up using an auto-body filler such as Bondo. Just follow the instructions on the product label, then sand and paint the spot as described in "Blast!" at left.

# Hello, Old Paint

As every owner of a wood-frame house knows, it takes more than a garden hose to keep these babies looking their best. Every so often, the house all but speaks up and shouts "Paint me—*now!*" And there's no doubt about it: Even a vinyl- or aluminum-clad house gets a whole new lease on life when it's sporting a fresh coat of paint.

Even when you're hiring seasoned pros to paint your house, it pays to know a thing or three about the process. After all, when you pride yourself on being a cheapskate, you sure as shootin' want to make sure that your work crew is covering all the bases!

## GIVE IT THE BRUSH-ON

Never spray-paint your house. Exterior walls need the protection of a thick, brushed-on coat. To get paint to come out of a sprayer, you have to thin the stuff so much that your walls wind up wearing more thinner than paint. Furthermore, sprayed-on paint doesn't adhere well to the surface, which means that within a year or so, you could find yourself forking out cash for a whole new paint job.

## DON'T SCRIMP

There are times when it doesn't pay to pinch pennies *too* hard, and paint-shopping time is one of them. Resist the temptation to buy a bargain-basement brand. Why? Because premium-quality paints hold up better and longer than their low-priced counterparts, and they're more likely to

## ODOR-B-GONE

\* \* \* \* \*

Even when you use them outdoors, oil-based paints and primers pack an odor wallop. But here's how to make that smell vanish like a quarter in a magician's hand: Just pour half of a small bottle of vanilla extract into the gallon can, and mix it in. The vanilla will reduce the paint odor dramatically. This formula works just as well with indoor paint, too.

give you the coverage you need in just one coat. And that's a bargain, if you ask me!

# ALWAYS SPEAK UP

**G**randma Putt used to say, "The only dumb question is the one you don't ask." Well, that's sure true of painting (and I've learned that the hard way!). If you're planning to tackle a paint job yourself and you're new to the game, find a paint dealer that caters to professionals. Then, drop by for a visit. Explain the project you have in mind, and ask for help in finding the gear you need. I've found that most of the people who work in these stores are happy to share their knowledge about materials, tools, and techniques. Here's a quartet of tips for getting the most out of asking for help:

1. Try to visit during the store's least-busy period. Normally, that's mid-morning or early afternoon on weekdays. Early in the morning, professional painters will be stocking up on supplies for the day. In late afternoons and on weekends, the staff will have their hands full helping your fellow do-it-yourselfers.

---

## ALL IN GOOD ORDER

\* \* \* \* \*

It's fine to apply latex over oil-based paint. But don't do the reverse, or you'll be asking for trouble because oil-based paint doesn't adhere well to latex.

---

2. Make it clear that you want a high-quality, long-lasting paint job, but you don't want to invest more money in the project than you need to.

3. Come prepared. Before you leave home, jot down the dimensions of the surfaces you'll be painting, as well as their composition (wood, vinyl- or aluminum-siding, stucco, or whatever), what kind of paint or stain (if any) is on them now, and what condition it's in. If you know when the walls were last painted, note that, too.

4. Buy your supplies from that dealer. Don't just take notes and then run off to the

discount store, thinking you'll save a few bucks. Not only would that be rude, but you'd be turning your back on a true bargain: the helpful service and working knowledge that can save you from costly mistakes. It's saved me a bundle on more than one occasion!

## AW, SKIP IT!

**H**ere's a neat trick I learned from a house-painter neighbor of Grandma Putt's: When you're painting stairs, like the ones leading to your porch, paint every second step. When those have dried completely, go back and paint the ones in between. That way, you'll be able to climb those stairs simply by taking two steps at a time, skipping over the wet ones.

## PRIME TIME

**A** good primer, properly applied, can mean the difference between a long-lasting paint job and one that gets flaky before its time. Before you (or your helpers) pick up a brush, keep these pointers in mind:

**Make 'em two of a kind.** For best results, use the same brand of primer and top-coat paint. Although all paint products of the same type are pretty much alike, each manufacturer adds its own set of ingredients to ensure performance factors like good surface adherence, mildew resistance, and shelf life. If you mix brands, some of those chemical additives could clash, making your paint job age prematurely.

**Surface matters.** If you'll be applying latex over old coats of oil-based paint, use an oil-based primer that's especially made to work with latex paint. (And make sure you wash and prepare the surface thoroughly before you begin.)

**It's all in the timing.** Try to paint your top coat within 48 hours of applying the primer. If that's not possible, just make sure you wait no longer than two weeks to finish your paint job. That timing is crucial because after about 14 days, compounds that form on the primer's surface will prevent the top coat from bonding well.

**Don't stretch it.** Most paints and primers cover about 400 square feet per one-gallon can.

If that's what the instructions on the label say, don't try to squeeze 425 feet out of the gallon. The coat will be too thin, and the top coat may not stick the way it should.

**Resist rust.** If you're painting anything metal, such as drainpipes or metal window frames, use a rust-inhibiting primer for the first coat. Follow up with any good exterior paint or enamel spray paint.

**Block it.** Cover stains, including wood knots, dark paint, old water marks, or mildew, with a stain-blocking primer. Different types are formulated to cover different kinds of stains, so read the labels carefully to make sure you get the right blocker for the job. Otherwise, you'll be throwing your money away.

# BUTTER UP!

Sure, paint thinner and turpentine will take paint off your skin, but there's a cheaper and much more pleasant alternative: Slice a small piece of butter, rub it on the paint spots, and then wipe it off. Those spots will be gone faster than you can say, "Strike three!"

# WHETHER THE WEATHER

There's no question that balmy weather makes outdoor work more pleasant. But when it comes to painting, weather affects a lot more than the painter's comfort level—it can spell the difference

## WHOOPS—THERE IT IS!

\* \* \* \* \*

Like most folks, I always wear my oldest, shabbiest clothes for painting. But once in a while, I accidentally rub up against wet paint or varnish when I'm wearing something that's not part of my painting wardrobe. I've learned, though, that those kinds of blunders needn't spell disaster—but you must act fast, before the spot dries. If the culprit is latex, just wash it out with soap and water. If it's oil-based paint or varnish, follow this routine:

Sponge the spot using the solvent recommended on the paint or varnish label. While the garment is still wet, put it in a solution of $1/4$ cup of dishwashing liquid and 2 gallons of water. Let it soak overnight, then wash it according to the care instructions on its label.

between an exterior paint job that will last for years, and one that will buckle up and peel off in no time flat. A painter can sum up ideal working weather in three words: warm and dry. Beyond that basic dictum, keep these guidelines in mind:

☞ Never paint exterior walls when the temperature is below 50°F or above 90°F, or when the humidity is above 85 percent. If you do, the coats of paint won't bond to each other properly, and you'll have peeling problems down the road.

☞ Don't paint right after a rain or early in the morning before the dew has lifted. Give the siding plenty of time to dry out completely, or the paint won't stick worth beans.

☞ Always try to paint in the shade. Hot, direct sunlight can cause paint to blister. Besides, painting is hard enough work as it is—you don't need to risk sunstroke to boot!

## PAINTING WITH THE PROS

Frankly, as tight with a dime as I am, house painting is one job that I'm happy to pay someone else to do. Not that I cast frugality to the wind, mind you. I always look around until I've found the work crew that will give me the best job for the most reasonable outlay of cash. The variation in prices can be *astounding*, and I've learned the hard way that the painters who charge the most

## NO STRINGS ATTACHED

When you need outdoor painting supplies, your county's solid waste/recycling/environmental services department could be your destination for one-stop shopping. In many communities, contractors and homeowners turn in paint, varnish, thinners, and solvents that they no longer need and that they can't legally dispose of. The appropriate department keeps the stuff until someone else comes along and asks for it. Check your phone directory's Blue Pages for the name and number of the local department in your county.

don't necessarily deliver the best performance. Here are a few ways that I've found quality work at fair prices:

**Check with student-employment offices.** Some of the best paint jobs I've seen have been done by young scholars eager to earn next term's tuition. Don't forget to also check with friends whose college-age sons and daughters will be coming home for the summer.

**Call a few churches.** Many youth and young-adult groups perform all sorts of chores, including painting, and donate the proceeds to charity. That means you may be able to get your house spruced up *and* do a good deed at the same time!

**Ask your neighbors.** When you spot a house with a beautiful, spanking-new paint job, ask who did it and how the crew was to work with. Even if the response is "I wouldn't hire those bums again if my life depended on it!" you'll be ahead of the game—you'll know who *not* to sign up for your job. But the answer just might be "They were great, and worth every dime I paid them." Then you've found your dream team—but act fast, before they're booked solid for the season!

# Through a Glass Lightly

**I once lived in a neighborhood where passing traffic kicked up so much dust and grit that keeping my windows clean could have become a second career! Fortunately, Grandma Putt rode to the rescue once again—or rather, her old-time know-how did. When I was a lad, washing windows was one of my routine chores around our house and, as usual, Grandma taught me just how to get the job done well—and quickly. That lesson has never left me, and now I'm passing it along to you!**

## WINDOW WISDOM

**H**ere's a collection of window-washing tips I learned at Grandma Putt's knee—or, I should say, on her stepladder:

★ Always wash your windows on an overcast day. Sunshine creates streaks.

★ Work from the top down, to avoid streaking and water spots.

★ If you do wind up with water spots on your windows, wipe on a little kerosene. Then rub with crumpled newspaper.

★ Use a sponge to get into corners where dirt and grit tend to build up.

For more tips on window washing, see pages 286–287.

## HAVE YOU HEARD THE NEWS?

**T**here's good news and bad news. The good news is that nowadays, many newspapers are

printed using soy-based inks, which are much less toxic than the old-fashioned, chemical kind. The bad news is that (for reasons I can't figure out) these new-fangled papers don't clean glass as well as the old-timers did. If you find that your newspaper isn't performing as well as it used to, don't write a letter to the editor—just invest in a good squeegee and use that, instead.

## REACH OUT

**B**esides cleaning more effectively than some newspapers, a squeegee has one advantage over all of them: You can fasten it onto a specially made extension rod. That way, you can get at those hard-to-reach windows without risking life and limb. You'll find these extension rods at hardware stores and home centers.

## LOOK, MA, NO SCRATCHES!

**G**ot light scratches on your windowpanes? The solution is probably in your medicine cabinet. (If it's not there,

---

### FANTASTIC FORMULA

**Classic Window Cleaner**

This was Grandma Putt's favorite window cleaner, and for my money, it's still hard to beat for routine washing.

10 parts vinegar

1 part water

Mix the ingredients together and pour the solution into a spray bottle. Then spritz your windows, and wipe them with newspaper.

you'll find it in the pharmacy section at the discount store.) It's toothpaste. Just squeeze a little mildly abrasive toothpaste—not the gel kind—onto a soft, cotton flannel cloth, and rub the scratches very lightly until they vanish. By the way, this technique works equally well on mirrors.

# SAVE ME!

Don't toss out that cracked window pane—at least, not until you've tried this trick: Put a drop or two of superglue in the center of the crack. The glue will spread along the length of the crack and, quite possibly, make it vanish. (Even if the crack doesn't disappear, the glue will seal the opening so that cold air can't get through.) Just make sure you close the window gently in the future—cracked panes, glued or not, will break more easily if the window is slammed.

# THE EYE OF THE STORM

When it comes to keeping Old Man Winter's ravages at bay, there are few more useful inventions than aluminum storm doors and windows. But if you don't maintain

---

## FANTASTIC FORMULA

### Heavy-Duty Window Cleaner

When you've got extra-dirty windows to contend with, mix up a batch of this potent formula.

1 pint of water
½ cup of rubbing alcohol
1 tablespoon of ammonia

Mix all of the ingredients together, and pour the solution into a clean spray bottle. Then spray and wipe. This mix will cut through dirt and grease, and what's more, it won't leave any streaks!

---

them, it doesn't take long before they look like heck. Fortunately, it's easy to do battle with the two biggest troublemakers on unpainted aluminum: corrosion and pitting caused by oxidation. Here are my methods:

✦ Remove corrosion by vigorously rubbing the affected area with steel wool dipped in paint thinner.

✦ To get rid of those ugly white oxidation pits, rub the frames with aluminum jelly, a product made just for this purpose that's available in hardware stores.

## FOILED AGAIN

**I**f your hardware store is fresh out of aluminum jelly (see "The Eye of the Storm," on page 323), don't despair. You can clean up oxidation pits on unpainted aluminum doors and windows by wadding up a ball of aluminum foil and rubbing it back and forth across the pitted areas. This won't make the oxidation disappear, but little bits of the foil will catch in the pits and make your door or window look better, at least for the short haul.

When it's time to buy window-cleaning equipment, don't head for the supermarket, or even the discount store. Instead, take your shopping list to a place that sells janitorial supplies. You'll find professional-quality gear—including squeegees and extension rods—that will last for years, at prices comparable to or lower than those at regular retail sources. You can also pick up heavy-duty soaps and cleansers in concentrated forms or giant economy sizes, and often for a fraction of what the same quantity would cost at a discount outlet.

# All Hands on Deck!

Decks as we know them weren't around in Grandma Putt's day—at least not in our part of the country. I sure as shootin' have one now, though, and if Grandma were here, I know that she'd enjoy it as much as I do. I also know that she'd treat that deck the way she did everything around our house—as though she intended to keep enjoying it for the next hundred years. Read on for some deck-keeping methods that she'd be proud to call her own.

## A CLEAN SWEEP

**L**eaves, branches, and other yard debris can spell disaster for a deck because they keep the wood moist, and moisture is an open invitation to decay. Sweep your deck frequently with a good, stiff broom, and make sure you get out all the pesky stuff that settles in between the boards. Get down on your knees and use a putty knife or a screwdriver to poke the debris from the cracks. Or, do what I do: Duct-tape that blade to an old broom handle, and do the job standing up!

# SALT O' THE BROOM

**A**s Grandma Putt always said, "A new broom sweeps clean." But it'll sweep cleaner and last longer if you soak the bristles in hot salt water before you use your new broom for the first time. I sure can't explain why, but believe me, it really does work! (Of course, this only applies to the old-fashioned, natural-bristle brooms. If you try it on a plastic-bristle broom, all you'll get is salty plastic.)

# SCRUB-A-DUB

**O**nce or twice a year, give your deck a good scrubbing with a stiff broom and my Down-Home Deck and Porch Cleaner, at right. It's not a hard job: Just wait until the sun's rays have passed, move furniture and container plants out of the way, and cover up anything that's planted near the deck. Then swab away. If you plan to stain or seal the deck afterwards, let the wood dry for several days.

## FANTASTIC FORMULA

### Down-Home Deck and Porch Cleaner

There are plenty of commercial deck cleaners on the market, but this works as well as any that I've tried. It's great for porches and wood fences, too.

2 gallons of hot water
1 quart of household bleach
1/2 cup of powdered laundry detergent

Mix all of the ingredients in a bucket, and scrub the deck using a stiff broom or brush. Then hose it down thoroughly.

# SEAL APPEAL

**E**ven if a deck is made of pressure-treated wood or a rot-resistant wood like cedar or redwood, you still need to coat it with a water-repellent sealer every couple of years. If you're not sure when it's time, here's a clue: If rainwater beads up on the deck's surface, you're good to go for another season. If the water soaks right in, sealing time is here. There are several good sealants on the market; I recommend that you use a product that's water-based, rather than solvent-based.

## NO STRINGS ATTACHED

Here's an easy and cost-free way to extend the life of your porch or deck: On a porch, always suspend your hanging plants from the outer—not the inner—edges of the eaves. If you attach planter boxes to your deck rails, make sure that they hang out beyond the deck surface. That way, when water drips from the containers, it'll land on the ground, not on your decking.

## LONG-LASTING COVERAGE

If you want to really ease up on the time and cost of routine deck maintenance, go a step further and treat your deck to one of these options:

**Stain it.** Once it's been sealed, a coat of exterior stain will keep your deck in good shape for another four years or so.

**Paint it.** Top your deck with a couple of coats of latex paint, and—except for an occasional washing—you can rest easy for the next seven or eight years.

## THE BARE TRUTH

Some folks think rugs or mats make a deck look nice and homey. Well, that may be, but they also trap moisture beneath them—and moisture spells early death for any wooden surface. So save floor coverings for your indoor rooms, not for your deck or porch.

## A Patio Primer

Surfaces that are made of stone, brick, or concrete are simpler to keep up than wooden ones—but that doesn't mean that you're home free with patios and terraces. Here's a roundup of frugal maintenance tips to help you keep those spaces shipshape and still have time left to enjoy them.

## HOLD THE SALT

Any lawn-keeper knows the harm that salt does to grass and other plants. Well, it does just as much damage to concrete, cement, and brick. When you wake up to an ice-covered patio or walkway, don't reach for rock salt, calcium chloride, or any other ice-melting product that contains salt. Instead, use sand, cinders, wood ashes, or clay cat litter. They'll cover the ice and keep you standing upright, without harming anything in your landscape.

# ICE BE GONE!

For times when I need to melt ice and send it on its way, I use one of these two remedies:

1. **Alfalfa meal.** This is a natural, nitrogen-rich fertilizer that does quadruple duty: Its gritty texture provides traction, the nitrogen it contains promotes ice-melting, and the resulting run-off is not only harmless to masonry, but also good for any plants it encounters.

2. **Fire power.** When you need to clear walkways on the double, fire up a propane weed torch, and take aim. But first make sure that you have a place for the melted ice to drain; otherwise, you'll just be moving your problem from one spot to another.

# A CLEAN SWEEP

Here's a neat trick: Before sweeping a concrete patio or floor, scatter slightly damp coffee grounds on the surface. They'll pick up the dirt and keep the dust down as you sweep.

# TO TOP IT OFF

If no amount of scrubbing makes your concrete patio or driveway come clean, you may want to consider investing in a

## FANTASTIC FORMULA

### Concrete Cleaner

When the concrete around your house starts looking a tad dingy, mix up a batch of this formula. It works well on patios, walks, driveways, concrete-block retaining walls—even the foundation of your house!

2 gallons of warm water
1/4 cup of washing soda (available in the laundry section at supermarkets)

Mix the ingredients together. Use a brush or stiff broom to wash the concrete, then rinse.

self-bonding resurfacing product, such as Top 'n Bond, to give the patio a new finish. Spread it on according to the manufacturer's directions. As long as the layer is no thicker than ½ inch, the coating will bond permanently with the concrete, and you'll have a new surface to display.

## NO STRINGS ATTACHED

If you're a backyard birdwatcher like me, you know this routine: You keep the feeder filled with sunflower seeds all winter long, and come spring, there's a small mountain of hulls on the ground under it. Well, don't just scoop 'em up and toss 'em out—there's gold in them thar hulls! Grind 'em up and sprinkle 'em into cracks in patios, walkways, driveways, or anyplace else that you want to keep weed seeds from germinating. I have no idea why this works, but trust me—it does!

# Set a Spell

**Remember all of those great outdoor-furniture finds I clued you in on back in Chapter 5? Well, now that you've got those chairs, tables, and barbecue grills home, I'm going to tell you how to keep them on the job—helping you relax in the great outdoors for many years to come!**

# TWEAK YOUR TEAK

If you've read Chapter 5, you know that my frugal furniture award goes to teak because, expensive as it is, it will stand up to decades of wear and tear with almost no maintenance. It does need one little bit of attention, though: Once a year, you should coat the legs with a water repellent (the ones made for decks work fine). Here's the simplest way I've found to do this chore:

Pour about 3 inches of water repellent into a clean coffee can. Place one leg of a table or chair into the can and leave it there for two or three minutes. Repeat the process until each leg of your deck or patio furniture has had its turn in the can.

# AN IRON-CLAD GUARANTEE

Like teak, iron is tough stuff. Well-made iron furniture will give you years of faithful service if you guard against its biggest enemy—rust. Give your pieces a careful inspection at the beginning and end of the summer. (Do this every few months if you live where the outdoor-living season goes year-round.) When you find spots where the paint has chipped off, tend to them immediately. Here's my simple, three-step technique:

**Step 1.** Wipe a coat of white vinegar over the entire piece and let it dry (no need to rinse).

**Step 2.** Repaint the worn areas with a high-quality, rust-resistant paint. I find spray paint the easiest to work with, but some folks prefer the brush-on kind.

**Step 3.** Dip a soft cloth in car wax, and rub the entire piece of furniture with it. Repeat this rubdown yearly, and your rust worries will be a thing of the past.

## ALL RAGS ARE NOT CREATED EQUAL

* * * * *

When you're a frugal soul like me and your clothes get too worn to wear even for painting and other outdoor chores, what do you do? Why, you shove 'em in the rag bag, of course! But pause before you shove, because not all fabrics make good rags. What I've discovered is that synthetics don't absorb water or even pick up dirt very well—and even at the price of $0, that's not a bargain in my book! That's why my rag bag is stuffed with worn-out flannel pajamas, T-shirts, diapers, old napkins, and anything else that's made of 100 percent cotton, linen, or wool. Those fabrics work hard and well, so they're what I stick with—and you should, too!

# BUT I DON'T WANT TO WEAR IT!

Aluminum furniture wins popularity contests for its light weight and reasonable price tag. Unfortunately, though, aluminum has one glaring flaw: Left untreated, the surface oxidizes and develops a powdery, white residue. This ugly stuff, in turn, leaves equally ugly, gray marks on clothes, tablecloths, and seat cushions. To ensure that your aluminum furniture keeps itself to itself, wipe it down with a solution of equal parts vinegar and water. Let it dry, then spray on a coat or two of either clear lacquer or exterior paint.

# SQUIRREL AND SNAKE STOPPERS

Squirrels love to munch on redwood furniture, and snakes like to hide out around any kind of wood—including your patio furniture. Here's how to keep these critters at bay:

---

## FANTASTIC FORMULA

### Grandma Putt's Wicker Preservative

To keep your wicker looking and performing its best, use this formula once a year.

1 part boiled linseed oil

1 part turpentine

First, remove all dust with a soft brush. Then mix equal parts of boiled linseed oil and turpentine in a wide-mouthed glass jar. Rub the solution into the reeds with a soft cloth, paying special attention to all the nooks and crannies. Then use a clean, dry cloth to remove any excess formula. Let the furniture air dry before use.

---

**Squirrels.** Keep them from dining on your redwood by rubbing the surface with chili sauce, then buffing with a soft cloth. The red color of the sauce will blend right into the wood, so you won't notice it, but when a squirrel takes a bite, he'll be off your deck before you can say, "Paul Bunyan!"

**Snakes.** Most snakes are entirely harmless to humans, but many folks still don't want to encounter one out on their deck. If you live in snake territory, sprinkle dried sulfur on the ground around the deck. The slitherers will keep their distance. (You can get dried sulfur at farm and garden stores.)

# WILD ABOUT WICKER

Every time I see an old-fashioned porch all decked out with wicker tables, chairs, and rockers, it takes me right back to my days at Grandma Putt's. Boy, did she love that wicker! When it came to looking after it, she was as fussy as a mother hen with her chicks. And, as always, she bestowed a lot of her know-how on yours truly. Here's what I've learned:

**Keep it under cover.** Wicker furniture can't stand up to the elements the way teak, redwood, and metal can. (See Chapter 5 for more about the ins and outs of outdoor furniture.) Even in its ideal summer home—a covered veranda—wicker needs more attention than tougher materials. So if you know that a storm is brewing, whisk your furniture indoors to avoid damage from wind and water.

**Keep it clean.** Once a year (or more often, if it's exposed to dust and grit), vacuum your wicker furniture with the machine's soft brush attachment, or brush it by hand with a soft brush. To keep white wicker bright without painting, mix ¼ cup of salt in 1 gallon of warm water. Dip a stiff brush into the warm salt water and give the furniture a good scrubbing. Then let it dry in the sun.

**Keep it moist.** Whether you've brushed your wicker or given it a good salt-water scrubbing, follow up with a dose of Grandma Putt's Wicker Preservative (at left).

# Great Grills o' Fire!

To keep your barbecue grill looking good and cookin' up a storm, give it the same care you give your outdoor metal furniture. That is, keep the casing clean, and when you spot dings or worn spots, paint them before rust has a chance to form. (Just make sure you use a high-temperature-resistant spray paint that's made especially for grills and stoves.) As for cleaning the business end— the grate that holds all that great food—read on!

# BAG IT

**A**n old friend taught me the easiest formula I've ever found for cleaning a grill. Just put the greasy rack into a black plastic garbage bag. (Only a black bag will do, because it will draw the intense rays of the sun.) Lay the bag down and pour in enough ammonia to cover the rack, then close the bag tightly with a twist-tie. Leave the bag lying flat in the sun for two or three hours. Then flip it over, and leave it for another two or three hours. When you open the bag, that grill rack will be clean as a whistle. Just rinse it off, dry it, and you'll be all set for your next barbecue!

## A CLEAN, MEAN, GRILLING MACHINE

If you're fresh out of ammonia, or if the sun chose not to shine on your festivities (see "Bag It," on page 331), you're still in luck—any of these methods will get your grill spankin' clean.

☞ Sprinkle 3 to 4 tablespoons of wood ashes on the cooled grill rack, then scrub away with a sponge or brush dipped in warm, soapy water.

☞ Fill a large tub with enough hot water to cover the rack, then mix in $1/4$ cup of dishwasher detergent and $1/4$ cup of vinegar. Let the rack soak for an hour or so, then rinse and dry. Some folks use the bathtub for this job. If you do that, just remember to drain and clean the tub right away, or you'll wind up with a nasty, greasy black ring!

☞ While the grill is still warm—*not* hot—crumple a piece of aluminum foil into a ball, and rub the rack with it. When you're finished, rinse the foil and toss it into the recycling bin.

## THE BIG COVER-UP

In between barbecues, keep your grill under wraps—that's the surest way to keep it cookin' with gas (or charcoal)

---

### OUT AND ABOUT

\* \* \* \* \*

Don't concentrate all of your cleaning efforts just on the inside of your grill—the outside needs attention, too, especially if you're one of those lucky ducks who lives near the ocean. That refreshing salt air can turn a slick metal grill body into a pile of rust in no time flat. To stay one step ahead of the salty reaper, every week or so, rinse the grill's outer surface with fresh water, and then dry it immediately with a soft towel. Even if you don't live near the ocean, you should still follow this cleanup technique to keep your grill looking its best; for land-lubbers, about once a month should do the trick.

for years to come. If you don't have a cover, you can order one from the manufacturer. That way, you'll be guaranteed a perfect fit, tailor-made for all of the contours. Otherwise, just drape a heavy tarpaulin over the grill, and tie a cord around the bottom to keep the elements from sneaking in.

# More Fantastic Formulas!

**We're not out of the yard (or garage) yet! Here are just a few more of my fantastic formulas to help you make the most of the great outdoors.**

## RUST REMOVER

Even with the best of intentions, you can wind up with rusty patches on your outdoor furniture. Well, for the price of a roll of aluminum foil (preferably from the dollar store!), you can make that chair or table look as good as new. Just cut a piece of foil and ball it up, then rub it over the rusted area until those flaky brown spots disappear. This technique works on any metal objects—grills, tools, fences—you name it!

---

**FANTASTIC FORMULA**

### Energizing Elixir

If Grandma Putt could walk through a supermarket today and see the price tags on those fancy "sports drinks," she'd have a fit! Back in her day, when folks took a break from working in the hot sun, they'd sit under a shady tree and drink this restorative elixir.

1 gallon of water
2½ cups of sugar
1 cup of dark molasses
½ cup of vinegar (either white or cider)
2 teaspoons of ground ginger

Mix all the ingredients together in a big jug. Then get your work crew out of the sun, and pour everyone a nice, tall glass.

---

## BLOCK THAT MOSS!

To keep moss from forming on roof or siding shingles, mix 2 capfuls of household bleach in 1 gallon of water. Sponge on the solution, and don't rinse.

To get rid of moss that's growing on stone or brick, spray the area with a half-and-half mixture of bleach and water, then wipe clean with a damp cloth.

## ODOR EATERS

**W**hen you're working or playing hard in the great outdoors, your foot gear can get a tad, um, aromatic. To make those boots or shoes wearable in polite company again, here's all you need to do: For each shoe, pour a few teaspoons of baking soda on a square of cotton cloth. Tie the corners of the cloth together tightly, tuck the ball into the shoe, and let it sit overnight. Come morning, your shoes will be fresh as daisies.

---

### FANTASTIC FORMULA

#### Wonderful Wood Cleaner

Here's my favorite formula for cleaning anything made of painted wood, including doors, window frames, fences, porch railings—you name it.

1 gallon of water
1 cup of ammonia
½ cup of white vinegar
¼ cup of baking soda

Mix all the ingredients together and pour the solution into a spray bottle. Use it to clean all your painted-wood surfaces—indoors and out. There's no need to rinse.

---

## ITCH RELIEF

**W**hen mosquito bites have you itching like crazy, don't scratch 'em—just reach for a bottle of Listerine. Moisten a tissue with the mouthwash, hold it on the bite for about 15 seconds, and kiss that ol' itch goodbye.

## CLEAN CONCRETE

**T**o get oil or grease off a concrete surface, use this technique: First, pour paint thinner onto the concrete, saturating the spots and an area 8 to 12 inches beyond them. Then spread a good, thick layer of cat litter over the whole area—thick enough that you can't see the concrete underneath. (I prefer clumping litter for this, because it absorbs better than the clay kind.) Let it sit for an hour or two. Then sweep up the litter with a broom. If the stain has been around for awhile, you may need to repeat the procedure. One note of caution: You must have good ventilation when doing this job, so if you're working inside the garage, be sure to keep the door open.

# CHROME ZONE

To clean the chrome on your car, barbecue grill, bicycle—or anything else—simply rub the surface with baby oil, club soda, or a piece of lemon. Wash with soapy water, then rub dry with a soft cloth. Now look at that shine!

# WAX REMOVER

Candles add a great touch to an evening barbecue, but melted wax doesn't—especially when it winds up on your deck. Fortunately, there's an easy trick for getting it off. First, scrape off as much as you can, using a credit card or a plastic scraper (don't use metal; it can gouge the wood). Then place a brown paper bag over the remaining wax and aim a hair dryer at it (set on high heat) until the paper has absorbed the wax.

# MILDEW CHASER

Fabric that's stored in a garage (or left there by accident) is a prime target for mildew. If this nasty spore has attacked your clothes, linens, or even favorite cleanup rags, try this formula: Paint the stains

## FANTASTIC FORMULA

### All-Purpose Weed Killer

This potent solution will rout weeds from wherever they're growing, whether it's the middle of your lawn, between the flagstones on your patio and paths, or through cracks in the sidewalk.

> 1 quart of water
> 5 tablespoons of vinegar
> 2 tablespoons of salt

Bring the water to a boil, then add the vinegar and salt. While the mixture is still hot, pour it directly on the weeds, and kiss 'em goodbye.

with lemon juice, sprinkle with salt, and place the item in direct sunlight to dry. Then launder as usual.

# PADLOCK PROTECTOR

To keep the latch and padlock on a shed door from rusting, try this old-time formula: Cut a piece of old inner tube that's big enough to cover both latch and lock. Nail it above the top edge of the latch. Then, when you want to reach the lock, simply lift the flap.

## CHALK UP RUST

To keep your tools rust-free, tuck a few sticks of chalk or chunks of charcoal into your toolbox. They'll attract the moisture that would otherwise cling to the metal.

## PLEASE PASS THE MAYO!

Good old mayonnaise can do a lot more than dress up sandwiches and potato salad. Use it to:

☑ Get grease, tar, or pine pitch off your hands, your car, or just about anything else. Just rub on the mayo, let it sit for a few minutes, and then wipe it off.

☑ Take tar out of clothing. Slather the mayo on the spots, let it soak into the fabric, then launder or dry-clean the garment.

☑ Remove crayon marks from wooden furniture (indoors or out). Rub on the mayonnaise, let it sit for a minute or so, then wipe with a damp cloth.

## POWER-TOOL PROTECTOR

To keep small hands—or unwelcome big ones—from starting up your power tools, get a tiny, suitcase-size padlock. Insert it through one of the holes in the prong of the plug and snap it shut. Voila! Thief-proof! Just be sure to write down the combination, or you'll be locked out, too!

## TIGHTEN UP!

Got a screw loose? Reach for one of these remedies:

★ Dip the screw in putty or glue before you screw it back into its hole.

★ Wrap a few strands of steel wool around the threads.

★ Shove a wooden matchstick into the hole to provide more grip for the screw.

---

### POP GOES THE BOLT!

\* \* \* \* \*

Got a rusted bolt? Not a problem—any carbonated beverage will loosen it up. Just soak a cloth in the soda pop, apply it to the bolt, and hold it there for a minute or so. Then, before that bolt is used again (or before you use a new one), coat it with petroleum jelly to prevent future rust attacks.

# VINYL SHINE

**K**eep your car's vinyl uphol-stery looking its best with this three-step routine:

**Step 1.** Clean the seats, dash-board, and other vinyl coverings with a damp cloth dipped in baking soda.

**Step 2.** Follow up by wash-ing with a mild solution of dishwashing liquid and water.

**Step 3.** Rinse thoroughly.

# ANTI-MOUSE MINTS

**W**hen it comes to munch-ables, there's nothing mice like more than car insula-tion—the stuff on the under-side of your hood and between the passenger compartment and the engine wall. And there's nothing mice hate more than mint. So put this secret to work for you by saturating a few cot-ton balls with peppermint oil

## FANTASTIC FORMULA

### Extra-Strength Windshield Cleaner

When heavy road gunk builds up on your car's windows, this formula will get it off in a hurry.

2 tablespoons of cream of tartar

1 cup of water

Mix the cream of tartar into the water, and stir to make a paste. Smear it onto the windshield, then rinse off with water. Finish by wiping with crumpled newspapers or—if dried-on bugs are part of the equation—use a handful of mesh onion bags. Then polish off the job with a clean, soft cloth.

and tucking them in the insulation. I guarantee that Mickey, Minnie, and their pals will find less aromatic quar-ters before you can say "Ears to you!"

# CHAPTER 14

# Pamper Your Pets for Less

Nowadays, it seems as though every time I turn on the news, there's some fancy new study showing that folks who have pets are happier and healthier than folks who don't. Well, if Grandma Putt were here, I know what she'd have to say about that! She'd shake her head at that old TV screen and say "Land sakes! Why are they wastin' good money doin' a study on that? Everybody knows there's nothin' better for a two-legged critter than a four-legged critter!"

One of the first things Grandma Putt taught me was how to take good care of our dogs and cats—and we had a lot of 'em over the years! So, it should come as no surprise that she also taught me to keep a tight rein on the pet-care budget. In this chapter, I'll share my collection of tail-waggin' tricks for beating the high cost of tender-lovin' critter care.

# Here's to Their Health!

And *your* bank account! If your four-footed friend has visited the vet lately, you know that even routine care doesn't come cheap—and the bill for just a minor problem can make a big hole in the family budget. Here are some ways I've found to cut down on those medical costs—without short-changing my pals one little bit.

## An Ounce of Prevention

It goes without saying that keeping your dog or cat well-fed, well-exercised, and out of dangerous situations will head off a lot of expensive medical bills. Well, here are some other, less-obvious tips for cutting the high cost of critter health care.

## YOUR BEST PAL'S BEST PAL

Sooner or later, almost every pet has a serious medical problem of some kind. When that time comes, you want to be darn sure you have a first-class vet on the job. And—for the sake of your pet's health, your peace of mind, *and* your bank account—the time to find that Superguy or Supergal is long before big-time trouble strikes. Why? For a couple of reasons:

1. When your veterinarian has treated your animal for routine matters, he or she knows your pet's overall health picture, which means it'll be much easier for the doc to diagnose and treat a serious problem. And that could translate into big savings for you.

2. When you have a good, ongoing relationship with your vet's office, the financial folks will probably bend over backwards to help you finance the cost of surgery or other major treatment.

## EASE 'EM IN

If your pets are anything like mine, a trip to the vet isn't exactly high on their list of fun things to do. To make it a bit less stressful, try to introduce your pets to their doctor *before* they're sick or in pain. Routine checkups and annual vaccinations are good places to start. And nail-trims are good, low-cost visits, too. But here's a free way to get your pet acquainted with the doc and staff: Stop by every so often to have your pet weighed. It's an especially good way to introduce a new puppy or kitten, or an older animal who's nervous about this doctorin' business. (Always call first to make sure the clinic isn't dealing with an emergency.)

## DON'T EVEN THINK ABOUT IT!

In any vet's office, Monday is the Day from You-Know-Where. That's when they're jammed to the rafters with pets who took sick or had accidents over the weekend and didn't get rushed to an emergency clinic.

### NO STRINGS ATTACHED

If you live near a veterinary school, you may be able to get free or very low-cost medical care for your pet—especially if you're a senior. What's more, if your four-footed pal has a serious problem that new, high-tech surgery might cure, a vet school's teaching docs will sometimes operate for next to nothing in the interests of research. So before you give up hope, pick up the phone and call.

Saturdays are busy, too, with both urgent visits and scheduled appointments. If you want the most attentive care for your pet, book your routine appointments for Tuesday through Friday morning.

## NO PENNIES FOR YOUR THOUGHTS

Did you know that pennies can be hazardous or even fatal to your pets? All one-cent coins minted after 1982 are made of copper plating around a core of zinc. If this toxic stuff is swallowed (by a critter or a human), it can cause kidney failure and damage to red blood cells. As if that isn't sobering enough, one single penny is enough to cause zinc poisoning in dogs or cats. So stash those coins in a good, secure piggy bank, folks! And, if you suspect that your pet has eaten a penny—or any other potentially toxic substance—call your veterinarian, *pronto.*

# POISON S.O.S.

**A**s we all know, our furry pals don't confine their unwise dining binges to regular business hours. For round-the-clock help, call the ASPCA Animal Poison Control Center's emergency hotline at 1-888-426-4435. (You will be charged a consultation fee.) The ASPCA Web site is also chock-full of information on poison prevention and advice on more critter-related topics than you can shake a Milkbone at. Check it out at **www.ASPCA.org**.

# GOTCHA COVERED!

**H**ave you ever wondered why there isn't health insurance for pets? Well, there is: For a tiny fraction of the cost of human policies, Veterinary Pet Insurance will cover your dog or cat for X-rays, surgery, hospital stays, lab fees—you name it. For a low additional premium, you can even get coverage for routine care, including an annual physical checkup, vaccinations, heartworm and flea-control medications, spay or neuter surgery, and teeth cleaning. This package will save you *big* bucks on pet health

**There are times** when only a conventional vet can solve your pet's health problem— for instance, you wouldn't rush him to an acupuncturist to treat a broken leg! But for routine care and for many chronic conditions, there are better— and much less expensive—alternatives to standard medical treatments. The Complementary and Alternative Veterinary Medicine Web site is a gold mine of information on new-fangled/old-fashioned (and low-cost) health care for pets, including homeopathic and herbal remedies. Check it out at **www.altvetmed.com**.

care. To find out all the details, log on to **www.petinsurance. com** or call 1-800-872-7387. (P.S. If you've got a bird, ferret, reptile, or even pot-bellied pig, there are policies for you, too!)

# HOLD THAT NEEDLE!

Some mail-order catalogs will sell you vaccines so you can give your pet his shots at home. Sounds like a great way to save money on vet bills, right? Wrong! One little slip-up—in vaccine selection, quantity, or your needle-wielding technique—could cause big-time harm to your pet and ultimately to your pocketbook. So, unless you've had a lot of experience and you *really* know what you're doing, leave this chore to the doctor!

# Chow Time

That old saying, "You are what you eat," applies to dogs and cats as much as it does to us humans—more so, in fact. Here are my budget-pleasing tips for keeping your furry pals sleek, well-fed, and out of the vet's office.

## Nutritious Nibbles

Most of us folks eat a pretty varied diet, so if we gobble up a candy bar now and then, it really won't hurt us. On the other hand, we feed our pets pretty much the same food every day, year in and year out. So, if their chow lacks nutrients that they need to stay healthy, or if it's packed with stuff that produces cancer in lab rats, it's bound to take its expensive toll sooner or later. Here's how to make sure your pet is eating right.

# BARGAIN HUNTERS, BEWARE!

**A**s you know by now, I'm one of the biggest boosters a store-brand product ever had. But when it comes to pet foods, it's a whole different ballgame. That's because the legal quality standards for pet foods are much lower than they are for human foods—and you practically need a Ph.D. in chemistry to understand the fine print on those pet-food bags and cans! At best, when you fork over your cash for a low-quality brand, you'll be paying for a lot of filler that isn't worth beans. At worst, your cat or dog could be chowing down on meat from diseased animals and mysterious "by-products" that could (and often do) cause serious and expensive problems. So don't be penny-wise and pound foolish—stick to the major pet-food brands.

# FIT 'N' TRIM

**B**eing overweight is just as bad for your pet's health as it is for your own. If your dog is packin' a few more pounds than he should be, you could switch him to one of those expensive diet dog foods. But my guaran-teed weight-loss two-step is cheaper, more fun—and a whole lot healthier:

1. Cut back on the daily dose of dog food, and make up the difference with cooked vegetables. Most dogs'll lap up any kind of veggie and never miss the kibble. (My pup is especially partial to broccoli.)

2. Go for a 2-mile walk every day—it'll put both of you in better shape!

# THIS IS YOUR LIFE!

**S**helf life, that is. When you buy a sack of pet food, you'll see a "Best if used by" date, just

## ALTERED STATES

\* \* \* \* \*

Besides being good for his or her overall health, altering your dog or cat can save you money on food bills. That's because a neutered male or spayed female needs 25 percent fewer calories than their unaltered counterparts. Of course, you'll have to make sure you cut back on the grub you dish out—otherwise you'll be spending more cash than you need to, and you'll have an overly plump pet, besides!

Corn is a big-time allergy-causer in dogs—and it's one of the most widely used ingredients in dog food. (See "His Allergies Are Killin' Me!" below.)
Before you start playing the expensive game of brand roulette, try any high-quality food that doesn't contain corn. That just might solve your problem lickety-split.

and other ingredients commonly used in grocery store pet foods—and even in some of the expensive brands that vets sell.

More and more pet foods are coming on the market minus the more common itch-causers. Just ask the folks at a pet-supply store or well-stocked kennel shop to recommend a high-quality, natural food that'll suit your pet's age, breed, and activity level. And let them know that you don't want to spend an arm and a leg. These nifty, new-fangled foods with old-fashioned ingredients come in all price ranges.

as you see on human foods. To make sure you're getting your money's worth, buy only as much as you know your critter will gobble up before that date. And store the stuff in an air-tight container, away from moisture and humidity, to keep it from losing nutrients.

## HIS ALLERGIES ARE KILLIN' ME!

If your dog or cat is scratchin' up a storm, before you fork out more money on vet visits or allergy meds, take a listen: The answer to Fido or Fluffy's problem could be right in his food bowl. A whole lot of dogs and cats are allergic to many of the dyes, preservatives,

## ALLERGY ALERT

If your pet is cuttin' any of these capers, the paw points to an allergy:

☞ Tail chewing

☞ Biting or licking paws

☞ Hair falling out in patches

☞ Dry, scaly skin

☞ A change in the coat, from dry to oily or vice versa

☞ Weeping eyes

☞ Unusual body odor

Try switching brands of food. If things don't clear up

after a week or so, take your pet in for allergy tests (see "Test Time," below).

# TEST TIME

**A** substance that's harmless to most critters can cause big-time, expensive trouble if your pet happens to be allergic to it. If a switch to a good, natural food doesn't cure your pet's woes, take him to a holistic veterinarian for an allergy test. (It's easier and faster than the kind conventional vets use. It'll still cost you a few bucks, but it'll be worth every penny.)

To find a holistic veterinarian, check the Web site of the American Holistic Veterinary Medical Association at **www.AHVMA. org**, or call (410) 569-0795.

# THE FOOD DID IT

**M** y dog was itching up a storm a while back. I dropped quite a bundle on skin medications, only to learn that my pup was allergic to rice, potatoes, and chicken.

So I switched him to a food that contained none of those ingredients, and bingo—no more itch! (And no more vet bills tryin' to cure the itch!)

---

**FANTASTIC FORMULA**

## Paw-sitively Pooch-Pleasin' Stew

When you run out of dog food—or if even the good stuff turns your pup's skin dry and itchy—try this healthy, easy, and cheap recipe. I make it up in big batches and then freeze it in individual portions.

1 tablespoon of vegetable oil

2 parts ground turkey*

1 part sliced sweet potatoes

1 part chopped vegetables (fresh or frozen, thawed)**

Water

Pour the oil into a large pot. Add the turkey, and stir until the meat is cooked through. Add the sweet potatoes, along with enough water to keep the ingredients from sticking to the pan. Stir to combine, then simmer until the taters are slightly tender. Add the vegetables, and cook until they're tender-crisp (about 3 minutes). Let the stew come to room temperature before you dish it out (in whatever amount your dog normally eats).

* Turkey is a safe choice for most dogs, but you can substitute any meat, veggies, or starch that you know he's not allergic to.

** Don't use corn unless you *know* that your dog's system can handle it.

## FANTASTIC FORMULA

### Pup-sicles

For hot-weather treats—or to keep a teething puppy from chomping on your favorite sneakers—stash a few batches of these in the freezer.

1 quart of beef or chicken bouillon

½ cup of finely chopped vegetables

½ cup of plain yogurt

Mix all of the ingredients together, and pour the mixture into ice cube trays. Then sock 'em away in the freezer 'til treat time rolls around.

# BYE-BYE BISCUITS

Even el cheapo dog treats can put a dent in the grocery budget if you buy them very often. What's more, most of 'em are chock-full of sugar and fat, and that's no better bargain for Rover than it is for you. So what do you do when it's snack time? Reach for some raw baby carrots, that's what! I'll bet bucks to biscuits

your pooch will go ape for the sweet taste and the tooth-pleasin' crunch. (Just don't tell him they're good for him.)

# CHEAP TREATS

Here are some other lip-smackin' snacks you can pull from the garden or the fridge. (A few cats I know go hog wild for these, too.) A word of warning, though: Raw fruits and veggies can cause serious gas in some dogs, especially dogs who are not used to "people food." So go easy on these treats at first—and don't stand behind your dog when he's eating!

★ Apples

★ Bananas

★ Berries

★ Broccoli

★ Cauliflower

★ Grapes

★ Green beans

★ Melons

★ Oranges

★ Tomatoes

★ Zucchini

## NIX THE ZITS

Sometimes, it's not food that causes problems, it's what you put the food in—namely, old plastic food bowls. Bacteria builds up in the scratches and makes cats and dogs break out with acne. (And you thought that only happened to teenage humans!) The simple, no-cost solution? Switch to ceramic or metal bowls. No law says they have to be traditional pet-food dishes, either. I'll bet you have some old bowls you haven't used in donkey's years that'll work just fine. If not, you can pick up a few for peanuts at a thrift shop or tag sale.

## MORE TROUBLE AHEAD

Too much chocolate might put extra pounds on you, but even a bite can be deadly for your dog. That's because it contains a chemical called theobromine which can cause severe, life-threatening diarrhea. Baking chocolate is especially dangerous because it's packed with almost nine times more theobromine than milk chocolate has. In fact, as little as 3 ounces of baking chocolate can kill a 25-pound dog. So keep those cakes, cookies, and baking supplies well out of paw reach!

## NO, THANKS

When your pooch bellies up to the salad bar, make sure he passes right on by the raw onions. Some dogs can handle small quantities, but in many cases, a mouthful can trigger fever, diarrhea, and vomiting—and neither of you needs that. So, why take the chance?

### FANTASTIC FORMULA

**Tuna Nip-sicles**

The next time you make yourself a tuna sandwich, whip up a batch of these frozen treats for your favorite feline.

1 can (6-ounces) of water-packed tuna
1 teaspoon of dried catnip, or several
sprigs of fresh catnip, chopped
Water

Drain the tuna liquid into a small pitcher or spouted bowl. Then, fill the sections of an ice-cube tray halfway with water, and sprinkle the catnip evenly into each section. Fill each compartment with tuna water, and put the tray into the freezer 'til the cubes are frozen solid. Serve 'em up, one at a time, in kitty's bowl.

# At Ease

**W**ant to have fun with your four-footed pals without breakin' your entertainment budget? The good news is that cats and dogs don't need fancy toys to play with. Read on for the lowdown on low-cost leisure, critter style.

## Toy Land

As we all know only too well, when human young 'uns hit school age, they start demanding all the latest, greatest gear their pals are totin'. Fortunately, dogs and cats don't give a hoot what their buddies are playin' with. Here's a roundup of gadgets that'll keep your pets amused, while keeping cash in your pocket.

## MARINATED MICE

**T**here's nothing my cat likes better than little toy mice stuffed with catnip. She just can't get enough of them—that is, until the catnip aroma wears off, which seems to happen in about a week. Then she wants nothing more to do with the boring things. Now, I love my cat, but I'm not about to keep her constantly supplied with new catnip mice! Instead, I bought a dozen at the discount pet-supply store, and I dole 'em out two or three at a time. The rest I keep "marinating" in a tightly closed glass jar filled with dried catnip. Then, when Kitty shows signs of boredom with her current crew, I pop the "stale" mice into the jar, take out a couple of fresh, odiferous replacements, and watch her jump for joy.

## WHEE!

**C**ats (and especially kittens) get a bang out of anything they can bat around or coax a little noise from. So why pay good money for toys? Give your favorite feline a few of these freebies to frisk with:

- ☑ Pens or pencils (unsharpened, of course)

- ☑ Practice golf balls or Ping-Pong balls

- ☑ Empty toilet-paper rolls
- ☑ Empty film canisters with a few dried beans inside
- ☑ Balls of crumpled-up aluminum foil
- ☑ Badminton birdies
- ☑ Paper grocery bags (with no handles that small heads could get caught in!)
- ☑ Cardboard boxes

# CUDDLE UP

**A**lmost every pooch I know is crazy about stuffed, plush animal toys. They sure don't come cheap, though! You can get around the high pet-store prices by heading for the toy department of your local thrift store, but look carefully before you buy. You want toys that are baby-proof. Otherwise, they may have sewn-on buttons for eyes, noses, and so forth. If one of them winds up in your dog's stomach, it could mean a trip to the emergency vet.

# GO FISH!

**M**y neighbor's cat goes bonkers over a fancy "fishing"

## FANTASTIC FORMULA

### Long-Last Leash Mix

If you take care of your pet's leather leash, it'll last a lifetime. Just take it from me—I'm still using the same leather leash my Grandma Putt had for her dogs, and it still looks as good as the day she brought it home from the store! Here's the formula I use:

> Neat's-foot oil (available at most leather-goods stores)
> Castor oil

Mix the ingredients in equal parts. Dampen a soft cloth with the mixture, and rub it into the leather. The longer you rub, the better that ol' leather will look. Wip off any excess with a clean, soft cloth. (This works great on new leather, too!)

rod that has a fish made of multicolored feathers tied to the line. My neighbor paid close to 20 bucks for the thing. I made one by pounding a tack into the end of a wooden dowel and tying nylon line to the tack. Then I tied a handful of feathers (available in craft and hobby stores) to the other end of the line, and presto! Fine feathered fishing, almost free!

## LEASH & COLLAR FIXER-UPPER

**W**hen you find a leather leash or collar for peanuts at a tag sale, don't pass it by because it doesn't look brand-spankin' new. It's a snap to make it look snappy again. Here's how:

☞ Wipe off any mildew with a solution of equal parts rubbing alcohol and water.

☞ Remove any white water spots by covering them with a thick coat of petroleum jelly. Wait a day or so, then wipe off the jelly with a soft cloth.

☞ Polish up brass buckles with Worcestershire sauce, ketchup, or toothpaste.

The American Kennel Club has a free booklet of tips on seeing America, or the whole wide world, with your canine cohort. To get a copy, log on to **www.akc.org**.

## ON THE GO

**T**ime to hit the road with Fido or Fluffy? Whether you're moving cross-country or just taking a family vacation, you'll save money—and enjoy the trip more—if you do your homework first.

Your local bookstore has dozens of titles on traveling with your pet. Here's what you'll discover:

★ how to gear up for the trip

★ what health records you'll need if you're going to another country

★ how to keep your pet safe and comfortable along the way

★ lists of thousands of hotels, motels, resorts, and campgrounds (in all price ranges) that welcome four-footed lodgers

★ lists of day-care kennels where your pet can romp or snooze, while you and the family see the sights

Just make sure that you get the latest edition of whatever book you buy; prices and policies can change from one year to the next.

# Whoops!

**Accidents happen. Whether your pet is the perpetrator, the innocent victim, or maybe a little of both, you know who has to deal with the aftermath. Here's a collection of tips for both heading off trouble *and* cleaning up the results.**

## CAT SCRATCH

If you've priced scratching posts lately, you know that they can cost almost as much as some of the furniture you're tryin' to protect from Kitty's claws. Here's a simple, no-cost alternative: Give your feline friend a piece of thick, bark-covered tree trunk to trim her nails on. Just make sure it's big and sturdy enough to stand up under your cat's weight—and before you bring that chunk of

> ### FANTASTIC FORMULA
>
> #### Hot Bug Brew
>
> 3 hot green peppers (canned or fresh)
>
> 3 medium cloves of garlic
>
> 1 small onion
>
> 1 tablespoon of liquid dish soap
>
> 3 cups of water
>
> Puree the peppers, garlic, and onion in a blender. Pour the puree into a jar, and add the dish soap and water. Let the mixture stand for 24 hours. Then strain out the pulp, pour the liquid into a handheld sprayer, and saturate the tree limb. Once you're sure the stump's pest-free, rinse it thoroughly with a garden hose—otherwise, the potent brew will send Kitty scramblin' away as fast as the bugs!

trunk into the house, spray it with my Hot Bug Brew (above) to get rid of any unwanted multilegged inhabitants.

## A LITTLE MORE CIVILIZED, PLEASE!

I know: Not everyone likes the rustic look. If a tree-trunk scratching post doesn't suit your decor (see "Cat Scratch," at left), you have other cheap choices: You

can scout tag sales and discount stores for a ready-made model, or make a fancier scratching post simply by fastening carpet scraps to a wooden box, plank, or fence post. Whichever route you take, though, keep these guidelines in mind:

1. Choose or make a post that's tall enough for your feline friend to stretch out fully against as he's scratching. Even if you have a kitten, get an adult-size post right from the start—that little scratcher'll be grown up before you know it.

2. Make sure the post has a sturdy, heavy base. If the structure topples, or even sways under your cat's weight, he won't use it again.

3. Stay away from textures that resemble those of your carpet or furniture. Otherwise, Kitty may not be able to tell the difference—and you'll be right back where you started!

# DOGGONE!

When it comes to damage to your domicile, a cat's nails can't hold a candle to a puppy's teeth! Here's a trio of the best gadgets I've found to keep those needle-sharp choppers safely occupied:

**Ice cubes.** Plain ones work just fine, but for added appeal, I sometimes make 'em out of bouillon or orange juice. Just make sure your dog eats them in the kitchen or on another easy-to-clean floor.

**Carrots.** For treats, I hand out the baby versions I talked about a few pages back (see "Bye-Bye Biscuits," on page 346). For teething purposes, though, big, fat carrots work better because they last longer and give the pup more of a chewing challenge.

**Frozen washcloths.** Rinse an old, clean one in cold water (make sure there's no lingering soap), and wring it out. Then roll it up tight, and twist it into a sort of spiral. Put it in the freezer till it's good and solid, then take it out, and give it to young Rover. Just make sure you whisk the cloth away as soon as it's thawed out; otherwise, the pup will recognize it for what it really is and figure that it's okay to chew on *all* washcloths!

## A BREATH OF CANNED AIR

**W**hen your four-footed young 'un is gettin' into mischief, here's how to stop him in his tracks:

Get a can of compressed air (electronics stores sell it for cleaning computers). Then, when the pup is chasin' the cat, or the kitten is stalkin' the bird, whip out that can and go "Pssssst." That blast of cold air works every time. And once they've learned to recognize the sound, that alone will do the trick—they don't even have to be close enough to feel the breeze. (Don't ever give 'em more than a short spritz, though: That air is *really* cold. And always be careful to avoid their faces, especially their eyes.)

## GET OUTTA MY HAIR!

**T**he next time your dog or cat has a run-in with a bush full of burrs and prickles, pour a few drops of vegetable or mineral oil on the stickers, then gently comb your pet. The stick-ums will comb right out.

### HAIR TODAY

\* \* \* \* \*

And gone in a flash. Here's a trio of ways to get cat and dog hair off your clothes and furniture:

**1.** Dampen a sponge, add a dab of glycerin, and rub the sponge over the hairy surface. (To de-hair a carpet, use a sponge mop.)

**2.** Use a scrap cut from an old Polar Fleece jacket or vest. The fuzzy stuff is one of the best hair picker-uppers I've found. (The downside is that hair also clings to the stuff when you're wearin' it!)

**3.** Wrap a strip of packing or masking tape around your hand, sticky side out, and run it over the upholstery.

## BARGAIN BLADES

**O**ne of the best ways to groom a long-haired critter is with a shedding blade. Pet-supply stores sell 'em in two sizes: small ones for cats and big ones for dogs. The dog versions are exactly the same as the ones used on horses—and you can get 'em at tack shops for about half the price the pet stores charge. Look in the Yellow Pages under "Riding Apparel and Equipment."

# SINGIN' IN THE RAIN

**I** have a friend whose normally fastidious cat developed a bladder condition (which has since been remedied). Before the problem was diagnosed, though, kitty let loose several times on a small—and valuable—Oriental rug. My friend was about to toss the rug out,

---

## FANTASTIC FORMULA

### Odor-Go Urine Remover

Here's what I use to clean and deodorize pet urine-damaged areas.

1 quart of water

2 tablespoons of white vinegar

1 teaspoon of liquid dish soap

Mix the ingredients in a pail, and use a scrub brush to brush the solution onto the problem spot. Say, "Out, out, danged spot!" three times and it will be—in a flash!

---

but instead decided to leave it outside for a while and see what happened. Lo and behold, after a couple of months in the fresh air and rain, all traces of urine smell had flown the coop. The moral of the story? When all else fails, turn to Mother Nature, and let her do her stuff!

# GOTTA GO!

**W**hen nature calls, critters do what they must, where they must—and that's not always where we'd like it to be. Here's my routine for getting rid of urine stains and odors:

**Step 1.** Blot, blot, and blot some more with paper towels or old rags. If the deed has just been done, this step alone will take care of 90 percent of the problem.

**Step 2.** Flush the spot with club soda.

**Step 3.** Brush on my Odor-Go Urine Remover (at left).

# AT-THE-READY POTTY TRAINING KIT

**A** puppy doesn't have full bladder control till he's almost 5 or 6 months old.

That's why, no matter how well he understands that his bathroom is outside and how hard he tries to contain himself, accidents do happen. The good news is that if you get there quickly enough, it's a snap to destroy the evidence. Before the pup even arrives on the scene, assemble this arsenal. Better yet, make up several kits and stash 'em around the house, so there's always one close at hand.

☑ 1 roll of paper towels

☑ 1 spray bottle filled with water

☑ 1 spray bottle filled with hydrogen peroxide*

☑ 1 pot-scrubbing sponge

When you see the pup start to tinkle, pick him up, say "Outside!" and rush him there. (Don't scold him, though; he's only doing what comes naturally.) Wait for him to finish his business, then tell him how ter-

* Test your carpet first; if it's not color-fast, use white vinegar. Whatever you do, don't use ammonia: You'll only be making a first-class trouble spot because to a dog, ammonia smells just like urine.

rific and smart he is. Then, bolt back inside and grab your gear. First, blot up as much of the liquid as you can with the paper towels. Don't rub. Next, spray the spot with water, and blot again. Finally, spray with peroxide, and gently rub it into the carpet fibers with the pot-scrubbing sponge.

# STAIN-BE-GONE DIARRHEA DISPOSAL

Short of keeping your dog in diapers, there's no way to avoid an occasional spill of, um, semi-solid waste. Here's the best way I've found to get the stuff out of the carpet. First, scrape off as much as you can using a plastic scraper or a piece of thin cardboard. Go easy—you don't want to rub any into the carpet fibers! Let the rest dry completely, then use a dull-bladed knife to scrape the carpet clean. If there's any lingering stain, this routine will get it out:

**Step 1.** Mix ¼ teaspoon of liquid dish soap with 1 cup of lukewarm water.

**Step 2.** Soak a towel in the

solution and blot the stain with it. Don't rub!

**Step 3.** Dampen another towel with ammonia, and apply it to the stain. Again, blot, don't rub.

**Step 4.** Repeat step 3, this time using white vinegar instead of ammonia.

**Step 5.** Sponge the spot with cool water.

---

## FANTASTIC FORMULA

### Spots Away

The only guaranteed way of preventing dog-urine spots on your lawn is to train your dog to go elsewhere. (My pup has his own private square of gravel behind the tool shed.) Until he gets the hang of using his own privy, though—or if neighbor dogs are paying visits—this formula will get rid of the spots.

> 1 gallon of water
> 1 box (8 ounces) of baking soda

Mix the water and baking soda in a watering can. Then search your lawn for spots, and saturate each one. The soda will cut the acidity in the urine, and the water will neutralize the excess nitrogen. Once you've mixed up this formula, use it pronto, before the soda settles to the bottom of the can.

---

# More Fantastic Formulas!

**We're not through yet, my friends! Here's a roundup of sure-fire, down-home recipes for happy petkeeping.**

# SUPER SKUNK DEODORIZER

When your frisky feline or cuttin'-up canine gets too close to the business end of a skunk, whip up a batch of this mix: 1 quart of 3 percent hydrogen peroxide, ¼ cup of baking soda, and 1 teaspoon of liquid soap in a bucket. Then corral your hapless pet, and soak him thoroughly with the solution. Rinse well, and towel him dry. That old *eau de skunk* will be gone faster than you can say Chanel No. 5!

# HIGH-INTENSITY URINE REMOVER

When you haven't made it to the accident scene as fast as you'd like—or if the urine odor is especially

stubborn, as it often is with cat urine—stronger measures are called for. Here's the high-intensity method:

1. Saturate the spot thoroughly with cold water.

2. Scrub in a half-and-half mixture of white vinegar and water.

3. Follow with a solution of water and a detergent for baby diapers, such as Dreft. Rinse with cold water.

4. Stand up and breathe deeply. No more odor!

# NEW-FANGLED TICK REMOVAL

The old-time way to get a tick out of a dog's (or a human's) skin was to douse the louse with alcohol or nail polish before pulling it out. Well, nowadays, the experts say that

could cause the varmint to regurgitate germs into the victim's skin. So, skip the pretreatment and use this simple formula: Grasp the thug with tweezers, and gently pull straight up. You may have to twist a little

## FANTASTIC FORMULA

### Toodleloo Tick Spray

Ticks can make life miserable for humans and pets alike. If these germ-totin' terrors are hanging out in your shrubs—one of their favorite hideouts—send 'em packin' with this spray. (The alcohol is the secret weapon here: It penetrates the rascals' protective, waxy covering, so the soap can get in to do its work.) Just make sure you wait 'til evening to blast the culprits—the alcohol in this spray will burn your plants if it's used in the sun.

1 tablespoon of Ivory liquid soap
1 gallon of rainwater or soft tap water
2 cups of isopropyl (rubbing) alcohol
6 gallon hose-end sprayer

Mix the Ivory liquid soap with the water in a hose-end sprayer jar, then add the alcohol. With the water pressure turned on high, spray your plants from top to bottom—and make sure you get under all the leaves. Repeat whenever necessary.

## FANTASTIC FORMULA

### Flee, Fleas Lemon Rinse

Here's a pet-pleasin' rinse that'll help keep fleas where they belong: off of Fido and Fluffy.

    1 lemon, thinly sliced
    1 quart of water

Put the lemon slices in the water and let the brew steep overnight. Once a day during flea season, groom Fido or Fluffy with a flea comb, then sponge on the lemon rinse.

if the creep won't let go. If you don't have tweezers handy, use your fingers—but first cover them with latex gloves, a plastic bag, or a couple layers of tissue. Whatever you do, don't touch the foul thing directly. Drop the tick into alcohol or soapy water, burn it in an ashtray, or flush it down the toilet.

If the tick has been guzzling for a while, the scene of the crime will resemble a mosquito bite. Dab it with peroxide and rub on an anti-septic cream. If the swelling doesn't go down in a couple of days, or if you suspect that the culprit was a deer tick (the spreader of Lyme disease), call your vet.

# FLEA-CONTROL

This safe, simple, and cheap routine will keep your pets happy and flea-free all summer long:

1. Make sure your pet is getting a good diet and plenty of exercise. (Tests show that critters in tip-top shape attract far fewer fleas than their less-healthy counterparts.)

2. Vacuum, vacuum, vacuum. Unless you keep fleas out of the house, you can't keep them off your pets.

3. Give your dog or cat garlic and/or brewer's yeast every day to repel fleas. (Some folks say this is an old wives' tale, but it's kept my dogs flea-free for years.)

4. If you live in big-time flea territory, or if your critter spends a lot of time outdoors, bathe him often during flea season. (Every two weeks for dogs or once a month for cats

should do the trick.) If regular cat or dog shampoo doesn't get all the fleas, add a cup of herbal oil, such as pennyroyal, eucalyptus, or peppermint, to the bath water. Just make sure you test the mixture on a small patch of Fido's skin to rule out allergies before you douse him with it.

5. In between baths, use the Flee, Fleas Lemon Rinse daily (see page 358).

# CLEAR SKIN ROUTINE

To get rid of a current acne outbreak on your cat or dog, soak a clean washcloth in warm water, add a few drops of pet shampoo, and gently pat the acne-infected area once or twice a day. If that doesn't send the spots packin' in a few days, use an over-the-counter product, such as Stridex, that's designed for human acne.

# HAIR OF THE CAT

Nowadays, there are special foods designed to prevent hair balls in cats, but any of these tricks will work just as well (if not better):

★ Put a dab of petroleum jelly on your cat's nose once a week. She'll lick it off, and when it reaches her tummy, it'll coat her stomach walls and prevent hair buildup.

★ Mix 1 teaspoon of corn oil or fish oil into your cat's food once a week.

★ Add 1 teaspoon of bran to your cat's food every day.

## FANTASTIC FORMULA

### Far-Away Feline Formula

When your cats—or somebody else's—are gettin' up to no good in your garden, safeguard your plants with this potent mixture.

4 tablespoons of dry mustard

3 tablespoons of cayenne pepper

2 tablespoons of chili powder

5 teaspoons of flour

Mix the ingredients in 2 quarts of warm water, and pour or spray the solution anyplace you want to set out the "Cats Unwelcome" mat.

## FANTASTIC FORMULA

### Dog-Be-Gone Formula

If the neighborhood dogs are runnin' roughshod over your turf, this potent elixir will send 'em on their way, right away!

2 small onions, finely chopped

2 cloves of garlic, finely chopped

1 jalapeño pepper, finely chopped

1 tablespoon of cayenne pepper

1 tablespoon of Tabasco sauce

1 tablespoon of chili powder

1 tablespoon of liquid dish soap

Combine the ingredients in 1 quart of warm water, and let the mixture sit for 24 hours. Strain out the solids, and spray the liquid anywhere Spot isn't welcome.

# BLOOD BUSTER

When you spend your life in bare paws, you're bound to cut a footpad now and then. For minor cuts, clean the wound with peroxide and apply an antiseptic cream; for major ones (of course), rush Rover or Puff to the vet. Then attend to the stains on the carpet using this formula:

Mix equal parts of meat tenderizer and cold water. Apply the solution to the stain, and let it sit for half an hour. Then sponge it off with cool water.

# Index

## A

Acne
    in humans, 301–2
    in pets, 347, 359
Advertisements, grocery, 13–14
Ahhh Aftershave, 301
Air conditioners, 69
Air fresheners, 168–69, 192, 279
Air travel
    as courier, 128–29
    discounts, 130
    fares, 124–27
Alcohol, safety with, 273. *See also specific types*
Alcohol-Free Mouthwash, 312
Alcoholic beverage stains, on furniture, 238–39, 240, 247
Alfalfa meal, as deicer, 327
Alfredo sauce, preparing, 176–77
Allergies, in pets, 344–45
All Eyes on You, 307
All the Tea in China, 290
Almond Joy Cleanser, 299
Almond oil, for skin care, 312
Almonds, for skin care, 299, 300, 308, 311
Alternative health care, for pets, 341
Aluminum foil
    in ovens, 212
    as pet toys, 349
    as scrubbers, 258–59, 324, 332, 333
Aluminum furniture, 120, 329–30
Aluminum jelly, 323

Ammonia, for cleaning
    all-purpose, vi, 284
    carpet, 356
    electronics, 230
    furniture, 240, 253
    glass, 249, 323
    grills, 331–32
    laundry, 194, 201
    ovens, 211, 231
    painted wood, 334
    safety and, 273
Anise seeds, for oral hygiene, 304, 312
Apples, 12, 300. *See also* Fruit
Appliance repair shops, 64
Appliances and electronics. *See also specific items*
    cleaning, 230–31, 273
    deal-making on, 62
    energy efficiency and, 60–61, 64, 65, 210–11, 215
    life span of, 62
    manufacturers of, 59
    no-frills models, 56–57, 61
    researching, 57–58
    scratched and dented, 61
    seasonal buys on, 55–56
    troubleshooting, 224–29
    used, 58–60
    warranties on, 63
Ashes
    for cleaning, 240, 332
    as deicer, 327
    as deodorizer, 141
Aspirin, for laundry, 189
Astringents, 307–8

Attics, storing clothes in, 181
Auctions, 92, 156
Auto-body filler, for siding repair, 315
Avocados, for skin care, 300

## B

Baby food jars, 259–60
Baby oil, 309, 335
Baby wipe containers, as toys, 261
Baby wipes, as stain remover, 205
Badminton birdies, 349
Baking soda
    as air freshener, 279
    brands of, 276
    for cleaning
        bathrooms, 277, 279
        dishwashers, 208
        floors, 275
        furniture, 230, 253
        garbage disposals, 209
        kitchens, 157, 272–73
        laundry, 194, 201
        office equipment, 231
        ovens, 211
        painted wood, 334
        stoves, 210, 230
        urine spots on lawns, 356
    as deodorizer, 334, 356
    freshness of, 273–74
    for hair care, 291
    for oral hygiene, 303
    for plumbing clogs, 285, 286